St Giles'

To all who have made St Giles' what it is and shall be.

St Giles'

The Dramatic Story
of a Great Church and its People

Rosalind K. Marshall

SAINT ANDREW PRESS
Edinburgh

First published in 2009 by
SAINT ANDREW PRESS
121 George Street
Edinburgh EH2 4YN

ISBN 978 0 7152 0883 0 (paperback)
ISBN 978 0 7152 0927 1 (hardback)

British Library Cataloguing in Publication Data
A catalogue record for this book is available from the British Library.

It is the publisher's policy to only use papers that are natural and recyclable and that have been manufactured from timber grown in renewable, properly managed forests. All of the manufacturing processes of the papers are expected to conform to the environmental regulations of the country of origin.

Typeset in Palatino by Waverley Typesetters, Fakenham
Manufactured in the United Kingdom by MPG Books, Bodmin

Contents

Foreword

The ease with which the reader is led through the chequered history of St Giles' will not prevent the more astute from recognising the scholarly precision with which Dr Marshall has conducted her survey of the available sources relating to the town church of Edinburgh. Her typescript work includes one thousand and eighty-seven footnotes. Her gift of engaging the reader without pompous or obscure language does not lead her to make judgements which she cannot justify, or present as definite those conclusions which are at best probable. The cornucopia of detail is not allowed to choke the fluent prose, and criteria of assessment from one century are not applied glibly to another.

With all the changes, in fabric and culture, of nine hundred years, the continuities deserve to be celebrated. Of course the words of a psalm or an epistle may be received with differing resonance and association from one period of history to another; but the same is true of four people sitting near each other at a service today. Yet the same Bible is read, the same psalms sung, the same sacraments administered. And today, as in the earliest days, people come in when no organised act of worship is about to begin, sit quietly or move around, light a candle, ask for particular help for themselves and others (these days by writing a prayer on a piece of paper).

One great change, from the heady days of the sixteenth and seventeenth centuries, is that then, not now, religious preferences and issues of church order were matters of life and death, intimately bound up with power and force and conflict. We will not long for those times ever to return, though we recognise that such links between conviction and conflict are readily found in parts of the world today. Whether we have gone too far in the opposite direction, and reduced the matters of life and death to optional, occasional, leisure time hobbies, could be debated endlessly, or at least until we became bored.

Another change is the move towards churches being run by church people, and the necessary money raised by church people. When we recognise that it is only in the last century, roughly, that St Giles' has been maintained by the 'members', I wonder if we should be slower to assume that that is the only right, Christian way for support to be given. The resident, living, congregation whose names are on the Communion Roll are deeply important to our contemporary life and witness; but St Giles' is an important place of pilgrimage and prayer at times when there are no members of the congregation present. The ways in which this building may be used in future years must be many and varied, and cannot be confined to the needs and wishes of one Church of Scotland congregation, who would, I believe, be delighted to share with others the use of St Giles' seven days a week, as well as sharing the responsibility of maintenance.

It is often said that we live in secular times, but times in which people are greatly interested in spiritual things. Some of us long for a healing of the Catholic/Protestant distinction, when our common heritage can assist us in balanced continuity and fitting innovation. To have so much information about St Giles', so readably and thoughtfully available, should remind us that the only constant thing is change, and that we should face the future with imagination and daring – and thank Rosalind Marshall with great appreciation.

GILLEASBUIG MACMILLAN

Acknowledgements

The Very Reverend Gilleasbuig Macmillan, Minister of St Giles', responded encouragingly when I suggested that it might be time for a new history of the Cathedral, and he kindly read the entire text. Professor Michael Lynch and Professor James Kirk gave me the benefit of their comments on the early chapters, Susannah Honeyman of St Giles' Renewal Appeal has been endlessly patient with my constant quest for information and John McLintock of the National Archives of Scotland provided me with valuable documentary references. I had many architectural discussions with Jo Penney, and Dr Margaret Sanderson and I continued to enjoy our long-running lunchtime conversations about sixteenth-century Scotland.

Others who supplied me with information, directed me towards promising sources or otherwise facilitated my work during the writing of this book are, in alphabetical order, the Reverend Helen Alexander, Elizabeth Baillie, Susan Groag Bell, Dr Louise Boreham, Dr Helen S. Brown, Morag Cross, Dr Elizabeth Cumming, Jeana Davidson, the Reverend John V. Gardner, Olive Geddes and her colleagues at the National Library of Scotland, Imogen Gibbon of the Scottish National Portrait Gallery, Dr John Hall, Michael Harris, Master of the Music at St Giles', Margaret Hilton, John Howard, Librarian of St Mary's Episcopal Cathedral, Edinburgh, Richard Hunter, Edinburgh City Archivist, Veronika Kallus, Visitor Services Manager at St Giles', the Very Reverend Dr Sheilagh Kesting, John Knight, Dr Anthony Lewis, Margaret Lumsdaine, Sheila Mackay, Maurice McIlwrick, Elaine and Dr Ruth McQuillan, Kirsteen Millar, Joan Noble, the Reverend Nancy Norman, Dr Sally Rush, David Scarratt of the

Museum of Edinburgh, James Simpson of Simpson & Brown, architects, Henry Steuart Fothringham, Sheana Stephen, artist jeweller, Gwenyth Telford, and Graham Tristram, of Campbell & Arnott Ltd, architects.

I am likewise grateful to all the copyright owners of quotations and illustrations. They are listed in the Sources of Quotations and the captions to the illustrations

R.K.M.

21 October 2008

Note

In writing the text, I have modernised archaic spellings for ease of reading. As for currency, in the mid-sixteenth century £1 Scots was worth one-quarter of £1 sterling, but by 1603 its value had fallen to one-twelfth of £1 sterling and it remained at that level until 1707, when the separate Scottish coinage disappeared with the Act of Union. A merk was worth thirteen shillings and four pence Scots. A shilling was worth one-twentieth of a pound and a penny was worth one-twelfth of a shilling.

List of Illustrations

Colour Plates

1   Central front panel of the Fetternear Banner, believed to have been embroidered about 1520 for the Confraternity of the Holy Blood, St Giles'.

(© National Museums of Scotland. Licensor www.scran.ac.uk)

2   *George IV at St Giles'* by J. M. W. Turner. The King stands beneath the canopy of the Royal Seat, on the right.

(© Tate, London 2008)

3   The St Giles' pulpit, designed by William Hay and carved by John Rhind in 1872–3.

(Photograph: Lars Strobel)

4   Memorial to William Hay, architect, died 1888, by John Rhind, in St Giles' Cathedral.

(Photograph: © Saul Gardiner)

5   Memorial to Lindsay Mackersy WS, Session Clerk, died 1902, by an unknown carver, in St Giles' Cathedral.

(Photograph: © Saul Gardiner)

6   Robert Burns memorial window, 1985, by Leifur Breidfjord.

(Photograph: © Peter Backhouse)

Black and white figures

CHAPTER 1

Lepers, Saints and Kings

*I*t was a late autumn afternoon when the young Australian tourist came into St Giles' Cathedral. The stained glass windows glowed in the mellow sunshine, the medieval stone pillars soared upwards to the shadowy Gothic arches of the roof, and the scarlet, yellow, green and blue banners of the Knights of the Thistle splashed the sandstone walls with colour. Cathedrals and great churches have a mysterious atmosphere all their own, the bustle of everyday life somehow intermingled with a stillness, a feeling of time suspended, and the visitor took a few steps forward then stopped abruptly, gazing around him, awestruck.

'But this is magnificent!' he exclaimed.

Seeing me standing nearby, he asked urgently, 'Is this building old?'

'Yes, it is,' I said with a smile. 'Very old.'

'How old? How old?' he demanded eagerly.

'Well, it was founded nearly nine hundred years ago,' I replied, 'and there was probably a church in this place several centuries before that. Of course, the original building has gone now, but much of what you are looking at dates back to the fourteenth and fifteenth centuries.'

Astonished, he shook his head in disbelief. 'I had no idea a building could be so old!' he exclaimed, adding excitedly, 'I must go and tell my friends right away!' and he literally ran out of the Cathedral to fetch them in.

Had our conversation continued for longer, he would probably have asked me, 'But who was St Giles? Was he a Scottish saint?' Not so. This holy man's connection with Scotland is not immediately obvious. Known in Latin as Aegidius, he was born in the seventh century AD and lived as a hermit and healer in the south of France. Many legends have grown up around these bare facts, giving all manner of circumstantial detail. These usually say that he was Greek, an Athenian who cured a sick beggar one day by giving him his cloak. Word of this miracle soon spread and Giles, finding himself the centre of unwanted attention, fled to France, going deeper and deeper into the forests near Nîmes, at the mouth of the River Rhône. There he stayed, with only a tame hind, a female deer, as a companion.

His peaceful life was shattered when Wamba, King of the Visigoths went hunting in the neighbourhood and shot at the hind. Pushing his way into a thicket in search of his prey, he came upon Giles, wounded by the royal arrow and holding the deer protectively in his arms. They spoke, and the King was greatly impressed by the holy man and the simplicity of his solitary life. Wamba returned many times after that, urging Giles to accept gifts of lands and riches, but Giles always refused. In the end, he managed to divert the King by suggesting that he use the royal resources to found a monastery instead. This Wamba did, but he insisted that the reluctant hermit accept the office of abbot, and there Giles lived out the rest of his life, greatly revered. He was subsequently canonised, is usually depicted with the hind and the arrow and became the patron saint of lepers, the lame, blacksmiths and nursing mothers.

Leprosy was perhaps the most dreaded medieval illness. A chronic infectious disease of the skin and eyes, leading to disfigurement and permanent disability, it gave rise to feelings of horror and dread similar to those evoked by AIDS in the late twentieth century. Easily treatable today, leprosy was incurable in the Middle Ages, and the unfortunate sufferers were shunned, forced to live in isolation, ringing a handbell when they ventured out, to warn passers-by to keep away. Prayers to St Giles on behalf of lepers were believed to be particularly effective and his shrine became a popular place of pilgrimage, not least because it lay on the main pilgrim routes to Santiago de Compostela in Spain and to the Holy Land. Crusaders carried home the legends about his life, and in England alone more than 150 medieval churches were dedicated to him. In Scotland, one other survives, in Elgin, its records going back to 1224.

We do not know when Edinburgh's St Giles' was founded, for no relevant charter has been preserved, but the earliest stone church on the site is generally thought to have been established about 1124. If we accept the date of 1124, the founder must have been either Alexander I, who died that year, or his brother David I, who succeeded him. Their parents were Malcolm Canmore, an energetic and effective King of Scots and his wife St Margaret, who was canonised for her determined work for the Church. Links between Rome and the Scottish Church became closer during their time, and several of their large family shared their pious preoccupations. Matilda, their elder daughter, married Henry I of England and, amid her many cultural and charitable activities, she founded in London in 1117 a leper hospital dedicated to St Giles. David I, her youngest brother, was sent as a youth to live in her household to complete his knightly training.

Going into her chamber one evening, he found her not only washing but kissing the feet of a group of lepers. Aghast, he urged her to stop, telling her that if her husband knew what she was doing he would never kiss her again. Matilda merely smiled. She had a good relationship with Henry I and, for her, comforting these poor people took precedence over all other considerations. She suggested that David should join her in the task but he ran off in horror. In later life his critics would scorn his piety, saying that he was far too holy to make a good king, but at that time his thoughts had not yet turned to religion. Nevertheless, this episode made such an impression on him that he recounted it in detail to Aelred of Rievaulx the chronicler, and it seems to have stayed in his mind. It may well have been he who founded St Giles', selecting its site and choosing to dedicate it to the patron saint of lepers.

Edinburgh was not yet Scotland's fixed capital, although the King often stayed there, and it was, of course, far smaller than it is now. There was no Royal Mile with overcrowded closes, no elegant New Town, no spacious suburbs. The Castle, perched on its craggy rock, had been a fortress since prehistoric times and the first settlement had grown up close by, in its protection, a huddle of wooden houses occupying the upper stretch of a long ridge running eastwards with a deep valley at either side. A market had been established in the centre, where the street called the Lawnmarket is now to be found, and beyond that stood St Giles', on the very eastern edge of the town, just within the line of a deep boundary ditch. The rest of the ridge was gradually developed after David I founded the Abbey of Holyrood at the foot of it in 1128, giving the Abbot permission to build houses up the ridge towards St Giles'.

An able and energetic monarch, David I erected Edinburgh into a royal burgh, with all the trading privileges that implied, and created a parish for St Giles', from the lands of the existing parish of the even older St Cuthbert's Church. If in a thirteenth-century ecclesiastical taxation roll

St Giles' was assessed as having an annual value of only twenty-six merks (a merk being worth thirteen shillings and four pence), just one-sixth of the value of St Cuthbert's, that was probably because its parish was much smaller. St Giles' was also provided with a grange, a stretch of agricultural land to the south of the town, where serfs would grow crops under the supervision of the clergy. David ruled over Northumbria as well as Scotland, and at some unknown date he granted St Giles' to the hospital of Harehope there. There was nothing unusual about that. It was common enough for a parish church to be appropriated to another religious institution, to increase the revenues of the recipient. Harehope was run by friars belonging to the Order of St Lazarus of Jerusalem, and the special role of that Order was to care for lepers.

Was David thinking of his sister Matilda when he made this arrangement? Perhaps. Certainly his intention was to benefit the Order financially. As in the rest of Western Europe, the parishioners of St Giles' would pay a fixed proportion of their income to support their church and its clergy. The annual payments were known as teinds (tithes), and they came in the form of a tenth of the annual grain crop, a tenth of the beasts born that year and a tenth of the butter, cheese, milk and eggs produced. After the gift to Harehope, all or most of the teinds would go there, although some were probably kept back for the vicar of St Giles'. In granting St Giles' to Harehope, David was in no way diminishing its status. In fact, at about the same time, he decided to give it an important new role. From that time onwards it would be the official burgh church, and the burgh authorities would take a close and proprietorial interest in it.

So what did St Giles' look like in those days? High up on the interior wall of its St Eloi's Aisle is the scalloped top part of a small pillar. Glaring with bulging eyes and beaky nose from the north aisle of the chancel is a grotesque mask of the same period, while a small, grinning face leers down from its place near the chancel roof, above the eighteenth-century coat of arms of George II. These three stones are the only identifiable remains of the twelfth-century church, rescued during building work centuries later and placed in their present positions. Apart from that, the complex Gothic structure we know today, with its many alterations and additions, gives us little clue. However, judging by other twelfth-century churches, the St Giles' of that time would have been a small, rectangular structure probably standing on the site of the present nave. It would have consisted of a nave and a chancel, possibly with a semicircular apse at the east end. Sometime before the mid-thirteenth century, an additional aisle was built on the south side, perhaps indicating an increase in population. There would have been narrow, round-headed windows and in the north wall was a highly decorative romanesque doorway which would survive until 1798. An engraved drawing of it shows the same sort of zigzag patterns, animals and grotesque faces familiar to us from churches at, for example, Dalmeny in West Lothian and Leuchars in Fife.

Figure 1
Early medieval doorway to St Giles', no longer in existence, from an engraving by
J. Armour, 1799. (© Edinburgh City Libraries. Licensor www.scran.ac.uk)

John is the first vicar of St Giles' whose name we know. Surnames were not yet in common use and he seems to have had none. He was there from about 1208 until at least 1243, when he must have taken part in an impressive ceremony performed by David de Bernham, Bishop of St Andrews, in whose diocese St Giles' was situated. Services could not be held in a new church until it had been consecrated by the bishop of its diocese. This set it apart for sacred use, dedicating it to the service and worship of God. The anniversary of the consecration was celebrated each year as a feast day, but many of the churches in Scotland had no record of their original consecration and Bishop de Bernham had been appointed in 1241 at a time when there were complaints from Rome about this unsatisfactory situation. He therefore set out on a visitation of the many churches in his diocese, determined to dedicate or rededicate as many as he could. Indeed, in the course of nine years he achieved the surprising total of about 140 consecrations.

We know this, because he wrote the details in the front of his pontifical, the book containing the prayers and ritual instructions for the ceremonies he performed. The volume is preserved in the Bibliothèque Nationale in Paris and it notes the consecration of St Giles' on 6 October 1243. Two consecration crosses still to be seen on the interior Cathedral walls may possibly date from that occasion. This was undoubtedly a rededication. It would be unthinkable for a church with a royal founder not to have been consecrated as soon as it was built. It is puzzling to discover that at St Giles' in later years the anniversary of its consecration was celebrated not on 6 October but on 3 November. Could that have been the date of the original consecration in about 1124? Probably not, for if the very first consecration had been recorded, there would presumably have been no need for a rededication. The explanation may lie in the fact that less than a hundred years after Bishop de Bernham's ceremony, the twelfth-century church apparently vanished and St Giles' was completely rebuilt, with perhaps a third consecration service when it was complete. So what had happened?

According to a persistent tradition, the little Romanesque church was destroyed by the English. Robert the Bruce, now Robert I, King of Scots, had triumphed over the English in 1314 at the Battle of Bannockburn during Scotland's Wars of Independence, but the relationship between the two countries remained tense and on 1 July 1322, Robert invaded England, laying waste to large areas as far south as the county of Lancaster. The following month, the English retaliated. On 12 August, Edward II marched into Scotland with a large army and moved towards Edinburgh, where he knew that Robert was staying. The Scottish King made a strategic withdrawal from the town and when Edward's supply ships were prevented by bad weather from sailing north, he too left, but not before his soldiers despoiled Holyrood Abbey. That much the early chronicles tell us, and no more. There is no mention of St Giles', but conjecture has subsequently been translated into accepted fact and it is believed that before they departed the English also set fire to Edinburgh's parish church.

Whatever really happened, the burgh was intent on providing itself with a much larger church in the latest architectural style, pointed Gothic vaulting replacing rounded Norman arches. Once more we are frustrated by the lack of any documentary evidence, but archaeologists and architectural historians have patiently studied the building as it is now and they are agreed that its core – the nave, crossing, transepts and chancel – date from this rebuilding, as do the four great octagonal pillars and the tower they support. In other words, it would have had the traditional ground plan for a church, in the shape of a cross, with the transepts forming the arms. The masonry is of a quartz-rich sandstone, probably from a local quarry and the advanced architecture and sophisticated decoration unmistakably indicate the growing wealth and ambition of the Edinburgh burgesses.

Who, then, came to services in St Giles'? Theoretically, all parishioners were supposed to attend mass each week, but by the fourteenth century most people took communion only once a year, at Easter. For the rest of the time they attended as spectators rather than participants. If the mass is sung, it is known as high mass, if spoken, then it is a low mass. Services were all in Latin and the notion of coming weekly to listen to preaching was entirely alien. The few sermons heard were mainly on feast days, and most churches therefore had neither a pulpit nor fixed seating for the parishioners. When individuals did intend to listen to a sermon, they would bring their own stools with them, but for the most part they either stood or they knelt in prayer. The nave was their part of the church, separated from the chancel by an elaborate rood-screen with a large cross on top of it.

The chancel was the holiest part of the building, reserved for the clergy, choristers and important members of the laity. Mass was celebrated there each day at the high altar, which of course was dedicated to St Giles. Behind it would have been an elaborate screen known as a reredos and, behind that, a large area known as the sanctuary. When mass was to be celebrated, the ringing of the sanctus bell gave warning that the service was about to start. Those present in the nave crowded forward, peering through the screen's carvings to watch what was happening. If they had a poor view, they would at least hear the chanting and the Latin words of the priest, but it was very important for them to see if they possibly could. They believed that, even if they were not participating in the service, the very sight of the consecrated bread would bring them important benefits. Having seen it, they would feel no need for food for some time afterwards. Their eyesight would not fade, they would not age in the immediate aftermath, they would not be struck down by sudden death and angels would protect their every step.

In the early days of the Christian Church, mass was intrinsically a commemoration of the Last Supper, the final meal Jesus took with his disciples. Since then, a much more elaborate ceremonial had come into being as theological thought evolved. The Church now taught that when the bread and wine were blessed by the priest, these elements were transformed. Outwardly they remained bread and wine, with the same texture and taste, but in essence they had been irrevocably changed into the body and blood of Christ, so that he really was present in them. No longer a simple commemoration, the mass had become a re-enactment of Christ's sacrifice on the cross, a miracle charged with deep spiritual significance, and the fact that the chancel was screened off from the rest of the church intensified the air of mystery.

The priest now stood facing the altar, with his back to the congregation and the climax of the mass came when he lifted the large, thin, almost transparent wafer of bread high above his head, saying in Latin, 'This is my body'. The sanctus bell was rung again and extra candles on the altar were lit, to make sure that the Host (as the wafer is called) was visible to everyone. Priests swung censers, wafting incense through the chancel, and all those taking part clasped their hands in prayer. Everyone bowed to the Host, and the parishioners in the nave fell to their knees. Having consecrated the bread, the priest, with a less dramatic gesture, raised the chalice of wine, which only he would drink. Those who wished to take communion then came forward through a door in the rood-screen to receive a small, specially baked wheaten wafer embossed with a cross or some other symbol such as the letters IHS, an abbreviation of the Greek word for Jesus. Although most people now took communion only at Easter, that was not seen as a sign of apathy. It was, rather, a token of the supreme importance of the mass. Even those who had little interest in spiritual affairs were convinced of its profound effect. It was regarded as a particularly valuable source of assistance in time of trouble and people could pay for masses to be said for recovery from an illness, for a good harvest, or for curing sick animals.

When death did come, the most prominent members of the community were buried inside the church, as close to the high altar as possible. More ordinary parishioners were interred in the graveyard which lay immediately outside, to the east and south. Excavated bronze shroud pins from that area show that the burials were in shrouds rather than in coffins and the stone marking the grave of a knight, probably dating from the late twelfth or early thirteenth century, can be seen in the Preston Aisle, embedded in the east wall. At that time, St Giles' still belonged to Harehope Hospital, but during the 1370s the Lazarite friars chose to support the King of England against the Scots. As a result, they were forfeited and St Giles' reverted to the Scottish King, now Robert the Bruce's grandson, Robert II. In 1376 he granted the Grange of St Giles', along with some other lands, to his son and heir, John, Earl of Carrick. With such active royal patronage, the future for St Giles' looked very promising but in 1385 disaster struck once again.

France and England had long been at war with each other and the previous year a deputation of thirty distinguished Frenchmen had arrived in Edinburgh, hoping to persuade their old allies the Scots to create a diversion by invading England on their behalf. Robert II refused, but some of his more warlike knights were eager for the fray and, led by James, 2nd Earl of Douglas, they held a secret meeting in St Giles' to discuss the situation. As a result of their deliberations, they set off to raid the north of England. Predictably, the English once more retaliated. On 6 August 1385 their 18-year-old king, Richard II, marched into Scotland with a large army. The chronicler Walter Bower, Abbot of Inchcolm, described what happened. 'He burnt to ashes with consuming flames churches devoted to God and monastic sanctuaries (namely the monasteries at Dryburgh, Melrose and Newbattle) and the noble royal town of Edinburgh with its church of St Giles'.' Richard marched south again on 19 August.

Fortunately, the fine new Gothic St Giles' was not burnt to the ground. It must have been saved by the efforts of the townspeople. Wooden roofing and furnishings were no doubt destroyed in the blaze, but most of the building survived. A document of 1387 mentions the crossing and the nave, which were still there, as were the four great octagonal pillars supporting the tower. Indeed, during late nineteenth-century restoration work, it was found that these pillars bore the marks of the medieval flames. The town authorities were no doubt anxious to repair the damage. They would have set in hand the most pressing repairs as a matter of urgency, and then, two years later, they embarked upon a project to build a series of new side chapels. The resulting indenture is the earliest known building contract relating to St Giles'.

It records that on 29 November 1387, Adam Forrester, Andrew Yutson the provost of Edinburgh (Scottish equivalent of a mayor) and the local community made an agreement with three masons, John Primrose, John of Scone and John Squire, to build five new chapels on the south side of the church, running from the west gable to the south-west pillar of the tower. Forrester, a leading grain merchant, was probably contributing substantially to the cost. He and his colleagues had clear ideas about what they wanted. They had already sent the masons down to Holyrood Abbey, to look at the vaulted roof above St Stephen's altar there, and it was to be their pattern for the roofs of the new chapels. Four of these would have windows while the fifth would have a door as good as the western door of the church itself. The roofs of the new chapels were to be of stone slabs and they would have proper gutters to cast out the water. Very often, medieval gutters had carvings at the ends, so that the rainwater spouted from the mouths of gargoyles. These no longer exist at St Giles', but one such gargoyle, resembling a pig's head, was taken from the church in the early nineteenth century and built into the wall of the garden of Swanston Cottage, a few miles south of Edinburgh.

The town was to pay for everything, and the masons had to promise to work 'truly, without fraud, as true men ought to do'. They undertook to lay 1,200 hewn stones, and in return for all they did they would be paid 600 merks. The sum of £40 would be given to them in advance. Few people in those days could write, and so in customary manner they sealed the document instead. John Primrose and John of Scone did not have seals and so they had to borrow those of friends, but John Squire solemnly used his own. On the back of the indenture are inscribed their receipts, dated 1390 and 1391, with £286 still owed to them. When the five chapels had been built, a further series was erected on the north side of the church, one remodelled from an existing chapel, and a porch was put up over the old twelfth-century doorway.

Because of the many changes the church has undergone since, relatively little of its elaborately carved detail remains, but stone carvings high up on the walls and in the roof give ample evidence of the decorative quality. The Green Man is perhaps the most common medieval motif of this kind, showing foliage sprouting from the mouth of a head which was sometimes human, sometimes cat-like. This design can be traced back to Roman times, after which it was adopted as a Christian symbol representing revival and regeneration, the death of the flesh and the renewal of life at the Resurrection. There are no fewer than sixty-six Green Men in St Giles', some from the fourteenth century, some from the fifteenth, along with formerly painted roof bosses carved with foliage and flowers.

The level of craftsmanship of the masons is an indication that St Giles' was prospering, but it was about to undergo another ominous change. Robert II died in 1390 and his son John inherited the throne, taking the title Robert III. His father was buried at Scone Abbey, and the following day he himself was crowned there. A picturesque story describes what happened next. Both ceremonies had caused the Abbey a great deal of expense, not least because it was harvest time and the corn was trodden down and destroyed by the courtiers' horses. Complaints fell upon deaf ears and so the labourers and servants of the Abbey staged a protest. Armed with drums, pipes and other instruments, they gathered at night and sang and played noisily outside the King's apartments. One of the monks was brought to Robert's presence and questioned. They were celebrating the harvest with their usual songs, he remarked ironically, since the King and his nobles had spared them the trouble of gathering it in. Fortunately for him, the good-natured Robert was amused, and to compensate them he granted them the patronage of the church of St Giles'.

This anecdote is probably apocryphal, for the grant to Scone was not made until 15 December 1393, three years after their protest took place. There was no mistaking its provisions, however. In future, St Giles' would have a vicar pensioner, paid an annual salary, instead of a vicar perpetual whose income came from the teinds. These would go to Scone, and when the current vicar, James Lyon, died, the Abbey of Scone would have the right to appoint one of its own canons as his successor. The Edinburgh magistrates were far from pleased when they heard the news. They had ambitious plans for their church which would be considerably hindered by this new arrangement. Their complaints were ignored and Robert's grant was not only confirmed by Walter, Bishop of St Andrews, but ratified by a papal bull. Fortunately for St Giles', it never really became effective; James Lyon failed to die conveniently and make way for a Scone nominee and indeed he would still be vicar in 1423.

Determined to have the grant annulled, the townspeople went ahead with their ambitious building programme and an aisle of two bays was constructed on the north-west side of the nave in the first decade of the fifteenth century. The Albany Aisle exists to this day, its two bays separated by an elegant pillar bearing the coats of arms of two of the most powerful men in early fifteenth-century Scotland, Robert, Duke of Albany, from whom it takes its name, and Archibald, 4th Earl of Douglas. Albany was one of Robert III's younger brothers and, unlike the King himself, he had somewhat confusingly been baptised Robert. Perhaps this had given him ideas about his future role and indeed when their father in his later years became incapable of ruling for himself, it was Albany who governed the country for him, as lieutenant of the realm.

Even after Robert III inherited the throne, Albany continued to exercise considerable power. Robert, tall and genial, with a gentle nature, was already 53 when he became king, an old man by medieval standards, and ever since a kick by a horse several years earlier he had been seriously disabled by lameness. As a result, much of the business of government was left to Albany, who earned a reputation as a domineering and un-scrupulous individual. It is only recently that research has revised his image, demonstrating that he was an energetic and effective leader who stepped in when his ill or feckless relatives lost control of affairs.

Albany's personal interest in St Giles' seems to have begun quite early on. At the very start of Robert III's reign, it was decreed that whenever the lord chamberlain's court met in Edinburgh, the fines exacted for breaches of trading regulations would go towards the building work being done at St Giles'. The sums were not large – £29 in 1391 and £26:13:4 four years later – but they were a valued token of royal favour. The granting of the fines is usually seen as an act of benevolence on the part of the King, but it is surely not without significance that the lord chamberlain of the time was none other than the Duke of Albany and the initiative may well have been his. During the following decade, the Albany Aisle was constructed. No building contract or foundation charter for it exists and so we do not know who paid for it or why it was erected. According to legend, however, it came into being in distinctly sinister circumstances.

Robert III had two sons, David and James. As time passed, people grew increasingly dissatisfied with the King's ineffectual rule, but his wife, Queen Annabella, was determined that Albany should not gain power again. In 1399, her elder son David reached the age of 21, and through her influence he was made lieutenant of the realm. People seem to have had their doubts about him, though, and there were conditions to his appointment. His term of office was limited to three years, he would be answerable to parliament for his behaviour and he would govern with the advice of a council headed by his uncle, Albany. At first all went well but, after the death of his mother, David's behaviour changed. Spurning the advice of his council, he reverted to his previous frivolity, according to the chronicler Bower, who considered him to be both dissolute and indolent.

The situation went from bad to worse, he constantly flouted his uncle's advice and in 1401 Albany had him seized and imprisoned in St Andrews Castle. By this time David was married to the sister of Archibald, 4th Earl of Douglas, and Douglas was his chief supporter. After consultations with Douglas, Albany moved David to the dungeons of his own castle of Falkland, where the Prince later died. According to contemporary rumours, he had been starved to death by his wicked uncle. An official enquiry in May 1402, two months after his demise, exonerated both Albany and Douglas and Albany was once more appointed lieutenant of the realm. That did not stop the rumours, of course, and it is usually assumed that the Albany Aisle must have been founded by the Duke and the Earl in penitence for their supposed crime.

Whether the two men were guilty or innocent, the burgh authorities were evidently untroubled by the lurid stories, for they sought and found in Albany a powerful ally in their struggle to free themselves from their link with the Abbey of Scone. Circumstances favoured their cause when Robert III's only surviving son, Prince James, was seized at sea by English pirates in the spring of 1406 and held prisoner. The shock was too great for Robert's weakened constitution and he died a fortnight later. The Duke of Albany would once more rule Scotland, this time as lord governor for his captured nephew, James I. Enlisting his support, the Edinburgh magistrates petitioned the Pope to dissolve the link between St Giles' and Scone. Their request was granted.

As for the Albany Aisle, we shall probably never know the real reason for its foundation. It may have been inspired by guilt but there is an alternative explanation. In June 1409, Albany and Douglas, who had fallen out with each other, decided to put an end to their differences and agreed a bond of mutual friendship, with Albany's second son marrying Douglas's daughter Elizabeth. Apart from Albany's connection with St Giles', Douglas was the valued patron and protector of various abbeys including Holyrood and Melrose and so the new aisle might well have been seen by them as a suitable way of marking their reconciliation and their new relationship. Whatever the truth of the matter, once the aisle was finished there must have been a lull in the construction work for, according to Abbot Bower, in 1416 storks built their nests on the roof of the church.

CHAPTER 2

Burgesses and Chaplains

One day during the early 1450s, Sir William Preston set off on an important mission to France. He owned the lands of Gorton, now called Craigmillar, on the edge of Edinburgh and he may have been a relative of Thomas de Preston, who was a bailie of the burgh at about that time. His journey, however, seems to have been made entirely on his own initiative and certainly at his own expense. He was going to see if he could acquire a relic of St Giles. This would be a wonderful gift for the church, for any surviving body parts or pieces of clothing belonging to saints were carefully preserved and placed in elaborate reliquaries. Objects of great veneration, they attracted large crowds of pilgrims to those churches in which they were displayed.

Now, St Giles himself had been buried in the south of France, and the possibility of obtaining a relic must have seemed remote. However, Sir William had good contacts and with 'diligent labour', great expense and the assistance of the French King, Charles VII, he succeeded in gaining possession of what was believed to be an arm bone of the saint. Returning triumphantly to Scotland, he died shortly afterwards and was buried in the Lady Aisle, which lay to the right of the high altar. He bequeathed his precious relic to 'our mother kirk of St Giles', where it was kept in a suitably ornate gold reliquary in the shape of an arm and hand, a diamond ring on the little finger. He attached no conditions to this bequest and, in gratitude for his generosity, the provost and bailies of the burgh on 11 January 1455 promised his son William that they would build a special aisle in his father's memory, to the right of the Lady Aisle. Sir William's coat of arms would be displayed on the stonework and, complete with service book and silver chalice, a chaplain would sing masses for his soul at the altar. It was dedicated to St Thomas the Apostle, 'Doubting Thomas', Jesus's disciple who was sceptical about the Resurrection until he saw the risen Christ for himself. The dedication is not recorded in the documents of the time, but an account of expenditure a hundred years later mentions that a new panel of glass was placed in a window of St Thomas's Aisle 'called Preston's Aisle'.

As well as building the Preston Aisle, the burgh promised to place an embossed memorial brass over Sir William's grave and there would be a separate brass tablet with an inscription recounting how he had brought the relic to Scotland. Whenever the arm bone was solemnly borne in procession, as it would be on St Giles' Day (1 September) each year, Sir William's nearest relative would have the honour of carrying it. The construction of the new aisle was to be undertaken 'in all possible and goodly haste', and the intention was that it would be finished within six or seven years. As is the way with building projects, it seems to have taken a far longer time than anticipated, because set into the roof is a decorative stone with the coat of arms of Lord Hailes, who was not provost of Edinburgh until 1487. Be that as it may, Sir William's carved coat of arms of three unicorns' heads can be seen in his aisle to this day, even though the reliquary and the altar are long gone, destroyed at the Reformation.

Praying for the dead had become a very important activity. Lives during the Middle Ages were shockingly brief. Any available statistics relating to life expectancy are very incomplete, but it is usually estimated that, on average, people could expect to die between the ages of 30 and 35. A significant number of mothers perished in childbirth, as many as half of the babies born failed to survive to adult life and illnesses which today can easily be treated by drugs such as antibiotics were all too often fatal. The Black Death had come to Scotland in 1349 and the parishioners of St Giles' had twice suffered English invasions in just over sixty years, watching their parish church go up in flames. It was hardly surprising if they worried not only about life's dangers but about what would happen to them after death. The Roman Catholic Church taught that the souls of men and women who die without having done sufficient penance for their sins must wait in purgatory, where they are purified by suffering, before they are finally allowed to enter the presence of God. The prayers of those left behind are believed to help in this process of purification, and masses for the dead were believed to be even more effective.

There was a practical problem with this, however. A chaplain could say mass only once a day at his altar, so how could every eager applicant for a memorial mass be satisfied? He either had to found a new altar himself or arrange for a new chaplain to say or sing mass at someone else's altar. Such endowments were known as chantries, from the French 'chanter', meaning to sing. That is the reason why there were at least eighteen side altars in St Giles' by 1466, some in their own aisles, others in existing aisles or bolted to the great pillars which lined the nave. Apart from the high altar, the oldest was the one dedicated to the Blessed Virgin Mary. It stood in its own Lady Aisle. As the mother of Christ, the Virgin is believed to possess great powers of intercession and so it is not surprising to find that parishioners were in the habit of donating money to her altar, in return for prayers for themselves and dead relatives.

Most of the early parishioners have long since faded into anonymity, but in a list of donations drawn up by John Rollo, common clerk of the burgh in 1369, we can catch a fleeting glimpse of some of those who had probably lived two or three generations earlier. Malcolm, son of John, contributed two shillings a year from his land near the Common Vennel, the street leading to St Giles'. His neighbour, John the goldsmith, and Matthew, son of Juliana, who had some property on the north side of the burgh, gave a similar amount.

Scotland might lie at the very northern edge of the known world but most of the early altars in St Giles' were dedicated to saints revered throughout Western Europe. Some were familiar biblical figures, like St John the Baptist, the prophet who had proclaimed the coming of Christ, and St John the Evangelist, the Galilean fisherman who had become a disciple, but there were also exotic figures like St Catherine of Alexandria. If few people today know anything about her, she was one of the most popular medieval saints. She had been an outspoken critic of the Emperor Maxentius, a notorious persecutor of Christians, in the early fourth century. He tried to silence her by proposing marriage to her, but she refused him, saying that she was already the bride of Christ. She suffered martyrdom as a result. Maxentius had a special wheel prepared on which her body was to be broken, but the wheel shattered, and instead she was beheaded. Even so, the 'Catherine wheel' has remained her symbol. She became patron saint of all craftsmen who worked with a wheel, such as potters and spinners, was especially popular with urban elite women and, later on, the name was even given to a firework.

Interestingly, the fifteenth century saw a small flurry of dedications in St Giles' to saints who had a specifically Scottish connection. There were altars to St Andrew, Scotland's patron saint; St Kentigern (Mungo), first bishop of Strathclyde and patron saint of Glasgow; St Ninian, traditionally believed to have converted the Picts to Christianity and St Duthac, a somewhat shadowy figure whose shrine was in Tain, a small royal burgh north of Inverness. Finally, there were three altars which were dedicated not to saints but to important symbols of Christianity: the Holy Cross altar immediately to the left of the high altar, the Holy Blood altar near the north door and the Trinity altar in St Catherine's Aisle.

The very wealthy, like the Duke of Albany, built entire aisles known as chantry chapels for themselves, but that was beyond the resources of the merchants and tradesmen who were Edinburgh's burgesses. As it was, setting up a new altar required a considerable financial outlay, and even arranging for a chaplain to be attached to an existing altar was a complicated business. We have no details of the exact procedure for establishing an altar, but we do know what the prospective founder of a chaplainry had to do. First of all, he had to obtain permission from the burgh authorities, because this was very much the burgh church and they were responsible for its fabric. The donor had to prove to them that he had sufficient funds to pay the chaplain, not just at the present time but for years and even centuries to come.

He would give a piece of land or a series of yearly payments known as annualrents from his various properties, or a combination of the two, and his hope was that his altar could be as near the high altar as possible. He then had to seek the approval of the Bishop (after 1472 Archbishop) of St Andrews, which was usually given as a matter of course. Once all this had been done, the donor would employ a notary to draw up a charter listing the lands and annualrents which he was donating, describing the various masses he desired and laying down a set of rules for the conduct of his chaplain. After that, there would be a small ceremony at which he formally made over the land and annualrents to one of the burgh representatives, and finally he would ask the King to confirm his charter, which the Edinburgh dean of guild put for safe-keeping in the church treasury.

Even so, keeping track of all the revenues involved was no easy task, and in 1386 William Guppild, alderman, a senior member of the burgh council, was complaining that, 'due to the dangers of wars and the continual mortality of men and ignorance of youth', many of the previous donations had been diverted to secular purposes. In future, he decided, he would keep a proper register of the lands and annualrents, and although he noted, with tantalising vagueness, that the altars had been built 'by the gift of burgesses' he did not say who they were. He was, after all, concentrating on noting the current sums of money due and the lands from which they came. The only founder whose identity seems to have been preserved was John Gray, Master of Arts and Medicine. A canon of Aberdeen and rector of the church of Kirkliston, near Edinburgh, it was he who in 1451 established the altar dedicated to St Kentigern.

By the mid-fifteenth century, not only individuals but the craft guilds were founding altars in St Giles'. These were groups of tailors and bakers and goldsmiths and other craftsmen who had banded together to protect their trading rights and the standards of their craft. They looked after their members who had fallen on hard times, their widows and orphans, worried about the status of their incorporation and already contributed to the building work at St Giles' by passing on some of the fines paid by those members who broke their rules. By the fifteenth century, they too were eager to found altars in the parish church. The skinner craft, for instance, in 1451 set up their own altar to that popular protector of travellers, St Christopher. Seventeen members, three of whom bore the surname of Skinner and three who did not have surnames at all, bound themselves to support their chaplain financially. In addition, whenever a master skinner took on a new apprentice, he would have to pay five shillings to the altar and its services, and as soon as the apprentice was fully trained, he too would contribute, according to his ability.

Like the founders of altars, those who established chaplainries were mainly burgesses, men like Roger Hogg, a leading Edinburgh merchant who traded with England, and Sir John Forrester of Corstorphine, son of Adam Forrester the grain merchant who had been involved in the building of the five new south chapels in 1387. Wives were sometimes associated with their husbands in their charters, and a few of the founders were ecclesiastics. John Laing, Bishop of Glasgow, formerly secretary to Mary of Gueldres, wife of James II, established a chaplainry at St Duthac's altar and Thomas de Lauder, master of the famous monastic hospital at Soutra, established another at the altar of St Martin and St Thomas in the Holy Cross Aisle. A graduate of the University of Paris, he later became Bishop of Dunkeld. Business frequently brought people like these to Edinburgh for weeks at a time, particularly when the court was in residence.

So what did the donors expect in return for their contributions? Many of them were anxious to have a burial place for themselves and their families as close as possible to the altar where the prayers for them were said. In 1392, John de Whiteness, his wife Katherine and their children were granted the privilege of being buried in front of the Holy Cross altar because a relative had established a chaplainry there some years earlier, and in like manner Patrick Donald, a member of the bakers' guild, was in 1456 the proud possessor of a gravestone and burial place in front of their altar of St Hubert. The stone may have been there already because it marked the grave of a kinsman, or perhaps Patrick had ordered his own in advance and put it in position to make sure that no-one else usurped that particular spot.

Securing an advantageous burial-place for one's body was important, but of course the services conducted by the chaplain were what really mattered. At first, people asked for a mass on the anniversary of their death, but by the fifteenth century many wanted a requiem mass said every day, or on specific days of the week. With so many altars in the church there had to be a fixed time for each mass, so that the voices of competing chaplains at adjacent altars would not drown each other out. At the appointed hour, the chaplain therefore arrived at the altar and tried to draw in anyone who happened to be standing nearby or passing through the church. The more people who joined in the prayers, the more effective they would be. This done, he would say or sing mass and then proceed to the all-important prayers for the dead.

At one time it had been thought that a mass was most effective if it was for the soul of one person only, but that was obviously not a consideration at St Giles'. The chaplain began with the current king and queen, who would be named, along with a brief indication that all the royal ancestors and successors were also included. Next the founder himself and his immediate relatives were enumerated – his wife and any previous wives, his children, parents, siblings, ancestors and descendants. Sometimes his close friends and his influential patrons were mentioned too. John de Alncorn was obviously a protégé of the Douglas family, for he required prayers to be said for William, 1st Earl of Douglas, his wife Countess Margaret and Sir Archibald Douglas. Finally, the list was rounded off with the provost, bailies and community of Edinburgh, and all the faithful dead. The mass on the anniversary of the donor's death was more elaborate, sung rather than said, with the help of extra chaplains, and a bell was rung through the streets as well as in the church to alert people to come along and take part.

John de Hill, John Earl, Robert Coats and all the other chaplains would have been familiar figures in and about St Giles', but we know little of them. We can only recreate their circumstances from a few stray references and from what we know of chaplains in general. Often a chaplain was a relative of the founder of his chaplainry. Kinship was very important in medieval Scotland and the hope was that a family member was more likely to be reliable than a total stranger. Founders were always wracked by fears that their masses might somehow be discontinued or interrupted, thereby increasing their own time in purgatory. There were all too many instances of chaplains who were lazy and neglectful, went off elsewhere or accepted additional positions which distracted them from attending to their proper duties and so the founder did everything he could to make sure that this did not happen.

Whether or not they were relatives of the founder, most chaplains came from burgess families. They had to be priests, of course, ordained at the age of 24 and probably taking up their position soon after that. Few of them were graduates. In the Middle Ages, a graduate prefixed his name with the title 'Master' but Robert, the two Johns and the majority of their colleagues did not do so. There were no special seminaries at that time for the education of priests and instead they would have gone to the local grammar school to learn Latin and then been trained by a local priest. When a chaplain was appointed, he was solemnly admitted to his office at a small ceremony where a representative of the burgh handed him a ring, his vestments, the service book for his altar and the silver cup for communion. He was expected to live near St Giles', told not to go away anywhere without permission and he was certainly not to employ a substitute. Forfeiture was the penalty for those who broke the rules.

A chaplain was poorly paid and if his founder had granted a piece of land for his support, he either had the hard labour of working it himself or he would, with the founder's permission, rent it out to someone else. John Bryden did this in 1429 with the croft of St Nicholas and it became an increasingly common practice. If annual payments from the founder's properties were the chaplain's source of income, he had to go round collecting them himself. It was no easy task. Sooner or later the property concerned would change hands, when the founder either sold it or died. The new owners would be well aware that they were obliged to pay the yearly sum to an altar but, even if they were churchgoers, they were often reluctant to do so. The result was that the chaplain frequently had to take them to court before he could extract any money from them.

Saying masses for the dead on a daily basis was a depressing occupation and quite a few chaplains tried to relieve the monotony and at the same time improve their financial position by taking on work as notaries, drawing up marriage contracts and wills, and sorting out quarrels about debt. Even so, their position was not good and it was very difficult for them to gain promotion to a more promising benefice. When they did depart, one way or another, the founder's heirs were supposed to supply a successor as soon as possible, often within a specified time. Master John Gray the Aberdeen canon seems to have been fairly relaxed about the matter, for in his founding charter he said that up to forty days could elapse before a new chaplain at his altar of St Kentigern was installed. Alan de Fernley, however, anxiously insisted that his heirs should replace his chaplain at the altar of St Ninian within eight days, otherwise the patronage of the chaplainry would be transferred to the provost, bailies and community of Edinburgh. The Master of Soutra Hospital was, for his part, wary even of the provost and bailies. Perhaps with good reason, he harboured the dark suspicion that at some future date they might move the altar of St Martin and St Thomas from the Holy Cross Aisle to some other part of the church. His charter forbade them to do so, but he obviously did not have much faith in their compliance, for he added that if, in spite of his instructions, they did move it, his heir should have the right to re-establish the chaplainry elsewhere in St Giles'.

Funded by his founder and employed by the burgh, the chaplain was also responsible to the vicar perpetual of St Giles' for the conduct of his professional duties and the vicar was a man of a very different calibre. Despite the past efforts of Scone Abbey, he continued to be nominated by the King and as the years went by, increasingly prominent men were given this important position. William Foulis, vicar in the 1430s and early 1440s, was Keeper of the Privy Seal of Scotland. So too was his successor, William Turnbull, later Bishop of Glasgow and founder of Glasgow University. John Methven, who followed him in the 1450s, was a graduate of St Andrews University and particularly expert in canon law. During an illustrious career he was not only secretary to James II but Master of the Rolls and Clerk Register. On several occasions he was even sent as a royal envoy to the courts of France and England.

Nicholas Otterburn took over after his death and he too acted as an important emissary. Clerk Register, Clerk of the Rolls and secretary to the King, in 1448 he negotiated James II's marriage to Mary of Gueldres and collected her dowry from Philip, Duke of Burgundy. Obviously, these vicars were far too busy elsewhere to celebrate high mass every Sunday and feast day, take baptism, marriage and funeral services or attend to the pastoral care of their parishioners. Instead, a curate would be appointed to carry out these duties but, whatever his shortcomings in the performance of his role, the often absent vicar perpetual added to the lustre of St Giles' by the dignity of his other offices.

The status of their parish church meant a great deal to the burgh. The provost and the magistrates were proud of its fine building, its royal connections, and its growing number of clergy. They were ambitious for it too, and by the early years of the fifteenth century they were eager for it to gain a special status. St Giles' was worthy of being far more than a mere parish church. It could not, of course, become a cathedral. A cathedral was the principal church of a diocese, and the place where the bishop had his throne. St Giles' lay in the diocese of St Andrews which had its own bishop and cathedral, and nothing seemed likely to alter that. There was another possibility, however. Why should it not become a collegiate church?

In spite of the name, a college in this context had nothing to do with education. Its principal function was to supply facilities for masses for the dead and its administration mirrored that of a cathedral, which was run by a dean and a chapter of canons. A collegiate church also had a dean, known as its provost, and a chapter of prebendaries, so called from their prebends, the lands and rents which supported them. More than forty collegiate churches were established in Scotland between the mid-fifteenth and the mid-sixteenth centuries. Some had been founded as private chantry chapels by noblemen, but most were former parish churches which had been granted this additional status. Surely this was an appropriate role for St Giles'?

Of course, people could not simply declare their church to be collegiate. Only the Pope could erect a collegiate church and when he received an application he passed it to a special committee to investigate whether or not the church in question met the necessary criteria. It must occupy a dignified place in the community and possess numerous clergy, a large and beautiful building, splendid vestments, impressive church plate and a sizeable enough income to support its new position. St Giles' seemed to possess all these requirements and on 19 June 1419, Archibald 4th Earl of Douglas, with the provost, bailies and community of Edinburgh, sent a petition to Pope Martin V, asking him to grant the church of St Giles' collegiate status. They pointed out that they already had thirteen perpetual chaplains who could easily be transformed into prebendaries and they laid stress on the fact that they had spent no less than five or six thousand gold crowns on their building during the past few years. Moreover, they promised to provide a further 100 crowns each year in future.

Disappointingly, their petition was not granted and although they were still trying in 1423, they did not receive the reply for which they were hoping. There is no record of why their requests were turned down, but perhaps the Abbey of Scone may yet have been laying some sort of claim to St Giles'. On the other hand, it may have been because the applicants could not show that they had royal support. One of the clauses in their petition proposed that, in future, the chapter of prebendaries instead of the King should nominate the church's provost, something which would hardly be popular with any monarch. Whatever the explanation, the burgh tried again in 1429 after the death of James Lyon, the perpetual vicar. James I had by now been released at last from his long captivity in England and was ruling Scotland with vigour and determination, but there is no evidence that he took any personal interest in Edinburgh's parish church. Indeed, intent on restoring royal rights after his enforced absence, he certainly would not have supported any attempt to remove the patronage of St Giles' from his control and once again the petition to the Pope was rejected.

The burgesses of Edinburgh were determined not to give up. They would bide their time and sooner or later the situation would surely change in their favour. When James I was assassinated by some of his discontented subjects in Perth in February 1437 he was buried in the Carthusian Priory there but a solemn requiem mass for him was celebrated in St Giles' with the Scottish exchequer paying fifty shillings for the white wax candles. His son, James II, was only 6 years old when he inherited the throne, but when he grew up there was an important new phase of building work in St Giles', designed to make it an even more obvious candidate for collegiate status. There is no evidence that James initiated this programme of improvements. He was more interested in fortifications than in modernising churches or even royal residences but it is possible that his wife, Mary of Gueldres, inspired some of the changes.

The daughter of Arnold, Duke of Gueldres, whose lands formed a fertile province in the East Central Netherlands, Mary had been brought up in Brussels, at the elegant and sophisticated court of her great-uncle, Philip the Good, 3rd Duke of Burgundy. Charles VII of France had a hand in arranging her marriage to James II in 1449. Bride and groom seem to have been delighted with each other, and they went on to have four sons and two daughters. During her time in Brussels, Mary had frequently attended services in the great Church of St Gudula, now the city's Cathedral, and the Church and architecture seem to have been two of the leading interests of this able and energetic queen consort. She and Bishop Kennedy of St Andrews established a Franciscan friary in Edinburgh and later on, in her widowhood, she founded beside it the Collegiate Church of the Holy Trinity, built Ravenscraig Castle in Fife and employed a royal carpenter to make a new chamber and stables for her at Falkland Palace.

During her years in Scotland, an army of masons and wrights was at work on St Giles'. It used to be thought that during the 1450s the east wall of the church was moved much further east, enlarging the chancel, but archaeological excavations in the 1980s revealed that the east end was extended only slightly in that direction. What was dramatically different was that the entire chancel was heightened. Higher arches were built to support a superb, elaborately vaulted roof. A row of windows forming a clerestory was inserted above the arches at either side and elegant new, fluted pillars were put up in the two bays nearest the east wall. Finally, a great bell was purchased from Flanders. It was made in 1460 by John and William Hoerhen and it is hard to believe that Mary of Gueldres did not facilitate its acquisition. Although it was officially commissioned by the provost and bailies of Edinburgh, it had the arms of Guelderland on its side, along with devices of the Virgin and Child. A Latin inscription recorded the date and makers' names and announced, 'I mourn the dead: I call the living' adding, in accordance with a common medieval superstition, 'I disperse the thunder'. The new bell was triumphantly brought back by sea, and hung up in the church tower.

James II died that same year, killed by an exploding cannon at the siege of Roxburgh. His son and heir James III was still a child and so Mary of Gueldres ruled Scotland on his behalf, advised by a council led by Bishop Kennedy. Possibly it was during her regency that the building work was finished and four carved, painted and gilded coats of arms were put up on one of the new pillars at the east end. The first is James II's, the second is his Queen's, the third belongs to James III and the fourth has the fleur-de-lis of the French King, Charles VII. The fact that James II's shield lacks the customary tressure or border across the top has suggested to heraldic experts that he was dead by the time it was erected. Nearby is a matching Town's Pillar, with the arms of Edinburgh, along with those of Bishop Kennedy, Nicholas Otterburn the vicar of St Giles' and that famous benefactor, Sir William Preston of Gorton. Otterburn died in 1461, Mary of Gueldres two years later. Whatever part these individuals played in the alterations to the chancel, the St Giles' they left behind them had become arguably the most beautiful burgh church in Scotland.

In 1466, the burgh authorities confidently petitioned the Pope once more for collegiate status, having taken the precaution of issuing a charter promising that the Crown would always have the right to nominate the church's provost. Edinburgh, their petition said, was the place where the King of Scots, and very many of the bishops, abbots and nobles spent most of their time, not to mention the crowds of people who visited it every year. St Giles' enjoyed royal patronage, had numerous clergy and an ample income. In other words, it met all the necessary criteria. The petition was taken to Rome and the following spring word reached Scotland that, on 22 February 1467, Pope Paul II had issued the much desired bull transforming St Giles' into a collegiate church.

In November 1469 James III, at 17, began to rule for himself. Six months after that, on 30 April 1470, another petition about St Giles' was sent to the Pope, this time by the King. He pointed out that he was living for most of the year in Edinburgh and 'bears a peculiar devotion to the said church, as honoured by his own presence'. He intended to endow it with many privileges but he was concerned in case Patrick Graham, Bishop of St Andrews, whom he disliked, might infringe these new rights. He therefore asked the Pope to exempt St Giles' from the Bishop's jurisdiction and instead take it under his own protection. This was not an unusual procedure with regard to collegiate churches and, on 30 April 1470, Paul II issued another bull, granting James's request. In return, the provost and prebendaries of St Giles' promised to pay to the Holy See each year, on the Vigil of St Peter and St Paul the Apostle, one ounce of pure gold.

With the papal bull, the chaplains of St Giles' were transformed into prebendaries, supported by their previous revenues, and Master William Forbes the vicar became the first collegiate provost, with a stipend of 220 merks a year from the teinds and other church revenues. A graduate of St Andrews University and formerly an Aberdeen canon, he would be no absentee priest. Unlike his predecessors, he was never called upon to occupy any important office of state, nor was he sent off on ambassadorial missions. Instead, he devoted himself to his task of organising his chapter and administering his church for almost forty years. Officially collegiate at last and gratifyingly independent, St Giles' had entered a new period of importance and prosperity.

CHAPTER 3

The Collegiate Church

James III's personal devotion to St Giles' seems to have lasted for the rest of his life. When his 18-month-old son Prince James was betrothed to the 3-year-old English Princess Cicely in 1475, he stipulated that the dowry be paid in annual instalments in St Giles' and, when the English decided later to break the match, their chief herald, Garter King of Arms, appeared in the porch at the south door and read out a parchment to that effect. It was James III who made Edinburgh the fixed capital of Scotland, bringing many benefits to the town as a result, and when he granted its sheriffship to its provost, bailies and council, he ordered them to give some of the profits to St Giles' in return, not for any building work but for the celebration of the services.

They were also told to sing a requiem mass each year on 3 August, the anniversary of his father's death, with additional prayers for his own soul and his prosperity. James's arbitrary methods of rule were by this time earning him more and more enemies in his realm. If it was true that, as one of his critics alleged, he spent more time singing and playing on instruments than he did in the defence of the Borders and the administration of justice, then the St Giles' services with their fine choral singing must have brought this strange, enigmatic monarch some quiet moments of solace. His reign lasted until 1488, when his subjects rose against him, his army was defeated at the Battle of Sauchieburn and he was assassinated as he fled the field.

James III's son, the affable, multilingual James IV, succeeded him and continued the royal connection with St Giles'. In an effort to promote

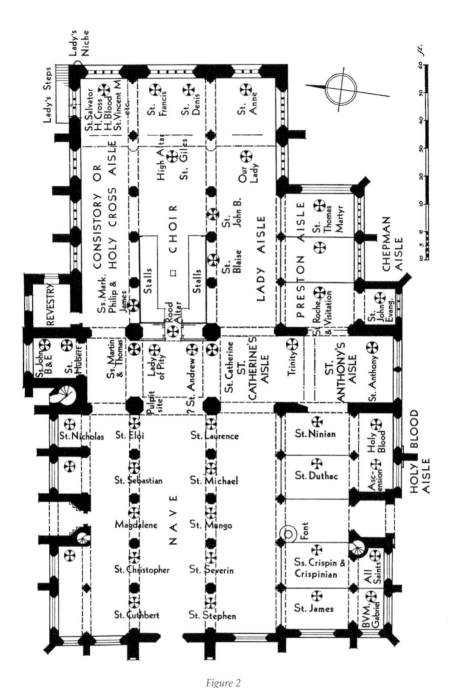

Figure 2
Plan of St Giles' before the Reformation, by George Hay, from his article
'The Late Medieval Development of the High Kirk of St Giles', Edinburgh'
in *Proceedings of the Society of Antiquaries of Scotland*, volume 107 (1975–6), page 255.
(© Society of Antiquaries of Scotland)

peace with the neighbouring kingdom, he married Henry VII of England's daughter Margaret in 1503. When he brought her to Edinburgh, the provost and clergy of the collegiate church came in procession to meet them, bearing the reliquary with the arm bone of St Giles', which the King solemnly kissed. By that time, Master Gavin Douglas, the accomplished and energetic son of Archibald Douglas, 5th Earl of Angus, had succeeded William Forbes as provost. Passionately interested in humanism, Douglas was a distinguished poet who spent most of his leisure hours at St Giles' translating the whole of Virgil's *Aeneid* into Scots. He finally completed it in 1513, just days before Scotland suffered a terrible disaster.

Despite the treaty of perpetual peace, Scotland and England were at war again. Henry VIII had attacked France, and the French persuaded James to support them by invading England. This he did, only to be killed leading the charge at the Battle of Flodden. His army was routed and the Archbishop of St Andrews, the Bishop of the Isles, nine earls and fourteen lords died with him that day. When the devastating news reached Edinburgh, the great bell of St Giles' tolled, summoning the remaining men to defend the burgh against a possible invasion, while the women were advised to go to the church and pray. Requiem masses for the King were sung in St Giles' and, two years later, Alexander Chalmers the painter was supplying 140 painted coats of arms for that year's memorial mass.

Memories of the national disaster were slow to fade, and in 1528 Walter Chepman, the prosperous merchant who had introduced printing into Scotland under James's patronage, decided to commemorate the dead monarch. Chepman had already founded the new aisle in St Giles' which still bears his name, with an altar dedicated to St John the Evangelist. Now he established another chapel at the foot of the churchyard. It was dedicated to St Salvator, the crucified Christ, and in his foundation charter Chepman gave instructions for masses for the souls of 'our late most powerful lord, King James IV, by the grace of God King of Scotland, and the souls of those most noble and faithful followers who, with him, were slain in defence of the safety of their country, in conflict with the English at Flodden'.

The new king, James V, was only 17 months old when his father was killed, and although when he grew up he was not noted for his personal piety, he continued the family tradition of sending offerings to the altars, while his devout French wife, Mary of Guise, was a regular visitor to the church. By their day, the population of Edinburgh had grown considerably and St Giles' was no longer at the eastern edge of the town but at the centre, surrounded by other buildings. At its north-west corner stood the

Tolbooth, a formidable stone structure where parliament and the courts of justice met, and wrongdoers were imprisoned. Immediately in front of it were goldsmiths' shops, and the High Street was tightly packed with more shops, houses and taverns, interspersed with the entries to the long narrow lanes called closes which ran off it at right angles. Noblemen and leading ecclesiastics had to spend a considerable amount of time in the capital and so they rented or built houses there, the size of holding rather than location indicating the status of the proprietor. Burgesses found themselves living next door to Robert Blackadder, Bishop of Glasgow, and William Gill's small tavern stood beside Hew, Earl of Eglinton's mansion in its spacious grounds. Crammed in between the High Street and St Giles' was a further line of luckenbooths (locked booths, in other words, shops) known as Booth Row. An unpleasant lane ran between it and the north wall of the church. Bluntly termed 'The Stinking Style', it led eastwards to the market cross and Our Lady's Steps, which formed a short passageway and was so called because of the statue of the Virgin Mary in a niche on the church wall above.

James III had built a royal mint at the east end of St Giles', where the Thistle Chapel now stands, and so burials now took place on part of the long, south-facing slope leading down from the church to the street called the Cowgate. Bounded on the east by a more reputable lane, the Common Vennel, where a number of the prebendaries and chaplains lived, the churchyard was enclosed by a stone wall intended to keep out stray animals. Access for parishioners was by means of a gate and several stiles. In the churchyard stood a cluster of buildings. There was the song school, where boys were trained for the choir, with a house called The Gallery, there was a stable for the provost's horses and there was the hospital of St Giles'. Very little is known about this last establishment, beyond the fact that the curate acted as its almoner and the Abbot of Kilwinning was patron of one of the beds. Whether its patients were lepers is unknown, but perhaps not, for there was already a leper hospital in Edinburgh, in St Mary's Vennel. On the lower reaches of the churchyard, the burgh built about twenty shops which they rented out to the local shoemakers, the revenue going towards the support of the church.

Adjoining the west side of the churchyard was the glebe of the provost of St Giles', with his manse standing in its spacious garden. The garden had been even more spacious at one time, but twice sections of it had been taken over by the churchyard. In 1478 William Forbes had parted with a stretch of it, noting that 'my parishioners daily multiply and increase, and when they die can obtain no place of burial either within or without the church'. Almost twenty years later, in 1496, he sacrificed the north part of his garden for that same purpose, in return for a promise by the burgh authorities that when he died they would establish an annual mass at the high altar in his memory. He was no doubt buried close to that altar.

Overlooking churchyard and manse was the main door of St Giles'. The church had four doors, one on each side of the building, but it was the south door with its large porch that was the principal entrance. It was opened at five o'clock in the morning in summer for matins, the first service of the day, and at six o'clock in winter, when it would still have been pitch dark. The goldsmiths' chaplain had to be there at that early hour to celebrate his weekly mass at their altar, in accordance with his foundation charter. The church closed again after the last evening service. Pilgrims by now came from far and wide to see the arm bone of St Giles'. Crowding in past the font, which stood on a paved area just inside the south door, they found themselves in a large, bright, imposing space. Even on dark days, there was light from the large chandelier which hung in the very centre of the building, there were candles on all the window sills, a candle on the pulpit and of course there were candles on the altars.

Beneath the visitors' feet, particularly round about the altars, much of the floor was paved with tombstones. Some of these would simply be incised stones, but many had memorial brasses with inscriptions and very often with the figures of those they commemorated: a solitary tradesman, perhaps, with the tools of his craft, or a couple, the wife in a long dress, the husband in an equally long gown.

In part, the brass was a proud recognition of the importance of the deceased, but its main purpose was to encourage those who passed by to say a prayer for the souls of those interred below. Because of the limited space inside the church, people were now inheriting burial places from their fathers. Women often did not need their own graves because they would be buried beside their husbands, and so in 1522 Isobel Fyfe resigned the stone of her father, John Fyfe the flesher, into the hands of the dean of guild, the burgh magistrate who supervised the expenditure on the fabric of St Giles'. He then transferred it to John Cunningham and his wife. Others seem to have been dissatisfied with the position of their family grave. Sir Thomas Tod had been pleased enough with his future grave and stone in front of the altar of St Francis, behind the high altar, but in 1522 his son exchanged them with John Marjoribanks, who owned a position not far away, on the north side of the altar of the Blessed Virgin. The new owners of a brass would either alter the inscription on it or have it removed from its stone, turned over and an appropriate design engraved on the back.

Lamplight and candlelight would have cast a glow on the memorial brasses, and when the sun shone the walls and probably the roof vaults of the church would have reflected light too, because they were plastered and limewashed with white in the customary manner of the time. High above the heads of visitors were vividly painted and gilded carvings, while brightly coloured images of saints would have stood in niches in the walls. Even the great stone pillars were colourful. During late nineteenth-century conservation work it was found that those at the east end had layer upon layer of red, blue and green paint which the architect and masons judged to be 'hundreds of years old'. The green may have dated from the post-Reformation period, but the red and blue would have been earlier.

As for the windows, there is tantalisingly little information about the medieval glass in St Giles'. During excavations in the early 1980s, tiny fragments were discovered in the soil and some of these have been set into the upper parts of windows in the Lower Aisle. However, fewer than 10 per cent of them show any sign of painted decoration. Two of the little pieces may have been from thirteenth-century grisaille work, the name given to glass which had geometrical patterns and leaves in shades of grey. Otherwise, there was a tiny leaf, a possible piece of script and what could be the furry edge of a heraldic beast. Judging by the magnificence of the internal furnishings, it could well be that there was expensive, imported, multicoloured stained glass in the windows, but in the later Middle Ages there was an increasing preference for grisaille, because it gave more light, and this may have been the case at St Giles'.

Walking towards the high altar, pilgrims had to weave their way among all the side altars in the nave and at the crossing, some partitioned off by stone or timber walls, others with curtains. By 1500, there were at least twenty-nine side altars and by 1560 there were almost fifty. This was a sign not only of people's continuing concern with prayers for the dead, but of the wealth of the St Giles' benefactors. By way of comparison, St Mary's Church in Haddington is a very similar size of building, but it had only seventeen side altars. The Virgin Mary continued to be the most popular dedication in St Giles' and in addition to her altar in the Lady Aisle there were eventually altars of the Visitation of the Virgin and St Roche, Our Lady of Pity and the Virgin and St Gabriel. The latter was founded by Sir

Alexander Lauder, provost of Edinburgh, shortly before his death at the Battle of Flodden in 1513.

Sir Alexander's widow, Dame Janet Paterson, subsequently made a series of donations to the altar of St Sebastian, where her father had established a chaplainry. Women benefactors were increasingly founding chantries. They were usually wealthy widows, like Dame Janet or Isabel Williamson, one of the best-known female merchants in Scotland, who had supplied the royal household with imported velvets and satins in the 1470s. St Giles' also had altars now to St Margaret of Scotland and to Thomas à Becket, the martyred Archbishop of Canterbury. Founded in 1503, his may have been established in connection with James IV's marriage to Princess Margaret of England. More of the crafts had altars too – St Anne for the tailors, Saints Crispin and Crispian for the shoemakers and St Mark for the clothmakers, shearers and bonnetmakers.

Each of these altars was furnished as richly as possible. There are no paintings or drawings from such an early era to show us what they looked like, but the records of the Incorporation of Hammermen of Edinburgh present a vivid picture of their particular altar in the first half of the sixteenth century. It was dedicated to their patron, St Eloi, and it stood at the left side of the nave, not far from the present position of the pulpit. Made of wood, it was covered with a red and green cloth, its green frontal decorated with silver crests. Above it hung a large, rectangular canopy trimmed with lace and red ribbons, the underside made of red and yellow buckram. The curtains at either side were changed to suit the seasons of the Church year.

The principal feature of the altar was a statue of St Eloi, presumably of carved and painted wood, carrying a hammer, for he had been a goldsmith before he became a preacher in Flanders and a founder of monasteries. Symbols of the hammerman's craft were suspended from an iron rod above his head: hammers, crowns and triangles. A carved wooden angel stood at each corner of the altar, and three candles on it were lit for services. A simple tabernacle placed in the centre contained the reserved sacrament, those consecrated wafers left over from the previous mass and reverently kept for distribution to the sick. Above it hung the obligatory lamp which was never extinguished. Cruets with silver vessels for wine and water stood on the corporal, a special square of cloth, in this instance embroidered with red silk and gold thread, and there were earthenware jars of fresh flowers by way of decoration.

Most splendid of all, of course, was the high altar. It had probably been moved further east by this time to make room in front of it for the choir stalls which faced each other across the chancel's central aisle. Even so, it was not right up against the east wall, for behind it were the altars of St Francis and St Denis. Any complete description of it is sadly lacking but we do know that it had a very ornate reredos (screen) with carved or painted and gilded scenes from the life of Christ. In customary fashion, a canopy was suspended over the altar to protect it from dust falling from the high roof, and beneath the canopy hung the pyx, the container for the reserved sacrament. It would have been in the shape of a dove or, in French style, a small tower and made of precious metal. The large candelabrum above the altar may have been the cause of an alarming fire in 1498 when the canopy caught light and both reredos and reserved sacrament were destroyed.

The altar was covered with the customary piece of tapestry, which was cleaned with a sponge specially purchased for the purpose and, after the fire, the reserved sacrament seems to have been kept in a very large and elaborate tabernacle known as the Eucharist, which stood on the altar cloth rather than being hung above it. Made of silver gilt and weighing seven pounds and two ounces, it was set with a sapphire, two pearls and other precious and semi-precious stones. Four gold bells hung from it along with a heart set with pearls and a little gold bell enamelled blue. Lower down there was a smaller gold heart, a great cross set with three pearls, a little cross with three pearls and an image of the Virgin Mary.

The other ornaments of the high altar were also of silver, the cross with its heavily weighted base, two cruets, the chalice, the paten (the plate on which the Host was carried to and from the altar), a spoon, two candlesticks and two great candlesticks, along with two censers and a vessel in the shape of a boat for incense. A 'round Eucharist' weighing twenty-three ounces would have been the coffer, the small round box in which the reserved sacrament was actually taken to the sick. The reliquary with the arm bone of St Giles may have stood on the high altar too. Certainly it always heads any list of church plate at the time. Weighing five pounds three and a half ounces, it was set with forty pearls and seventeen other precious stones as well as the diamond ring on the little finger. The church also had a very large statue of St Giles himself, vividly painted and wearing a cloak of crimson velvet trimmed with gold.

When the statue was carried through the town on St Giles' Day, that was always a great occasion. In preparation the church was dusted, swept and washed outside and in, and the interior was decorated with flowers and greenery. Brass work was scoured, the organ was tuned, the arm bone reliquary was polished and the statue of St Giles was freshly painted. In 1556, the sum of six pence was paid for 'bearing him to and from the painter', Walter Binning, who lived beside the churchyard of the Blackfriars and was frequently employed by the Queen Regent, Mary of Guise. When 1 September finally arrived, minstrels preceded the image of the saint as it was carried through the streets on a wooden stand, followed by clergy, monks, friars, town dignitaries, harpers, trumpeters, drummers and players on the shawms, an early form of oboe. There was even a bull led along at the end of a tow, possibly in imitation of a similar French custom whereby a prize ox was taken through the streets in procession. The arm bone was also publicly exhibited on Relic Sunday. No details of that occasion appear to have survived, but it seems that people paid to see it, augmenting the church revenues.

We have no knowledge of the craftsmen who created the statues, angels, the church plate or the heavy brass lectern which stood in the chancel and weighed over ninety-three stone, but many of those items would have been imported. Scottish merchants regularly brought back altarpieces, tapestries, books of hours and statues of saints, vestments and memorial brasses from France and Flanders. Indeed, soon after 1526, the deacon of the goldsmiths, Thomas Rhynd, came home from the continent with a statue of Our Lady of Loretto for their altar. It stood in St Eloi's Aisle, which they had recently acquired from the merchants. Rhynd then sent to Flanders for brass pillars which would possibly have separated the Aisle from the rest of the church, and one of his successors imported a Flemish tapestry woven with a design featuring Our Lady of Loretto.

Not only were the furnishings at the side altars ornate, but the masses were becoming increasingly elaborate. Donors now gave instructions about the number of candles to be lit on the altar in question and told the chaplain to go and sprinkle the founder's tomb with holy water after the mass was over. The anniversary high masses were even more impressive, with as many as ten, sixteen or even twenty chaplains taking part and it had become customary to encourage the poor to join in the prayers for the dead by promising them food and drink. Bread, meat, fish, butter, cheese and wine were placed on a table nearby before the mass began, and were distributed afterwards. Additional portions were sent to the Friars Minor and the leper hospital in St Mary's Vennel.

Matins, high mass and vespers were, of course, celebrated at the high altar itself. The large organ in the organ loft was played for services there, with the prebendaries and choirboys almost certainly singing polyphonic choral music by composers such as the early sixteenth-century Scot, Robert

Carver. The visual splendour of these services must have been considerable too, particularly on feast days, because of the magnificence of the vestments worn by the officiating clergy. The best set, with garments for three priests, was made of cloth of gold and there was another cloth of gold set known as 'Dame Lauder's stand', no doubt the gift of that generous donor, Dame Janet Paterson, widow of Sir Alexander Lauder. Other sets were made of white damask, red velvet, black velvet, blue velvet, cloth of silver and green damask, all no doubt elaborately trimmed with gold and silver braid and intricately embroidered. The altar cloth, the chasuble worn by the priest and the banners on the walls were changed to suit the seasons of the liturgical year: white for Christmas Day and Easter, violet for Lent, green for Trinity to Advent and red for various saints' days.

Not all services were conducted at one of the altars, however. As we have seen, baptisms took place near the main door, for the baby's entrance into the Christian community. Fonts of the period were made of stone or wood, with a lead basin and some, like the St Giles' font, had a cover. Precautions always had to be taken to make sure that no-one purloined for purposes of witchcraft the holy water remaining after a baptism. On dark days the font was lit by three candles in an iron candlestick. As for marriages, banns for the wedding were read out in the parish churches of bride and groom on at least three Sundays before the marriage ceremony and then on the wedding day bride, groom, relatives and guests assembled at the south door, where the vows would be exchanged, for the couple too were entering into a new life.

The bride would not be wearing white, but her best clothes. If she had never been married before, her hands would be bare, but if she was a widow, then she would be wearing gloves. In the presence of the officiating priest, she and the groom swore on the Gospels that there was no reason why they should not marry. The bride's father gave her away and the priest placed her right hand in the right hand of the groom. The groom said, 'I take thee to my wedded wife', she replied, 'I take thee to my wedded husband', they both repeated, 'In the name of the Father and the Son and the Holy Spirit' and then they kissed. After a pause, the priest enquired about the bride's dowry and the jointure, the sum of money the husband settled on her in case he died before her. Satisfactory answers given, the priest said a prayer and blessed them. Only after that did the company go into the church for nuptial mass.

Probably it was the curate who read out the banns and performed wedding services. He was the provost's assistant and although his title sounds a lowly one, he was also known as the vicar, the first prebendary and, even more grandly, the president of the collegiate church. He had his own chamber above the song school, an allowance of twenty-five merks a year in addition to his prebend and when the provost was away, it was he who officiated instead. There were fifteen prebendaries apart from the curate, and when a new one was chosen, he was formally admitted by the provost, who gave him his choir stall and his place in the chapter, while he in return promised to obey his superiors and keep the church's statutes.

Some of the prebendaries were graduates, and they would all have been expected to be skilled in Gregorian chant and polyphonic music. Two of them had specific roles. The fifteenth prebendary was the sacristan and the sixteenth was leader of the choir. The sacristan combined his role with that of parish clerk, but his main duties concerned the chancel. He was responsible for seeing that the organ was played and the bells rung: the great bell, the common bell, the curfew bell and the dead bell for funerals. One of these was also known as the Mary bell, but it is impossible to say which. He also looked after service books, the church plate in the jewel house and the garments in the vestry. There were other, more mundane tasks as well, and Henry Loch, sacristan in 1554, had to be firmly reminded of his duty to supply light, fire and water for all the chaplains as well as washing and sweeping the chancel once a week.

The leader of the choir was also master of the song school. There, the four official St Giles' boy choristers were taught, along with choirboys from other churches and boys hoping to become priests. They learned how to sing and play the organ and other instruments such as virginals. In the mid-sixteenth century, St Giles' had a master of the song school who was a distinguished organist and composer of church music. John Fethy had previously held similar appointments at Dundee and Aberdeen and had studied on the continent. Indeed, he is credited with having introduced into Scotland the skill of playing the organ with all ten fingers instead of using merely the middle three on each hand, as was customary. He retired in 1551, but four years later he was still being paid a fee for tuning the organ for St Giles' Day. The song school itself had fallen into a state of disrepair by then, but the new master, Edward Henderson, oversaw the building in the churchyard of a new school with a thatched roof.

Apart from their professional duties, we have little evidence as to the lifestyle of Fethy and his colleagues, but the situation of the canons at Glasgow Cathedral in the 1530s may be taken as being more or less comparable. There, forgetting his vow of celibacy, Master Adam Colquhoun the canon lived with the woman who was his wife in all but name and their children. We can see from his will that his house was luxuriously appointed, with Flemish furniture, velvet cushions, silver plate and a chiming clock. He even had a parrot and, like St Giles, a tame hind. Archery and hare coursing were among his worldly enthusiasms, nor did he always dress as a priest. He certainly had surplices, hoods and the other requisite vestments, but he also had a fur-lined damask gown, a crimson velvet doublet lined with scarlet and a velvet bonnet sewn with gold. By way of contrast, his friend James Houston the sub-dean at Glasgow gave most of his wealth to the Church, his will was short and simple and his few clothes were black.

These are two extremes, of course, but they do demonstrate the wide variations in behaviour which were no doubt to be found in Edinburgh as well as Glasgow. A religious vocation, real or assumed, was not seen by many priests as necessitating an austere life. It is well known that a significant number of churchmen ignored their vow of chastity and illicitly enjoyed the companionship of the otherwise perfectly respectable women bluntly termed 'concubines'. Even Cardinal David Beaton, Archbishop of St Andrews, had a permanent partner who was the mother of his eight children. In common with benefactors throughout Western Europe, most of the donors of St Giles' chantries now found it necessary to insert in their foundation charters a clause insisting that their chaplain should neither take a concubine nor waste his time playing at cards or dice.

The spiritual and the secular were intermingled in other ways too, and St Giles', like other parish churches, was not simply a sacred space where people came to worship. It also fulfilled the role of meeting place for the entire community. Friends came there to gossip, their babies cried, their children played on the floor and squabbled, the poor arrived eagerly hoping to find a table set out with food, young men and women flirted, stray dogs got in, snarling and barking and the only people to be turned away were miscreants who looked as though they were up to no good, and lepers and plague victims, who must not be allowed near anyone else.

People came on business too, for this was where they could find a lawyer, a notary who had set up his table in the nave and could give advice on debts and petty disputes and draw up marriage contracts and wills. Margaret Murray of Blackbarony's brother Andrew arrived in March

1530 at an unnamed altar in St Giles' to require her reluctant fiancé Henry Wardlaw, Laird of Corry, to implement their marriage contract and marry her. Whether he was successful is not recorded. On an even more dramatic note, Robert, Lord Maxwell appeared personally before the altar of the Virgin Mary on 5 February 1533 to beg the pardon of Robert Dalziel of that Ilk for having killed his grandfather. Reconciled, the two men promised to be friends in future.

Unseemly as it might appear to us, those who had mortgaged their land and now wished to redeem it were usually required by the original agreement to count out the money on one of the altars in St Giles', this being seen as an insurance against cheating. So, Thomas Wemyss made his way into the church on 18 May 1500, carrying two boxes. He had mortgaged some land to the Keith family, but now he had gathered together the necessary money to get it back. Opening the boxes, he counted out upon the high altar itself gold unicorns, French crowns, Scots crowns, ducats, rose nobles and gold angel nobles to the value of 120 merks. He then waited expectantly, but to his dismay Andrew and Gilbert Keith, his creditors, refused to accept the money. This was not because some of the coins were foreign, for the coinages of other countries were current in Scotland. They must have had some other objection. Thomas Wemyss protested but they would not budge, and so he angrily gathered up his coins, put them back in their boxes and retreated, declaring ominously that he would sue the Keiths.

He probably intended to take the matter to an important church court, the consistory court, which met in St Giles'. The Holy Cross Aisle in the north-west corner had been permanently fitted out for the purpose. Presided over by the representative of the Archbishop of St Andrews known as the Official of Lothian, a well-qualified judge, the court heard cases concerning marriages, wills, slander, disputes over money and goods, and crimes affecting churchmen. Indeed, it was there that a chaplain, not necessarily from St Giles', was tried for being involved in the murder of Cardinal Beaton in 1546. When the Consistory Aisle, as it was now known, needed a new roof in 1555, the dean of guild acted swiftly and twelve great joists were bought from a Dutchman, along with other timber and nails from different sources. Repairs were not always undertaken so quickly and, that same August, James Carmichael the dean of guild was complaining bitterly to the burgh provost and council that he had several times warned them about the state of the window in the east gable, which was liable to fall down at any moment, destroying St Denis's altar below it. A little expenditure would put matters right, but they had done nothing and he wanted his concern to be recorded in case the worst happened.

In spite of that, St Giles' was never neglected in the way that some churches were. Also in 1555, 3,900 slates costing £19:10/- were brought by sea from Dundee to re-roof 'the body of the kirk', from the steeple to the west door, and Patrick Gowan was regularly employed to 'dicht' (dust) the gutters. When the steeple clock stopped, it was carefully taken down to Leith in a covered cart to be repaired, and then painted with red lead when it came back, to prevent it from rusting. Peter Baxter was kept busy pointing the entire building and Thomas Watson the church glazier was paid four pounds a year for life to take down faulty glass in the windows and replace it with a mixture of old and new panels as well as repairing the leads, the dean of guild supplying the ladders and scaffolding that he needed. Most of this work was in the way of normal repairs, but on one occasion two panels of glass fifteen feet long in all had to be put in a window in the Consistory Aisle after thieves broke in through it.

The dean of guild also saw to the lighting, minor repairs to furnishings and the cleaning of the nave. He supplied ropes for lowering the large chandelier hanging in the middle of the church and the one in the chancel. He ordered locks for doors and for the choir's book cupboard and had a new lectern made for the choristers. Then as now, special efforts at cleaning were made before important occasions such as Easter and Christmas or a visitation from the Archbishop of St Andrews. The brass lectern and pillars were scoured, the wooden pulpit was waxed and, in April 1557, two dozen heather besoms were bought to sweep away the 'mouswabbis' (cobwebs) on walls and windows all over the kirk.

Most of the additions to the building were already in place by 1466, but one or two important projects were undertaken after that, notably the erection of the stone crown on the tower around 1500. Unfortunately there are no building accounts to give the details, but a list of rules laid down by the burgh in 1491 for the master mason and his men may well relate to that major undertaking. They were to work each day in summer from the stroke of five in the morning and 'continue busily' until the clock struck seven in the evening, with two half-hour breaks and a couple of hours off in the middle of the day. In winter they could work only during daylight hours, of course. If any of them neglected their tasks, they were penalised by a reduction in their wages.

Another aisle was added to the church in 1518. Increasingly, members of craft guilds were forming themselves into confraternities, religious organisations whose members wished to support a particular altar and receive various privileges in the way of special services in return. Some years earlier the prestigious Merchant Guild had formed the Confraternity of the Holy Blood with James IV himself as a member. St Eloi's Aisle was now too small for them and they probably paid for the building of their new aisle with its two bays on the south side of the church. High mass was sung there every Wednesday and when it was omitted on 27 February 1511 Gavin Douglas found himself in serious trouble with the burgh authorities. The Confraternity's altar, dedicated to the Holy Blood, was richly furnished with a silver-gilt chalice, a silver cross and other precious ornaments and vestments, probably including the famous Fetternear Banner which depicts Christ with all his wounds (see Plate 1). It is preserved to this day in the Museum of Scotland, a vivid reminder of the intensity of spiritual feeling in the early sixteenth century.

Finally, the 1550s saw some improvements at the east end of St Giles'. Walter Binning painted two great and eighteen smaller panels to be placed in the chancel, as well as two great coats of arms and two small ones. New stalls were provided for the prebendaries. The stalls on the north side may have been imported, but the row on the south side was made by Andrew Mansioun, a French carver probably brought over to Scotland by Mary of Guise. He had carved the cradle for her first short-lived Scottish son, he was employed by her husband James V at Stirling Castle and he would later work on the King's tomb in Holyrood Abbey. Once the stalls were finished, the burgh began refurbishing the Lady Aisle. In 1556–7 it was enclosed with stone partition walls panelled with wood, the gravestones in the floor were taken up, repaired and then carefully replaced, and brass pillars from the continent were erected.

Contributions towards the pillars came from James Carmichael the dean of guild and other local dignitaries who were rewarded by being allowed to display on them shields with their coats of arms. Andrew Mansioun then carved an elaborate new stall for Mary of Guise herself. At Easter 1558 it was carried to the high altar when she attended mass. There is no documentary proof, but it is tempting to speculate that it was she who had inspired the Aisle's refurbishment. James V was dead by now and, ruling as regent for their daughter Mary, Queen of Scots, she was determinedly trying to improve the administration of Scotland and strengthen its alliance with France. There was, however, growing opposition to her policies, and the Roman Catholic Church was under threat. Indeed, as long ago as 26 May 1535, Master Andrew Johnston, chaplain at St Andrew's altar in St Giles', had left the country because he was a heretic.

CHAPTER 4

St Giles' and the Reformation

One night in July 1558, a group of Protestants broke into the collegiate church and stole the large statue of St Giles. Surreptitiously they crossed the High Street and clambered down the steep slope beyond to the Nor' Loch. There they threw the image into the loch, 'to drown him', but seeing that this had done little damage, they fished the statue out again, presumably dried it off and set fire to it. Mary of Guise and the Roman Catholic authorities were horrified when they heard the news. Apart from the sacrilege involved, St Giles' Day was fast approaching and how could the celebrations proceed without the central figure?

The Archbishop of St Andrews sent a stern letter ordering Edinburgh's provost and magistrates either to find the remains of the old image and repair it or, if that were not possible, have a new one made at their own expense. He angrily threatened to excommunicate them if they did not obey, but the council appealed to the Pope and no action was taken against them. Meanwhile, the prebendaries knew that the Franciscan friars had a smaller image of the saint, and they asked if they could borrow it. The Franciscans were reluctant, fearing that they would never see it again, and prudently asked for a sum of money as security. Reassured by some silver coins, they handed over the statue and it was taken to St Giles' and nailed to the wooden frame on which it would be carried through the streets.

On 1 September, the customary procession set off to the sound of trumpets, drums and bagpipes. Fearing trouble, the Queen Regent

43

decided to lead it in person. Mary of Guise was in her early 40s now, a tall, commanding figure much hated by those of the Reformed faith. She was, after all, a daughter of the Guise family, cultivated intellectuals who had nonetheless earned themselves an unenviable reputation for their persecution of Protestants. It was twenty years now since she had left France to come to Scotland as the bride of James V and, as she said herself, she had not known as much as a month of rest since then. Instead of retiring to her native land after her husband's early death, she had determinedly stayed on. She sent her daughter Mary, Queen of Scots to marry the heir to the French throne, wrested the regency from the Scottish Earl of Arran and was now doing her best to modernise the country. To her enemies, however, it seemed that she was bent on making Scotland nothing more than a satellite state of France.

Behind the Queen Regent walked the St Giles' provost, prebendaries and chaplains, as well as monks and friars and other priests, with the statue of the saint on his frame, drums beating and ecclesiastical banners floating overhead. Crowds surged forward to see the spectacle as the procession slowly wound its way along the traditional route. Everything seemed to be going well, and at the Canongate market cross they stopped. This was where it had been arranged that several Protestants would formally give up their new faith that day. First, however, Mary of Guise had arranged to honour Sandy Carpenter, a wealthy burgess, by taking dinner in his house. She went inside, but no sooner had she disappeared from view than some Protestants pushed their way through the throng as if eager to help to carry the statue. Lifting it up on their shoulders, they shook it violently to try to dislodge it, but of course it was nailed in place and so, to shouts of 'Down with the idol!' they turned it upside down and dashed its head against the paving. All was confusion, and as the Queen Regent watched in disbelief from a window of Sandy Carpenter's house, a fight broke out and the priests in the procession fled. Once the commotion had died down, Mary's escort hurried her back to the safety of Edinburgh Castle.

Shocked as the Queen Regent, the Roman Catholic authorities and indeed some Protestants undoubtedly were by this unseemly occurrence, it was not the first episode of its kind. Discontent with the doctrines of the Church had been growing for a long time. Could the bread and wine really become Christ's physical body and blood at the mass? Did prayers for the dead do any good? What use were pilgrimages and relics? There were many other causes for dissatisfaction: absentee churchmen, monks and canons like Master Adam Colquhoun living in luxury, chaplains with their concubines. Pamphlets expounding the views of Martin Luther, the German Reformer, came flooding into Scotland, smuggled into Leith from the Low Countries and brought overland from England. In fact, Master Andrew Johnston, the fugitive St Giles' chaplain, had been distributing Lutheran tracts when he was found out and fled to the continent.

In October 1555, the burgh authorities had ceremoniously burned books in English just outside St Giles' at the market cross. The following September, some men had been accused of taking down and smashing images of Our Lady, St Francis and the Holy Trinity. The church concerned is not named in the records, but it was almost certainly St Giles'. Mary of Guise wrote to the provost of Edinburgh to complain. She and the Archbishop of St Andrews were well aware of the need to reform the Church from within, but progress in that direction was too slow for the opposition and in May 1559 supporters of the Reformed cause were given a new and powerful cohesion with the arrival back in Scotland of John Knox.

Knox is one of the most controversial figures in Scottish history. Hardly a week goes by but he is mentioned in the media as a sinister bigot whose narrow-minded views permanently blighted Scottish artistic life because of his disapproval of pictures and dancing and plays, yet until the middle of the twentieth century he was universally revered as the father of the Church of Scotland. Statues were put up in his honour, streets and schools were named after him and David Laing, the nineteenth-century editor of his works, was expressing the general opinion when he wrote, 'Well may Scotland be proud of such a man as Knox. His character rises superior to detraction, and will ever stand forth, worthy of admiration.'

In Laing's day it was thought that Knox led the Scottish Reformation single-handed, but that was an exaggeration. It was the nobility who carried it through. They, their fathers and their grandfathers had leased lands from the Church and had come to regard these as their own. Some were genuine supporters of the Reformed faith, but many simply feared the prospect of having to give their Church lands back one day and so they enthusiastically aligned themselves with the opponents of Roman Catholicism. Knox nonetheless played a vital part by preaching the Reformed doctrines. After all, how effective could Lutheran pamphlets be when less than a quarter of the male population and very few women knew how to read? A charismatic preacher was needed to explain in person why the Roman Catholic Church must be reformed, and how the Bible was the true basis of belief. Knox was the very man to do this.

At the time of his return to Scotland in 1559, he was about 45 years old, short, sturdy, with piercing blue eyes, a black beard and a ruddy complexion. Born in Haddington at some unknown date and orphaned at an early age, he had been sent to St Andrews University by his relatives and had become a priest. He converted to Protestantism in the 1540s, but after his mentor George Wishart was burned at the stake for heresy in 1546, his life changed even more dramatically. In danger of suffering a similar fate, he went into hiding, only to be seized along with a group of fellow Protestants when a French fleet sent to help Mary of Guise captured St Andrews Castle, where they had taken refuge. Carried off to France, he was forced to serve as a galley slave, chained to a rower's bench and fed on water, ship's biscuit and vegetable soup.

It was hard, physically exhausting work. He fell ill, and that may have been why he was released eighteen months later. He dared not to return home, and so he spent the following years in exile, as a highly successful pastor in Protestant England, as minister to a group of English exiles in Frankfurt and, more permanently, as friend and disciple of John Calvin the reformer in Geneva. There he was pastor of The Auditory, the little church behind the Cathedral of St Pierre where Calvin preached, and he also had time to study and write. In 1555 his friends urged him to return to Scotland, where more and more people were turning to the Reformed faith. He went, but his visit ended when his hopes of converting Mary of Guise were dashed. Back to Geneva he went, and settled down until another invitation came in 1558. Scotland was now on the brink of a religious reformation, he was told, and his leadership was urgently needed.

Knox was reluctant to leave Geneva. He liked his congregation, deeply appreciated the friendship of Calvin and had only recently published his best-known book, *The First Blast of the Trumpet against the Monstrous Regiment of Women*. Its title is often misunderstood. This was not intended as some sort of sexist tract. 'Monstrous Regiment' in sixteenth-century language meant 'unnatural rule', and he was attacking Mary I of England, who did persecute Protestants, and Mary of Guise, who did not. However, they were equally culpable in his mind, and he actually urged their subjects to overthrow them. He was planning a *Second* and a *Third Blast* (which he never did write) and, his career apart, he did not want to disrupt his happy family life with his English wife Marjorie and their two small sons. However, when spring came he sailed from Dieppe and landed in Leith on 2 May 1559 to find his native land in a state of ferment.

Figure 3
Detail of full-length statue of John Knox, in St Giles', by Pittendrigh Macgillivray, 1906
(Photograph: Lars Strobel)

On 11 May he delivered a stirring sermon in St John's Kirk, Perth, against images and idolatry. He attracted a large congregation and the service passed off without incident, but a short time afterwards a riot broke out and people began tearing down the statues not only in St John's but in other Perth churches too. Mary of Guise sent forces to Perth to restore order and the Lords of the Congregation, as the leading Protestant members of the nobility were known, raised their own army. Waiting in trepidation to see what would happen next, the population of Edinburgh heard at the end of June 1559 that the Congregation's army was marching on the capital. Well aware of the destruction in Perth, the burgh quickly took measures to protect St Giles', ordering the sacristan to hand over the church silver to John Charteris senior, dean of guild, for safe keeping. Charteris protested, saying that he was aged and sickly and had only his wife and serving women with him to protect the valuables. The council thought again, and on 27 June they decided that the ornaments and vestments should be distributed among leading members of the community for greater security.

Significantly, the treasures were not given solely to devout Roman Catholics like Charteris. In fact, the list of recipients was headed by James Barron, a leading Protestant merchant and a friend of Knox since 1555. He received custody of the magnificent Eucharist. Thomas Makcalzean, future provost of the burgh and another early Protestant, was to take care of the reliquary with the arm bone of St Giles'. James Lindsay, the town treasurer and a convinced Roman Catholic, would guard the sacrament cloth and the gold embroidered cloak of the St Giles statue, John Charteris the younger kept the candlesticks and tapestry of the high altar while the deacons of the various guilds took charge of the rich velvet and cloth of gold vestments. The Edinburgh councillors then hired sixty soldiers at thirty pence a day to guard the church and its expensive choir stalls. At three o'clock in the afternoon that same day, 29 June, the army of the Congregation marched into Edinburgh and John Knox preached in St Giles' for the first time. A week later, Protestants in the town met in the Tolbooth and publicly elected him minister of Edinburgh.

The 'purging' of the church interior began a week after that, under the supervision of the Lords of the Congregation, led by the Earls of Argyll and Glencairn. The elaborate altars were to be dismantled and the statues taken down and destroyed. Still agitated about their choir stalls, the burgh council hastily moved them next door to the Nether Tolbooth for safety. The situation was far from stable. Neither side had a large enough army to defeat the other, and the ensuing months would see marches, counter marches and abortive negotiations as Mary of Guise waited impatiently for French reinforcements, and the Lords of the Congregation entered secretly into correspondence with Elizabeth I.

In July, Mary of Guise offered to allow the people of Edinburgh to choose whichever form of religion they wished, Roman Catholic or Protestant. The Protestants could hold their services in St Giles', while mass would be celebrated at Holyrood. Both the burgh council and Edinburgh's Protestants refused the offer of a referendum, but the Lords of the Congregation signed a truce with the Queen and agreed to leave Edinburgh. Six days later, Knox preached again in St Giles'. That autumn, the Lords decided to take their campaign further. The French had sent some reinforcements to Mary of Guise and, fearing more, the Lords officially deposed her as Queen Regent and began to besiege Leith, now occupied by French soldiers. Siege ladders were hastily constructed in the aisles of St Giles'.

Mary of Guise ignored her deposition, Leith held out, the Lords began quarrelling among themselves and their soldiers began to drift away. Seizing the opportunity, the Roman Catholics reoccupied Edinburgh and took possession of St Giles' once more. Believing that the church had been defiled by the Reformed services held there, the Archbishop of St Andrews on 9 November 1559 conducted a service of reconsecration, in the presence of Nicholas de Pellevé, Bishop of Amiens, a French emissary sent to Mary of Guise. Most of the altars were still in place, for dismantling them had been slow work, and masses resumed. However, it was not long before the situation changed again. Less than three months after the service of reconsecration, on 27 January 1560, Elizabeth I signed the Treaty of Berwick with the Scottish Protestants, promising to send them both men and money. An English fleet sailed north and an army of 6,000 English foot soldiers and 1,700 cavalry crossed the border into Scotland at the end of March. The Protestants jubilantly took possession of St Giles' once more and in April John Knox returned to his church. Each time he entered the pulpit he preached vehemently against Mary of Guise.

Jean de Monluc, Bishop of Valence then arrived, sent by the French to mediate. He went to see the Queen in Edinburgh Castle and found her in want of health and almost everything else except greatness of spirit and good understanding. Indeed, she remained undaunted by all her troubles, almost as if she had all the forces in the world at her disposal. In fact, she was waiting desperately for further French assistance, and although she negotiated determinedly with the English commanders in a tent erected on the castle outworks, she was suffering from chronic heart disease. By 1 June 1560 she could no longer eat or lie down in bed, finding it easier to spend her nights propped up in her chair. In the late afternoon of 8 June she dictated her will. That night her speech failed. She lingered on for a little longer, but died half an hour after midnight on 11 June. Five days later, the Treaty of Edinburgh was signed, agreeing that all foreign soldiers, French and English, should leave Scotland at once. Matters of religion must be referred to the Scottish parliament.

The Reformation Parliament, as it came to be known, first met on 10 July and, nine days later, Knox preached at a service of thanksgiving in St Giles'. Parliament reconvened on 1 August and began passing a series of acts concerning religion. The Archbishop of St Andrews sat and listened grimly as papal authority was abolished in Scotland and the celebration of mass was forbidden. Anyone attending mass would have their property confiscated for a first offence, they would be banished for a second offence and condemned to death for a third. Legislation continued, and from 24 August 1560 Scotland was an officially Protestant country. St Giles', Roman Catholic for more than 400 years, was now unquestionably of the Reformed faith.

Since his return to Edinburgh, Knox had been working with a group of other ministers to compile the First Book of Discipline, outlining the future policy of the Reformed Scottish Church. There would be no hierarchy, no Protestant archbishops and bishops. Instead there would be ten or twelve superintendents who would each be in charge of a diocese, preaching and supervising the ministers there. They would be ministers themselves, but paid a larger stipend, though they were not to be allowed to live 'as your idle Bishops have done heretofore'. To make sure of that, they would be directly answerable to the General Assembly of the Church of Scotland, a gathering of ministers and laymen who met from 1560 onwards to direct the policy of the Church. In fact, only five superintendents were ever appointed.

The First Book of Discipline likewise dealt with such matters as the abolition of saints' days, holy days, abbeys, monasteries, friaries and nunneries. It laid down the procedure for the election of ministers and elders, urged the repair of church buildings and outlined the ambitious but financially unachievable ideal of a school in every parish. The statement that churches must be repaired was included because many church buildings had been neglected as a result of their revenues having been diverted elsewhere. That certainly did not apply to St Giles', but all its internal fittings would have to be removed and the resulting empty space converted into something suitable for very different services.

The burgh council decided that the church silver and the vestments should be sold and the proceeds put towards the necessary work.

Presumably the Protestant John Barron had no qualms about handing over the Eucharist and Thomas Makcalzean quickly produced the arm bone reliquary with its diamond ring. These and various other items could be melted down and so they were sold to John Hart and Michael Gilbert, two leading Edinburgh goldsmiths, raising the sum of £854:7:6. However, some of the silver, the furnishings and the vestments were slow to come in. The silver-gilt chalice and other ornaments of the Holy Blood altar were not returned until early in 1561, after repeated requests, and as late as 1569 David Somer was still being urged to return the great cloth that used to hang on the back of the high altar.

In May 1560 it had been decided that the Mary bell should be taken down from the steeple, ostensibly because three bells were enough for future purposes, one to be rung for prayers, one to serve the clock and one to be 'the common bell'. Sometimes known as the Lady bell, the Mary bell was no doubt chosen to be the one to go because of its name. The only medieval bell to survive intact to this day, it may be the small one which sits in the nave and is engraved with the words, in Latin, 'O Mother of God, remember me'. Somehow it escaped its intended fate, perhaps because of its small size. The original plan was for it, the brass lectern and all the brass pillars from Lady Aisle and St Antony's Aisle, weighing 218 stone, to be melted down and, if possible, made into artillery for the town, but in the autumn, after several public auctions, they were sold to the highest bidder, the Protestant Adam Fullerton. In a similar mood, in June 1562, the council had the figure of St Giles cut out of the banner with the town coat of arms and replaced by a piece of white taffeta with a thistle on it. As elsewhere in Scotland, however, there is no hint that there was any thought of changing the church's name.

Long before the proceeds were available to pay for it, work had begun on the building. On 1 May, within days of Knox's return, ten workmen started to take down all the altars and the rood-loft with the aid of a great ship's mast brought up from Leith to act as a crane. The gravestones which paved the floor were taken up, cleaned and relaid. No fewer than sixty-six brooms were purchased for sweeping the floor, which was then plastered over. From June until at least October 1560 an ever increasing army of workmen was employed inside the church: masons paid from twenty to thirty shillings a week, wrights at twenty-four to thirty shillings, sawyers at sixteen shillings, barrowmen at twelve shillings, plasterers and painters at varying sums and a water wife to carry pails of water to them at three shillings a week.

Meanwhile, the roof was being inspected, because whenever it rained, water kept running down the great south pillars supporting the tower. A careful examination showed that this was happening because the wind was driving the rainwater back under the roof and much of the wood had rotted. Large quantities of imported Scandinavian timber were brought up from Leith, some of it by means of carriage horses, some of it carried on men's backs. New lead gutters were installed, all the slates above both the west end of the church, the chancel and some of the side aisles were stripped off, a great deal of rotten wood was replaced and the slates were put back on again, while one of the masons and his men repaired various holes in the stonework beside the tower where the rain was coming in.

The Reformers objected to stained glass windows which had representations of Christ, the Virgin Mary, the saints or indeed any other biblical figures, but evidence for any change to the St Giles' windows, any smashing of stained glass, for example, is vague. An enigmatic entry in the town treasurer's accounts in November 1560 speaks of a payment of two shillings 'for bringing of the windows forth of the Kirk and having of them again', but the size of the payment does not suggest a major operation. There was a purchase of lime in January 1561 'for pointing the windows after the breaking', but that could have been accidental. The window above the clock had been broken by the wind that same winter. Similarly, repairs to the window of the former Holy Blood Aisle in November 1561 seem no different from the type of work done by the pre-Reformation glaziers. Thomas Watson, still employed, replaced it with the usual combination of new glass (249 and three-quarter feet) and old (257 feet), so the situation remains inconclusive.

The interior of St Giles' was now ready for redecoration. Chalk was purchased from Andrew Lamb the prominent Leith merchant at eight pence a stone for whitewashing the walls and then Walter Binning was employed once more. No longer required to paint the vanished statue of St Giles, he would apply green paint to twenty-five pillars at eight shillings each. Green and white were the customary colours for Protestant church interiors. The texts of the Lord's Prayer and the Ten Commandments were then painted on the walls. As to furnishings, the principal item in future would be the pulpit. A new one had been brought to the church ready-made for John Knox at the end of April 1560, and while all the cleaning was going on it was carefully protected from the dirt by six ells of old canvas. We do not know what it looked like, but it had an outer and an inner door, both with locks, and an ell of French green cloth was bought for it. Nearby was a wooden lectern.

As for the parishioners, instead of wandering in and out, pausing to watch mass at one of the altars, they would in future be expected to listen to lengthy sermons, and so seating had to be provided. On 19 June 1560 James Barron, now dean of guild, was ordered to have seats, forms and stools made from some suitable timber lying in the vault under the Tolbooth. Could this have consisted of plain parts of Andrew Mansioun's intricately carved choir stalls, taken there for safety in 1559? Perhaps, for they were never seen again. Seating was in fact to be an all-consuming issue for centuries to come. Everyone who was anyone wanted to sit near the pulpit, but not necessarily to listen fervently to Knox preach. There were those who were more anxious to show the rest of the congregation that they were people of importance. At any rate, the pulpit at that point seems to have been immediately to the east of the crossing. One of the accounts for 1564 records that a large stone had to be placed in 'the steeple wall above the pulpit for resisting the great wet that fell down there'. Immediately in front of the pulpit were seats for children and close by were the marriage seats, presumably occupied by the bride, groom and their friends, for weddings no longer took place at the south door.

Now, of course, there were no prebendaries occupying the best seats in the church. Instead, the noblemen took pride of place, and a loft was constructed for them, bolted to a couple of the pillars in the chancel. Like the pillars, it was painted green. Deprived of indicating their status by having their own craft altar and being buried close to it, members of the trades turned their attention to where they would sit. The tailors were indignant to find that the dean of guild had constructed a seat at the site of their former altar, St Anne's. On 1 August 1560 James Norvell their deacon demanded that it be taken away so that he and his fellow members could sit there but he was sharply rebuffed. 'In respect of the godly order now taken in religion, all title and claim to altars and such other superstitious pretences are and should be abolished', the provost and town council told him.

Three years later the provost, bailies and council gave themselves a special seat at the crossing, conveniently near the pulpit. Outside, the churchyard was also causing problems. The walls had to be repaired with stones from the Dominican and Franciscan friaries because animals were once more managing to stray in and children were playing there. The doorway leading to what used to be Walter Chepman's St Salvator's

Chapel was blocked up, people in the locality were given a solemn warning about keeping their beasts on their own land and any children found playing in the churchyard were to be whipped with wands and then imprisoned.

Purging the church and tidying up the churchyard was difficult enough, but what was to happen to the former personnel? It has been estimated that in Scotland generally at the time of the Reformation, a quarter of the priests conformed and became ministers of the churches in which they had been vicars or curates. That was not possible at St Giles' of course, where Knox had already replaced all the many priests. So what was to happen to the rest? The new Protestant council of Edinburgh told the burgh treasurer on 8 May 1560 to stop making any payments to prebendaries and chaplains, and less than three weeks later they instructed everyone who owed annualrents to chaplainries to stop paying them in future. However, parliament had not attempted to legislate for a new financial structure for the Reformed Church and most of the priests went on drawing at least some of their previous income.

It was not intended to persecute them. It was hoped that they would convert. They were expected to attend special sermons to this end, but if after three months they refused to abandon Roman Catholicism, they were banished from the town. Even then, they would be allowed back if they changed their minds. This obviously did not have the desired effect, because six months later the council decided that public shaming was necessary. Recalcitrant priests would be carted through the town and branded on the cheek before banishment took place, and the most stubborn who refused to conform were held in 'the priests' prison', above the north door of St Giles'.

Lacking any personal correspondence from those concerned, it is difficult to estimate the effect of the cataclysmic changes in their church on the clergy and parishioners. Gone with the altars and the statues were all the old certainties, the emphasis on good works, the comfort of prayers for the dead, the intercession of the Virgin Mary and the saints. Faith was what mattered now, and the Word of God, as reported in the Bible. Some people must have welcomed the changes with great enthusiasm, others must have felt that their lives had been shattered. As a distinguished historian remarked, there was a good deal of scepticism about religion generally at that time, and so this may have meant that more people could acquiesce in the changes without too much difficulty. One of the prebendaries of St Giles' certainly proved to be wonderfully adaptable.

Edward Henderson had been master of the song school. He continued in this capacity after the Reformation at a fee of £10 a year, but instead of training young choristers to sing at high mass his task was to 'learn the town's bairns in the art of music', as his successor was told to do, and on Sundays lead the singing of the psalms. This did not occupy all his time, however, for Henderson acted as master of works for many of the building projects at the church in the 1560s. He oversaw the repairing of the churchyard walls and all the work on the church roof, arranging transport to bring the materials up from Leith and counting and numbering all the new slates to make sure that none was stolen. He even superintended improvements to John Knox's lodging and one of his payments came in the form of a grant for life of the defunct chaplainry of St Kentigern, so that he could draw its annualrents. He was described in 1570 as being still 'a papist' but that seems unlikely.

He lived until 15 August 1579 and his lengthy testament gives us an invaluable insight into the life of this ordained priest at a time of great change. He must have married at least twice, for he left bequests not only to his children Gilbert, Alexander, Michael, James and Agnes but also to 'my last wife's bairns, Matthew and Elizabeth Henderson'. He had been comfortably off, leaving them furniture, bedding, napery, a monocord (a stringed instrument resembling a clavichord, the ancestor of the piano), and some rather fine clothing. His friend Robert Lekprevik was to have his slippers, his leather shoes and his satin bonnet while the Laird of Braid would inherit his silver spectacles in their brass case. He must have been a widower when he drew up his will, and his sister Agnes was apparently living with him. She would have the furniture in her own room, and she was to look after the younger children, making sure that James and Matthew continued their schooling. Sadly, the stress of her altered circumstances seems to have been too much for her, for she committed suicide a few months later.

Henderson, however, had founded a dynasty of musicians. In 1582 his son James was granted the office of master of the song school and a year later James's elder brother Gilbert was appointed to lead the psalms. By 1597, the second son, Alexander, was master of the song school. When he resigned in 1602, his son Samuel took over and was eventually succeeded by his brother Patrick who later became session clerk. Patrick was still alive in 1657 when, considering that 'their aged servant' was 'now stricken in years and finding many infirmities daily creeping upon him', the burgh employed an able young divinity student to help him keep the registers of baptisms and marriages. William Henderson and his son Ralph, joint session clerks and leaders of the praise in 1689, may well have been members of the same family.

CHAPTER 5

John Knox at St Giles'

C rowding into their freshly decorated green and white church to the tolling of the Great Bell and sitting down on their unfamiliar benches, the congregation of the reformed St Giles' found themselves experiencing an entirely new type of service. The familiar saintly images, gleaming silver and rich vestments had vanished. The walls were bare and John Knox wore plain, dark, everyday clothes beneath his black Geneva gown. The elaborate choral music had gone, and so had the choristers. Everything was in English, and everyone had to join in the singing of metrical psalms, unaccompanied, because the organ had been taken away. Musical instruments were now regarded as being a distraction from the biblical words and so, when a psalm was announced, Edward Henderson in his new role as leader of the praise stood up and sang one line at a time, which the parishioners repeated after him. In this way, they would gradually learn the psalms by heart. Literate members of the congregation who could afford to acquire their own Bibles and psalters would have been encouraged to do so.

Church services were now conducted according to the Book of Common Order, drawn up by Knox and his colleagues during the months he had spent as pastor to a group of English exiles in Frankfurt. He had subsequently used it with his congregation in Geneva and it was approved by the General Assembly in 1562. Popularly known in Scotland as 'Knox's Liturgy', it resembled the English Book of Common Prayer in some of its passages and was often bound with the metrical psalms. The Reformed service frequently began with the repetition of the Ten Commandments and moved on to a selection of psalms, prayers and biblical readings. The Lord's Prayer was included, as was the Apostles' Creed, while the Doxology, a short hymn of praise to God, was usually sung after the psalms. The lessons from the Bible and some of the prayers were read out by John Cairns who was not an assistant minister but a reader, so called for obvious reasons. He sat immediately in front of the pulpit, facing the congregation, and his presence allowed Knox to concentrate his energies on the sermon, now the main part of the service.

Protestant sermons were meant to be delivered without notes, giving the opportunity for the preacher to be divinely inspired as he went along, and most of them lasted for at least an hour. Some rambling ministers went on for much longer, in which case it was not uncommon for people to fall asleep, start whispering to each other and even engage in noisy arguments with their neighbours, but there was little opportunity for that in St Giles'. Knox was a forceful and entertaining preacher, now alarming his hearers with thundering threats, now entertaining them with his biting humour. Sermons at that time were in three sections. They began with the chosen biblical text, moved on to a detailed exposition of it, and ended with a discussion of its relevance to people's daily lives. The construction may be similar today, but the rhetorical style of delivery was very different. The minister would sigh over his parishioners' shortcomings, denounce their sins, hurl out threats of eternal damnation, plead with them to change their ways, groan and even weep, deliberately setting out to provoke an equally emotional response in them. The shedding of tears by the congregation was regarded as a desirable reaction.

After the sermon there were prayers, and more psalms to be sung before everyone went home. Even then the parishioners' time was not their own. In the afternoon they had to hurry back for the second service, and in the evening they were meant to go over the sermons in their minds, discussing them with their families, reading the Bible, singing psalms and praying. Sunday was intended to be a holy day, but the legislation of the burgh council shows that not everyone was ready to give up secular pleasures. Owners of shops and taverns frequently had to be reminded not to open on Sundays and parishioners were all too often to be found playing games and bowling, with 'hussies, bairns and boys' running about the High Street when they should have been sitting in church.

Although the Reformed Church had no hierarchy, a full system of presbyterian church government had not yet been introduced. However, as we have seen, the General Assembly existed from 1560 and St Giles' had its kirk session, a group of respected members of the community known as elders, along with deacons who were financial officers. All were men, elected at that point for a year at a time. The elders assisted Knox in administrative and pastoral duties and, while services were taking place, some of them would have gone round the houses in the parish to seek out and fine any adults lurking at home without a good excuse. Occasionally the reverse problem occurred, with people going into the church who should not have been there. In 1584 a poor man would run naked through St Giles' shouting 'God save the King!', but he was dealt with kindly, given a set of clothes and a pair of shoes and told that he must not behave in that way. John Philip the leper was also in the habit of going into the church although that was forbidden, for fear of infection. The council agreed that he should be given thirty pence a week for his sustenance, but only if his father made sure he did not set foot in St Giles' again. The burgh also gave orders that the church doors were to be kept locked except during services, to prevent adults and children from going in, dirtying the benches and seats and committing other 'ungodliness'.

At the start of his ministry, Knox preached twice on Sundays and three times during the week, a demanding schedule which saw the burgh council grant him an assistant in 1562. John Craig, a former Dominican friar, had occupied the influential position of Master of Novices at Bologna and had narrowly escaped death at the hands of the Inquisition after converting to Protestantism. According to stories circulating in the town, he had managed to hide in a forest and was saved by the providential appearance of a dog which ran up to him and laid at his feet a purse containing gold coins. With these, he was able to make his way back to Scotland, bringing with him the dog and the remainder of the coins. Whatever the truth of the matter, Craig was now available to deputise for John Knox whenever Knox was called away, and of course he also helped with the many services.

Baptisms took place after the Sunday morning service, for the First Book of Discipline was insistent that these should be held in the presence of the congregation, preferably on the Sunday after a baby was born. The ceremony no longer took place at the south door of St Giles', however. Following what had become the accepted practice, there was no standing font but a baptismal basin attached to the pulpit by an iron bracket and the minister was thoughtfully provided with a linen cloth on which to dry his hands. The baby's parents would have been questioned beforehand about their knowledge of the Creed, the Ten Commandments and the Lord's Prayer, and when the father and godparent presented the infant at the baptismal basin, they had to answer further questions from the minister before promising in a loud, clear voice to bring up the child in the Christian faith.

Marriage services had also undergone a transformation. They now took place inside the church, before the entire congregation, and there were no questions about the financial provisions involved in the match. These were dealt with in the marriage contract drawn up by a notary. Instead, the minister began by reminding his hearers that God had fashioned Eve from Adam's rib to be his helper and by telling the bride that it was the wife's duty to 'study to please and obey her husband, serving him in all things that be godly and honest'. For his part, the groom was warned that he had no power or right over his body without his wife, for God had knitted them together for the procreation and upbringing of children.

The minister then asked if there was any impediment to the marriage and, if no-one spoke, the couple took their vows, the groom promising to forsake all others and live in holy conversation with the bride, she in return promising subjection and obedience to him. Everyone sang Psalm 128, 'Blessed are they that fear the Lord', and after the benediction the wedding party went home to celebrate. Ideally, the Reformers would have preferred marriages, like baptisms, to take place immediately after the Sunday service, but no-one was willing to give up the feasting and dancing afterwards and so weddings usually were held on other days.

Funerals were different too. There was to be no more praying for the dead. People were told to discard the idea of purgatory. Replacing it was the doctrine of predestination which said that, at the moment of birth, a person was chosen by God to be either one of the elect, who would go to heaven, or one of the reprobate, who would go to hell. There was nothing anyone could do about it. Of course, the parishioners were not supposed to sit there smugly convinced that heaven was their ultimate destination. No-one knew whether he or she was one of the elect or not, and many devout people were tormented with worry as to which category applied to them. This difficult doctrine had not been invented by the Reformers. In the Bible, both Jesus Christ and St Paul had spoken about 'the elect ones' and 'the chosen few', but it was St Augustine who had fully developed the idea in the fifth century and now it was becoming a central tenet of the Reformed faith. It may not have been believed quite as rigidly in Knox's time as it was in the seventeenth century, but Knox himself had written an indigestible book about it and he no doubt preached on the subject often enough.

The Reformers decided that there should no longer be any funeral service and instead the body should be carried to the grave by relatives and friends, with no ceremony whatsoever. They were also adamant that there should be no more burials inside churches, but this rule was broken from time to time when a small number of very prominent men such as the Regent Moray and Robert Crichton, a long-lived former provost of the collegiate church, were buried inside St Giles'. People were, however, very loath to do away with the comforting funerals they had known and so a sermon of thanksgiving was allowed after an interment had taken place. Indeed, Knox himself preached such sermons on various occasions. By this time, the churchyard had become very overcrowded and in 1561 the burgh decided that in future almost all burials would take place in Greyfriars' churchyard, about five minutes' walk away.

The most important service of all was, of course, communion. John Calvin had tried to introduce weekly communion in Geneva but had failed and at St Giles', as in the rest of Scotland, it was held three times a year, in the spring, summer and winter, on varying dates but avoiding what were regarded as the popish observance of Christmas and Easter. Although all parishioners were supposed to attend church each Sunday, they were not automatically admitted to communion. In fact, they had to undergo a lengthy period of preparation. The elders visited every household and questioned the members about their behaviour and their knowledge of church doctrine. Only if their replies were satisfactory would the parishioners be entitled to receive a communion token, a small lead disc stamped with the name of the parish. Without it, they would not be admitted. In the days leading up to communion, people were supposed to fast, and on the Saturday before there was a special sermon focusing on the need for repentance and the reconciliation of members who had fallen out with each other.

Communicants arrived at St Giles' early in the morning on Communion Sunday, to find that six long trestle tables covered with linen cloths had been set up in the nave, with forms to sit on at either side. At the top was a short table for John Knox. In winter, the nave was lit by candles and torches and the area was enclosed by specially erected wooden barriers made from borrowed planks, keeping out those who did not have a communion token. There was no question now of kneeling before an altar to receive a wafer from the priest. The Reformers were determined to return to what they saw as the purity of the early Church, and the communicants would sit, as people pictured Christ and his disciples sitting to eat and drink at the Last Supper. The service began with the usual readings, prayers, psalms and, of course, sermon. The Reformers insisted that communion was not to be celebrated without an accompanying sermon, and indeed in subsequent years the sermon tended to become the dominant part of the service although the Eucharist was central to the faith.

After he had preached, Knox would come down from the pulpit and move to his table while the first relay of communicants took their places at theirs, relatives sitting together as if for a meal, everyone equal in the sight of God. To the accompaniment of readings from the scriptures, basins of bread and cups of wine were passed along the tables, for the wine was no longer reserved for the clergy. Everyone was allowed to receive it and, in fact, an early instruction for Church of Scotland communion services told participants to 'sit well back and take a deep draught', possibly to emphasise the point.

In spite of its changed nature, however, communion was far from being a mere commemoration of the Last Supper. The *Scots Confession* of 1560, which laid down the doctrines of the Reformed Church, clearly stated that during communion, 'Christ Jesus is so joined with us that he becomes the very nourishment and food of our souls.... The faithful, in the right use of the Lord's Table, do so eat the body and drink the blood of the Lord Jesus that he remains in them and they in him'. The belief in the real presence of Christ had not been discarded, but it was no longer considered to be in the elements, as the bread and wine are called, since his glorified body was in heaven with God. Instead, Christ is taken to be present in the communion service itself, which symbolises his sacrifice and unites believers with him through faith.

When those seated had received both bread and wine, they would go back to their places in the church and a second wave of communicants would come forward. If many communicants were present, communion could last for most of the day, and that must have been so in the 1560s, when it has been estimated that the total number of participants was in the region of 1,300. Afterwards, the tablecloths were washed by women who were paid eighteen pence for their work, the tables and forms were carried away to be stored until the next time and the wooden barriers were given back to their owners. The following day there was a special service of thanksgiving, which everyone was supposed to attend.

No St Giles' communion silver survives from this period, possibly because in most churches ordinary drinking vessels were used, to emphasise the difference from the Roman Catholic mass with its elaborate chalices. There is no indication in the accounts that flagons and cups were purchased or borrowed, although of course they might have been freely lent by some of the goldsmiths in the congregation. As for the elements, at the first communions in St Giles' six gallons of wine sufficed, but this rose to ten and then twelve in subsequent years, presumably indicating a greater number of communicants. Similarly, two dozen pieces of bread soon had to be increased to three and then four dozen. All expenses, including the bread and wine, were paid for not by the congregation but by the dean of guild on behalf of the burgh.

Among those unable to obtain a communion token were parishioners who were in trouble with the church for what were described as the sins of harlotry (promiscuity, prostitution), adultery and fornication (any other sexual intercourse outside marriage). Before the Reformation, those found guilty of such offences had been forced to stand beside the high altar during mass, clad in penitential linen garments. The high altar had gone now, and so wooden pillars of repentance were supplied instead. Wrongdoers would have to stand there throughout the morning service for several consecutive Sundays, wearing linen or sackcloth, according to the seriousness of their misdemeanour, and on 1 February 1567 David Binning was paid five shillings to paint upon a pillar in St Giles' the words, 'This is the place appointed for public repentance'.

If the accused still did not repent after this public humiliation, he was consigned to the jail previously occupied by recusant priests and fed on bread and water. Women offenders were kept in the roof-space above the kirk, next to the steeple. The Reformed Church's intervention in people's private lives may seem to us today to have been intolerable, but Margo Todd the historian has argued persuasively that, apart from haranguing the alleged wrongdoers, the minister and kirk session were acting very much like a combination of modern social and marriage counselling services. Certainly John Knox, ridiculed in our own day as an intolerant monster, had been known to his parishioners during his English years as a kindly and understanding pastor and there is no reason to suppose that he earned a different reputation in Edinburgh.

The provost and town council were well aware that in Knox they had an outstanding minister and they were anxious to do everything they could to make him comfortable so that he would not move away. He was not paid on the ordinary salary scale of a minister but was given £200 a year, the stipend of a superintendent. Some of his stipend initially came from the sale of the church vestments. Payment of their ministers' stipends was always a struggle for the burgh, because it had been agreed in 1562 that pre-Reformation bishops and other Roman Catholic benefice holders would continue to draw two-thirds of their accustomed income. The other third would go partly to the monarch and partly to pay the stipends of the Reformed clergy. Apart from the inadequacy of this funding, it was as difficult as ever to collect the various annualrents from the townspeople who were supposed to provide them.

There was also a problem with the manse, which was unavailable because it was still in the possession of the last provost of the collegiate church of St Giles'. However, the burgh gave Knox the use of the mansion formerly occupied by the Abbot of Dunfermline. It was conveniently situated in Trunk Close, one of the narrow lanes near the church, on the north side of the High Street, and they made him a warm study leading from his bedchamber, with shelves, lecterns and seats. On one unfortunate occasion when rain leaked through his chamber ceiling on to his bed and his books, the burgh lost no time in replacing the faulty slates, and when Knox had to travel to Angus in December 1561 on Church business, Alexander Guthrie, the dean of guild, went with him, not only to pay all his expenses but to 'haste him home again'.

The previous year, Knox had suffered a cruel blow in the death of his young wife, Marjorie, described as the most delightful of wives by John Calvin when he heard the news. She had joined Knox in Edinburgh with the two little boys and was exhausted helping him to deal with all his correspondence and papers. We do not know the cause of her death, but as the minister's wife she would have been buried in St Giles' churchyard. When they were old enough, Knox sent their two sons south to her English relatives and in 1564 he married again. He and his second wife, Margaret Stewart, were happy together and had three daughters, but by that time, he was taken up with what he regarded as a devastating disaster: the return of Mary, Queen of Scots.

Brought up in France from early childhood, married to the French king, and now an 18-year-old widow, Mary had decided to come back to her native land. Her friends had warned her against doing this, telling her that, as a Roman Catholic, she would never be able to rule her newly Protestant kingdom, but she had refused to listen. This tall and majestic young woman received a surprisingly enthusiastic welcome from her subjects and, with the advice of her Protestant half-brother James, Earl of Moray, one of her father's many illegitimate sons, she ruled with toleration, allowing the Protestants to worship as they wished, as long as she could have her own Roman Catholic services at Holyrood.

Knox, although a friend of Moray, was appalled. He was convinced that Mary would restore Roman Catholicism, and relations between the Queen and Edinburgh's principal minister were notoriously difficult. From time to time she would try to seek his cooperation for political reasons, but she remained the symbol of everything he abhorred. Apart from his famous confrontations with her, when he criticised her religion, her family, her love of dancing and her choice of suitors and she wept, there were other more minor incidents which did not help. She ordered the release of one of his congregation, a local apothecary who had been put in the Tolbooth, no doubt at the kirk session's request, for having had a Roman Catholic wedding. She also allowed John Charteris the younger to have his child baptised by a French priest in her chapel at Holyrood Abbey. Week after week, Knox preached in St Giles' against her in language which could only be described as venomous.

Mary would never have attended his Reformed services, of course, but she was in part of St Giles' on several occasions. This came about because by 1562 the adjoining Tolbooth had fallen into a dangerous state of disrepair and the Queen ordered its demolition, telling the burgh authorities that they would have to supply temporary premises as a matter of urgency until they could build a replacement. In the event, the old Tolbooth was not completely demolished but the council provided what was intended to be temporary accommodation by dividing the west end of the church from the rest of the nave. After all, there was ample space because the interior was too big now to be the sort of preaching hall required, and it was impossible for any minister to make himself heard throughout the entire building. Stones from Walter Chepman's disused chapel in the churchyard were purchased from his heir, the partition wall was built, and what would in modern times be called a mezzanine floor was inserted. The court of session then met upstairs and the central criminal court and the town bailies' court held their meetings downstairs. As soon as the alterations at the west end were complete, the council used stones from the Old Tolbooth to build their New Tolbooth at the south-west corner of the church.

Work on the Outer Tolbooth, as the west end of St Giles' was now called, was completed just in time for the 1563 session of parliament. Held in the spacious session chamber upstairs, parliament was opened and attended by the Queen herself, as it was again in 1564 and 1567. Was Mary able to resist the temptation of opening a door and looking down into the church so familiar to her dead mother? No-one will ever know. Knox did allege, however, that wooden altars found in Holyroodhouse had been made on the Queen's orders and were intended for St Giles'. While considering the alterations to the west end of the church, the council had also discussed building a partition at the east end, to create rooms for a school beneath the east window. That would have the added advantage of concealing the place where the high altar used to stand. This was not specifically stated, but it was a fairly common practice in Reformed churches in both Scotland and England. However, it is doubtful if the east partition was ever built.

Some works did take place. In 1563, the old vestry on the north side of the building was converted into premises for the town clerk, providing two chambers for him, one above the other, linked by a turnpike stair brought from the former Dominican friary. All the burgh's charters and other documents were carried there in a great cupboard. When the clerk complained of the coldness of the earthen floor beneath his feet, a wooden one was hastily installed for him, but rain streaming down the wall of the upper chamber behind the great cupboard spoiled many of his documents before it was discovered. On a happier note, in April 1567 the old weathercock on the steeple was taken down and Alexander Honeyman was paid ten pounds for making a new copper one, with a body weighing fifteen and three-quarter pounds, and a tail weighing seven and a half pounds.

During her reign, the dramatic events in Mary's personal and public life impinged from time to time upon St Giles'. The banns for her marriage to the disappointingly petulant Lord Darnley in 1565 were proclaimed in the church and a few weeks after the wedding Mary sent her husband to attend morning service. A pillared throne with his coat of arms suspended above it was erected for 'King Henry' as he was now known. The occasion was not a success, which was hardly surprising, since Knox preached on the theme of wicked princes being sent as tyrants to plague their people, openly comparing Mary to 'the harlot Jezebel'. Worse still, the sermon was twice as long as usual, and when it was over Darnley flounced out, declaring himself unable to eat his dinner afterwards. Mary retaliated by having her privy council forbid Knox to preach while she and her husband were in Edinburgh, but the town council refused to prevent him from doing so.

Mary and Darnley's son, Prince James, was born in 1566 and a service of thanksgiving was held in St Giles'. However, his birth did not reconcile his by now estranged parents and Darnley was assassinated at Kirk o' Field early the following year. Already suspected of complicity in the murder, Mary made her greatest mistake when she decided to marry James, 4th Earl of Bothwell, the man generally believed to be the principal assassin. He had a wife already, Lady Jean Gordon, but she obligingly sent her lawyers to obtain a divorce from him in the commissary court, Protestant now, and meeting in the Outer Tolbooth. Denying that he was responsible for the events at Kirk o' Field, Bothwell pinned to the church door a paper challenging anyone who doubted him and on 9 May 1567 the banns for his marriage to Mary were reluctantly read out by John Craig, Knox having made a strategic withdrawal to England some months earlier.

Within weeks of her marriage to Bothwell, the Queen's Protestant lords rose against her, imprisoning her in Lochleven Castle and forcing her to abdicate in favour of her baby son, who was crowned James VI. She escaped from Lochleven in 1568 and raised an army, only to be defeated at the Battle of Langside. She then fled to England, where she found herself being held prisoner by Elizabeth I. Meanwhile, Scotland was ruled by a series of Protestant regents. The first was Knox's old friend the Earl of Moray. He and his wife, Lady Agnes Keith, had been married in St Giles' and now a throne-like chair with a green cloth cushion was set up there for him. He probably attended services regularly, but he was assassinated in Linlithgow in 1570 by one of Mary's supporters. Preaching the sermon at his funeral in St Giles', Knox reduced his congregation of more than 3,000 to tears.

Despite the rules about burial, Moray's coffin was placed in a vault beneath the church and his grief-stricken, pregnant widow erected an elegant monument over it. The epitaph was inscribed on the back of a medieval brass commemorating a Scottish merchant and his wife and although the monument was destroyed during nineteenth-century alterations, the plaque survived and is set into a replica of the memorial. Both assassination and funeral are depicted in the nineteenth-century stained glass window nearby. Unusually in an age of arranged marriages, Moray and his wife had been deeply in love and although she remarried after his death, she was buried next to him at her own request.

A few months after his friend's assassination, Knox suffered a stroke which left him permanently weakened, but he was soon back in his pulpit demanding the execution of Mary, Queen of Scots each time he preached. Her supporters were holding Edinburgh Castle for her and for a time they managed to gain control of much of the town, placing their artillery in the steeple of St Giles'. For safety, Knox was persuaded by his friends to withdraw to St Andrews, but after a truce was signed he came back, struggling to preach in a voice so weak that he could barely be heard. He took a few services in one of the smaller upstairs rooms in the Outer Tolbooth, but he knew that his life was drawing to a close.

On 9 November 1572 Knox managed to induct as his successor James Lawson, an eminent Hebrew scholar who was sub-principal of King's College, Aberdeen. However, his bronchitis turned to pneumonia and, having taken farewell of his friends, Knox asked his wife to read to him from the Bible. First he chose the passage from 1 Corinthians 15 with its famous verse, 'The trumpet shall sound and the dead shall be raised, incorruptible' and then he asked for the seventeenth chapter of St John, which had always meant so much to him. It recounts how Christ, on the eve of his crucifixion, prayed to God for his disciples and for all whom they taught, 'that they may all be one; as thou, Father, art in me and I in thee'. He died that same evening.

John Knox was buried in St Giles' churchyard, probably beside his first wife Marjorie, and James, 4th Earl of Morton, now Regent, pronounced the funeral eulogy, declaring him to be one who had 'neither feared nor flattered any flesh'. Knox's enemies rejoiced at his demise, but he was greatly regretted by his friends and colleagues who knew the sensitive and surprisingly humble man beneath the intimidating exterior. Calvin's successor, Theodore Beza, wrote, 'We have been afflicted beyond belief by the death of Master Knox' and when Adam Foulis, minister of Heriot, died the following year, he touchingly asked to be buried in St Giles' churchyard, 'beside John Knox's sepulchre, if it may be possible'. This was not merely a sentimental whim, of course, but a contemporary expression of that same desire which had made early Christians eager for burial near a martyr's shrine, so that the dead could show them the way to heaven.

James Lawson, Knox's successor, lived in a rented house until 1574, but by then the collegiate provost's house in the churchyard was available although in a dilapidated condition. Finding themselves 'superexpended', the council decided that it would be cheaper to repair it for the minister rather than build a new one and in 1580 part of the loft next to Lawson's study was fitted up as a library for the 268 theological books left to town and kirk by Clement Little, advocate. These would eventually become the nucleus of Edinburgh University Library. The previous year, a new burgh song school had been built in the churchyard with stones from Craigmillar and 2,500 slates, great and small, and in 1585 the clock of Lindores Abbey in Fife was purchased to replace the old one in the church tower. The Lindores clock came over the Forth by boat to Leith and was then brought up on horse-drawn sleds to the Council House. James Scott used butter 'to make her go' and Adrian Vanson the artist painted and gilded the boards which would form the two faces. The clock was then installed in the steeple, its mechanism placed so that one of the bells could strike the hours.

During these years the population of Edinburgh was steadily increasing and the council, having apparently abandoned their plan for a school at the east end of the church, took an important decision. They would make the interior of St Giles' into two self-contained churches. To do this, they built a partition wall cutting off the chancel from the crossing and the nave. The chancel would become what was known as the East (or Little or New) Kirk, while the crossing and the nave as far as the Outer Tolbooth were transformed into the Great (or Old) Kirk. Both would be equipped with balconies, called lofts, which would considerably increase the amount of seating available. By the autumn, masons and wrights were busy bringing in stones, building the wall and installing the first lofts. It could be dangerous work and when John Simpson's head was hurt during the erection of scaffolding, John Waddell the barber had to be paid six shillings and eight pence for 'curing him'.

Again in response to the rising population, the town council decided in the autumn of 1584 to divide Edinburgh into four separate parishes. The East Kirk would serve the north-west parish, the Great Kirk was for the south-west and residents of the other two parishes went to the Magdalen Chapel and Trinity College Church. Each parish had its own minister and three elders, and they all met as a single Edinburgh Kirk Session. It is not without significance that from then onwards the East Kirk, which was of course the former chancel, was always the most important in the town. By 1587, so many people were coming to the Sunday morning services there that the minister could hardly manage to push his way through the crowd to his pulpit and a special entrance had to be made for him. The Great Kirk, however, had the honour of possessing the royal loft for James VI. It was directly opposite the pulpit, and next to it was the special Adulterers' Seat with twenty decorative oak pillars. Much raucous hilarity was caused when a visitor one day mistook it for a rather superior pew and sat down there, 'till he was driven away with the profuse laughter of the common sort'.

In 1598, the council decided to transform the upper part of the Outer Tolbooth into a third self-contained church known as the Tolbooth (or West) Kirk. The former court of justiciary fittings were removed, the existing partition wall was demolished and John Watt the mason built a new dividing wall with stones brought from Craigmillar. It was set further east than the partition it replaced, at the next set of great stone pillars.

A painted loft was erected and a new wainscot pulpit made by Moses Scroggie the wright was covered with fringed green cloth. Somewhat pessimistically, not just one but four great pillars of repentance were then installed.

CHAPTER 6

St Giles' becomes a Cathedral

*I*n the spring of 1590 Robert Bruce, one of the ministers of St Giles', received an important letter from James VI. The King was out of the country. Twenty-three years old now, he had decided to marry Anne, daughter of the wealthy Frederick II of Denmark. There was talk of the wedding being celebrated in St Giles', but the Princess's ship was driven back by contrary winds and she got no further than Norway. When he heard the news her bridegroom, with uncharacteristic daring, resolved to go and collect her in person. They met for the first time in Oslo and he was gratified to find that she was tall, fair-haired and cultivated, if somewhat remote in her manner.

The autumn was already well advanced and so James decided that this was not the moment to risk the dangerous sea voyage home again. He would marry Anne in Oslo and they could spend the winter in Denmark with her family. The following April they finally set sail, after James had sent his message to Robert Bruce announcing his impending arrival. 'Waken up all men to attend my coming and prepare themselves accordingly', he wrote. He was determined that his homecoming should be a great occasion, 'a holy jubilee in Scotland', as he somewhat quaintly put it. Bruce would crown the new Queen at Holyrood on 17 May and two days later, when she made her official entry into Edinburgh, she would go to St Giles' for a short service.

The minister passed on the news to the burgh authorities, who at once began their preparations. The St Giles' weathercock was re-gilded and repaired because it had several holes in it, caused by people sportingly shooting at it. Twenty-one iron weather vanes were put up on the points of the crown steeple and two painters washed the clock. At this very wrong moment the roofs started giving trouble again and hasty repairs had to be made. Inside, urged on by the incentive of a new set of clothes each 'to give them occasion to be diligent in their work', John Workman, his brother and son whitewashed the walls and repainted the fittings of the East Kirk while his sister Janet stood by with the colours they used. Sheaves of flowers were brought in to decorate the lofts, violets from the gardens of Heriot's Hospital were strewn on the floor, tapestries were hung on the walls and Thomas Binning painted the coats of arms of the King and Queen. These were hung above the loft where the students usually sat but which would that day be occupied by the Queen.

Joiners toiled throughout the night to make sure that everything was ready in time, and two poor boys who held candles so that they could see what they were doing were promised two shillings and kept going with four quarts of ale and some bread. At last the great day arrived and Queen Anne rode into Edinburgh in her own coach, led by a procession of Scottish and Danish notabilities and followed by her ladies-in-waiting. The King stayed behind at Holyrood, for this was very much his wife's special day. Pageants and speeches greeted her all along the route, and when she reached St Giles' she found that a large platform had been erected immediately outside, with townspeople disguised as Virtue and her daughters waiting to make flattering speeches of welcome. Four of the town councillors stepped forward with a red velvet canopy on four long poles which they carried over the Queen's head as she entered the church, while the congregation sang Psalm 19, 'The heavens declare the glory of God ...'. Escorted to her loft, Anne listened to Robert Bruce preach a sermon, the congregation sang another psalm, and then she left.

This was not to be Anne's only visit. She came to the church from time to time and was occasionally a guest at weddings in St Giles' but, raised as a Lutheran, she disliked Calvinist services and was later rumoured to have converted secretly to Roman Catholicism. Her husband, however, was a regular attender. The only son of Mary, Queen of Scots and Lord Darnley, James VI had been crowned by the Protestant Lords shortly after his first birthday. His father was murdered at Kirk o' Field when he was still an infant and his mother saw him for the last time when he was only 10 months old. He was brought up in effect as an orphan and given a demanding academic education by the alarmingly stern neoclassical poet

George Buchanan, a bitter enemy of Mary, Queen of Scots. It was a lonely childhood, complicated by the attempts of ambitious noblemen to seize him so that they could exercise power, supposedly on his behalf. However, he emerged from all those difficulties a shrewd and highly educated intellectual with a keen interest in theology, a jocular familiarity with his subjects and a pithy sense of humour.

We do not know when James started to attend services in St Giles', but as a vulnerable 16-year-old he was reduced to tears by John Craig, formerly Knox's assistant, who rebuked him for neglecting his duties. That was the beginning of a long and tense relationship between the King and the ministers. It would be interesting to know what the congregation made of the frequent occasions when James sat in his painted and gilded royal loft in the Great Kirk, the ministers criticised him bluntly in their sermons and he rose to his feet to argue vigorously with them. Some parishioners no doubt relished these verbal battles, being fairly pugnacious themselves. In March 1589 the town council had been forced to pass an act promising punishment to the 'divers contentious and wicked people' who were causing trouble in St Giles' by 'injuring their neighbours, drawing of swords and shooting of pistols, and thereby abusing that place appointed chiefly for God's service'. The more peaceable members of the congregation were probably embarrassed, wondering how their ministers dared to criticise the monarch to his face.

John Knox had set a precedent, of course, by preaching constantly against Mary, Queen of Scots, although not in her presence, and since then an important new theory had been introduced into Scottish thinking by Robert Bruce's mentor, Andrew Melville. A native of Angus and a St Andrews graduate, Melville continued his studies in France before spending several years as a professor in Geneva. By the time he returned to Scotland in 1574 he was ready to put forward his views. Kings, said Melville, had no business interfering with the Church. Monarchs might believe that they had been chosen by God to rule over their kingdoms but that was far from being the case. As Martin Luther had argued, in any country there is not merely one kingdom but two, the spiritual and the worldly. Everyone is a member of the spiritual kingdom, including the King, and in that context everyone is equal in the sight of God – monarchs and ministers, beggars and noblemen. As to the worldly kingdom, God rules it through earthly governments, and so it is the godly monarch's duty to reign justly and restrain the wicked. If he fails in that duty, then the King is subject to the discipline of the Church like everyone else.

Confident in the theory of the two kingdoms, ministers had no hesitation in reprimanding James whenever they thought that he was going wrong and indeed on one occasion Melville had the temerity to catch him by the sleeve, telling him, much to his indignation, that he was no more than 'God's silly [i.e. humble] vassal'. James, of course, took a very different view of his role. As he saw it, there was only one kingdom, God was its head and he was the viceregent. There could be no subversive second kingdom, with impertinent church ministers trying to undermine his rule. The battle-lines were drawn and both monarch and ministers were all too ready to enter into debate on a Sunday or indeed any other day. Sometimes the subject was James's alleged tolerance of Roman Catholics, sometimes it was the ministers' rebellious attitude towards him, and on one occasion the quarrel related to Mary, Queen of Scots, still languishing in her English captivity. It was 1586, and she was in danger of execution because of her involvement in plots to set her free. James ordered Patrick Adamson, the Reformed Archbishop of St Andrews, to preach in St Giles' and pray for her. When the King arrived, however, he found John Cowper, one of Bruce's colleagues, already in the pulpit. Taken aback, James told the minister that he could stay where he was, provided he remembered Mary in his prayers. Cowper refused and the King ordered him to leave. He did so but, as soon as the Archbishop stepped into the pulpit instead, most of the congregation gave a loud shout and rushed out of the church in protest, 'especially the women', leaving the disconcerted monarch and a few of his lords sitting in their lofts. Mary, Queen of Scots was executed early the following year.

Perhaps the bitterest cause of controversy was the question of bishops in the Church of Scotland. Immediately after the Reformation, the Roman Catholic bishops had been allowed to continue drawing most of their former revenues, but they began to die off and in 1572 it was agreed that they would be succeeded by suitably qualified Reformed ministers. The new bishops would not, however, be allowed to sit in parliament as their predecessors had done. They remained ordinary parish ministers, answerable to the General Assembly. Even so, Melville and his supporters wanted to abolish them, replacing them with a Calvinist system of church courts: kirk sessions at local level, with elders now ordained for life; presbyteries; synods and the General Assembly. The King, on the other hand, was intent on strengthening the bishops' position.

In 1584, parliament made laws confirming the monarch's power over his subjects, both spiritual and temporal, and saying that the Archbishop of St Andrews and the bishops should direct all ecclesiastical matters. James Lawson and Walter Balcanquhall preached eloquently in St Giles' against these so-called 'Black Acts' and then had to flee to England to avoid arrest. In 1592, parliament passed an act officially authorising the presbyterian form of church government but in spite of that James's power was increasing. In 1597 he allowed the return of Robert Bruce, whom he had banished the year before for allegedly causing a riot in St Giles'. Bruce had to promise to serve the King, study his preservation and take no part in any attempt to touch the royal garments let alone the royal person. Three years after that, James appointed three new bishops who would be allowed to vote in parliament.

James VI's ecclesiastical policy was meeting with success but his regular appearances in St Giles' came to an abrupt end in March 1603, when Elizabeth I of England died and he inherited her throne. His lifelong ambition achieved at last, he lost no time in making preparations for his removal to London. On 3 April he came to St Giles' to hear a sermon. Once more he stood up in his loft but not, on this occasion, to argue. Instead, he made a parting speech, vowing to defend the faith and establish peace, religion and wealth in his kingdoms. He also promised to return to Scotland every three years. He then left at once for the south. The Queen, who was pregnant, was to follow at a more leisurely pace with their eldest son and daughter, but a miscarriage delayed her departure and it was not until 31 May that she too came to St Giles' with Prince Henry Frederick for their own farewell service.

James VI of Scotland and I of England was happy in his new kingdom, where his subjects treated him with suitable deference, church services were dignified and beautiful and bishops sat obediently in parliament. They would never dream of clutching his sleeve and haranguing him rudely. They were, he felt, vital to his rule and indeed, as he remarked on one occasion to a leading English Puritan, if the bishops were removed he knew then what would happen to his own position. 'No bishop, no King.' James and his Queen had drifted apart by now, but Anne too was reasonably content, with much enhanced resources to indulge her passion for fine paintings and elaborate jewellery. Meanwhile, Edinburgh had lost its royal court with the result that the nobility and everyone else seeking royal patronage had to spend several months each year in London. However, the Scottish parliament still met in the Outer Tolbooth, as did the court of session, and St Giles' remained the church attended by lords and ladies, judges, the town councillors and all the other notabilities.

Burdened with the upkeep of three churches in one, not to mention several others in the town, the council maintained the fabric as best they could. Interestingly, in 1596 the term 'High Kirk' appears in the burgh records as a convenient way of referring to the whole building, perhaps because the councillors wished to avoid the name St Giles' with its pre-Reformation connotations. At any rate, the 'High Kirk' features occasionally in connection with structural repairs from then until around 1615, after which the term seems to have fallen out of use. Incidentally, this name, also used elsewhere, does not imply anything about the importance of the church in question or its form of worship. It simply meant that it was geographically higher up in the town than the other churches.

Whatever name was being used for St Giles', the dean of guild almost despaired at the interminable problem of the leaking roofs, caused by what he liked to call 'the vehemency of the winds and weather'. In March 1599, a 'great number of drops of rain' had been running down the pillars again, and he decided in desperation to seek foreign help. He dispatched a deputation to the Low Countries to see if its members could find workmen with the necessary expertise to put an end to the difficulties once and for all. Richard Bannatyne spent forty-two shillings in Middlebourg drinking with a Flemish mason named Laurence and his servant Hans, but it was worth it for the pair were persuaded to come to Scotland that spring.

Even they were not able to solve the problem permanently, of course, and slaters and masons continued to labour away on the roofs. There was a troubling incident in 1615 when a workman with the unpromising name of William Slowman 'fell off the Kirk' and his medical expenses had to be paid, while a charmingly worded entry in the 1623–4 accounts reveals John Telfer at work 'mending of some raindrops in the Little Kirk'. Year in and year out walls had to be pointed and crumbling stone replaced. Small boys amused themselves by pushing stones into the door locks and the plain, diamond-paned windows were a constant expense, not least when the great east window had to be repaired after 'ane mekle dog dang forth and lap out at it' (a large dog burst forth and leapt out at it).

The church interiors were whitewashed regularly, with the royal loft carefully protected from splashes of white by a ship's sail brought up from Leith. The mechanism of the Lindores clock in the steeple was replaced in 1610 by James Smith the town clockmaker and then there was the ministers' accommodation to be kept up. Sometimes they lived in rented lodgings, sometimes in the three manses in the churchyard but, wherever they were, the town met their expenses. Robert Bruce was provided with a fine oak bed 'of the Flanders fashion', hung with fringed green curtains, a long settle and a box to keep his candles in. James Lawson was supplied with a gardener to plant herbs, seeds and flowers in his yard and Walter Balcanquhall's windows were quickly repaired in 1595 after they were blown out by the great wind and vehemency of the weather.

More than 300 miles away, King James boasted that he could rule Scotland with a stroke of his pen. He had not kept his promise to visit his native land every three years, but in 1617 word came that he intended to make the long journey north. The town councillors were immediately galvanised into action. The royal loft in the Great Kirk was looking distinctly dilapidated. It was extended and painters re-gilded it with 100 books of gold leaf, sixty-nine of which were imported from Holland. The loft was then lined with heavy green woollen cloth and the King's chair, cushions and carpets were brought up from Holyroodhouse to make it more comfortable. The pulpit was repaired, the Lords' Loft was freshly repainted green and Janet Carr supplied eight extra sheaves of flowers in addition to those she provided every week to decorate the church. James entered Edinburgh after his long absence on 16 May and immediately went to St Giles', where he heard a suitably flattering sermon by John Spottiswoode, Archbishop of St Andrews, preaching on Psalm 21, 'The king shall joy in thy strength, O Lord'.

In the midst of the excitement, the ministers of St Giles' were wary of their returned monarch's intentions. They suspected that he wanted to make their services more like those of the Church of England. It was well known that he did not care for Knox's Book of Common Order and indeed he had asked several ministers to draw up a new liturgy to replace it. These fears seemed to be justified when, as soon as he arrived, the English Book of Common Prayer was used in his Chapel Royal at Holyrood, with choral singing, surplices and organ music. Observers were even more shocked when communion was celebrated there on 8 June and the King, most of the bishops and various courtiers, knelt to receive the bread and wine.

James also took the opportunity of airing various controversial proposals which he had in mind. It was not that he deliberately wanted to impose English practices on Scotland, but he was always anxious to bring his two kingdoms closer together in every possible way. When he eventually went south again at the end of the summer, he left behind him an atmosphere of distrust and resentment. Nevertheless, his proposals were adopted the following year at the General Assembly, meeting in Perth, its members carefully chosen to exclude the opposition. Known as the Five Articles of Perth, these innovations revived the holding of services on Christmas Day, Good Friday and Easter, allowed private baptisms for sick infants and ordered people to kneel at communion. No more was heard of the new liturgy though, probably because James realised that he would never manage to persuade the Scots to accept it as well. The ministers of St Giles' obediently preached on Christmas Day, but the Great Kirk was reportedly so empty that dogs were able to play in the middle of the floor.

In 1622, a visitor from the continent came to St Giles' and was singularly unimpressed with what he saw. Father Alexander Baillie, prior of a small community of Benedictines at Würzburg in Germany, seems to have been sent to Scotland as a missionary on behalf of the Roman Catholic Church and he was deeply saddened to see the changes which had taken place since the Reformation. He gazed in dismay at the walled-off former chancel, the partitioned interior, 'bare walls and pillars all clad with dust, sweepings and cobwebs instead of painting and tapestry, and on every side ... the restless resorting of people treating of their worldly affairs, some writing and making obligations, contracts and discharges'.

Some were counting out money while others strolled around chatting about merchandise or the law and 'too many, alas, about drinking and courting of women, yea and perhaps about worse nor I can imagine'. It seems that, although in Knox's time St Giles' was kept locked except for services, medieval habits had reasserted themselves. People evidently had access to the building during the week and borrowers had reverted to redeeming their property in the church. They could no longer count out their money on a chosen altar but instead the revered Regent Moray's tomb had become the favourite place for doing this, a practice which went on until as late as 1720.

Alexander Baillie probably came just too soon to hear the pealing of two fine new bells. In 1609 it had been found that the common bell was cracked. Mariners from Leith, accustomed to climbing the rigging of their sailing ships, were summoned to take it down. Once it was on the ground, nineteen men lifted it and carried it to Charles Hogg in Potterrow, on the south side of the town, so that he could recast it. Unfortunately, when it came back and was hung, it did not sound right and the provost and council were forced to have it broken up. Nothing more seems to have been done until 1621 when the dean of guild shipped the broken metal and the curfew bell to Campveere in the Low Countries. There they were sold and with the proceeds a great common bell weighing 2,150 pounds was purchased from Michael Burgerhuys of Middlebourg, the well-known bell-founder who had already supplied a bell for the Great Kirk in Delft. A 'middle' bell weighing 768 pounds was also bought for St Giles'. These were brought back through Leith and on 29 November 1624 they rang out proudly to mark the marriage of James VI's only surviving son, Prince Charles. Less than four months later, the King was dead.

Charles I was a very different man from his father. Transformed into the epitome of elegance in his portraits by Van Dyck, he was small and thin, with a melancholy expression. Like his mother, he loved the visual arts, he was very fond of music and he was deeply devoted to the Church of England. In his relationships with people, however, he was far from adept. Where his father had a shrewd understanding of human nature in general and his Scottish subjects in particular, Charles had no personal experience of his northern kingdom, which he had left as a 3-year-old. This lack was unfortunately combined with an immoveable obstinacy once he had made up his mind about something, and he was already distrusted because he had married a Roman Catholic, Princess Henrietta Maria of France.

On 2 February 1626, Charles I was crowned in London. He was the first monarch to inherit the thrones of both Scotland and England simultaneously, and it was decided that he should have a second coronation in Edinburgh, in St Giles'. His Scottish privy councillors were told to inspect the building and as soon as they did so they could see that there was a problem. There was no proper precedent for a Reformed coronation because James VI had been a baby when he was crowned. However, during their coronations his Roman Catholic predecessors had always faced east, towards the high altar. If Charles faced east in St Giles', he would be looking not at an altar or even at the great east window but at the stone partition wall which separated the Great Kirk from the East Kirk. It would have to be removed. That was not as simple as it sounded, however, for it would involve emptying the East Kirk of all its expensive seats and fittings and, in any case, the town council had no desire to see its Protestant preaching halls returned to something resembling their pre-Reformation state. For all they knew, the King might even insist on setting up an altar.

After years of delay, Charles was finally crowned in Holyrood Abbey on 18 June 1633, with elaborate ceremonial. A crucifix had been put up, the clergy in their vestments genuflected before it, an organ brought specially from London was played and choristers sang. To add to the annoyance of the Scots, Charles's irritating ecclesiastical adviser, William Laud, Bishop of London, took a prominent part and as usual offended people with his lack of tact. Five days later, Charles attended his first service in St Giles', sitting in the royal loft in the Great Kirk in traditional manner, but he had no intention of hearing the customary Scottish service. The normal Bible readings had hardly begun when they were interrupted. John Maxwell, one of the ministers, suddenly came down from the royal loft and told the reader to make way for two English chaplains in surplices. The service was then conducted according to the English Book of Common Prayer. The congregation were horrified.

Undeterred by the visible resentment around them, Charles and his retinue were able to study the entire building for themselves. As Laud remarked, the East Kirk with its lofts looked for all the world like a square theatre. With a view to further enhancing the power and prestige of the Scottish bishops, the King was already encouraging repairs to Glasgow, Dunkeld and Dornoch cathedrals and he was even determined to restore the ruinous cathedral in St Andrews. His plans for St Giles' were equally ambitious. The town courts had moved into the New Tolbooth as soon as it was ready, the Old Tolbooth was being used as a jail, but the court of session and parliament were still meeting in the Outer Tolbooth at the west end of St Giles' and the vacated space on the ground floor was now used to store the burgh artillery and the early form of guillotine known as the Maiden. The provost and council were unhappy about this, but they had been unable to do anything about it because of shortage of money. However, the King was determined that intrusive secular activities should be moved out of the church as soon as possible and the town dared not disobey.

The councillors borrowed substantial sums of money, demolished the ministers' houses in the upper churchyard and began to build what became Parliament House on the site. When it was completed in 1639, the court of session and parliament at last moved out of St Giles', the town's armaments were transferred to the former adulterers' prison above the north porch and the west end of the church was once more available for spiritual purposes. This was very important to Charles. He was resolved to create a bishop of Edinburgh, and every bishop required a cathedral. On 29 September 1633 he issued a royal charter erecting the bishopric, transforming St Giles' into its cathedral and giving Edinburgh the status of a city instead of a mere burgh.

The new Bishop of Edinburgh, William Forbes, namesake of the first provost of St Giles' Collegiate Church, was consecrated the following January. An Aberdonian of ecumenical views who supported the Five

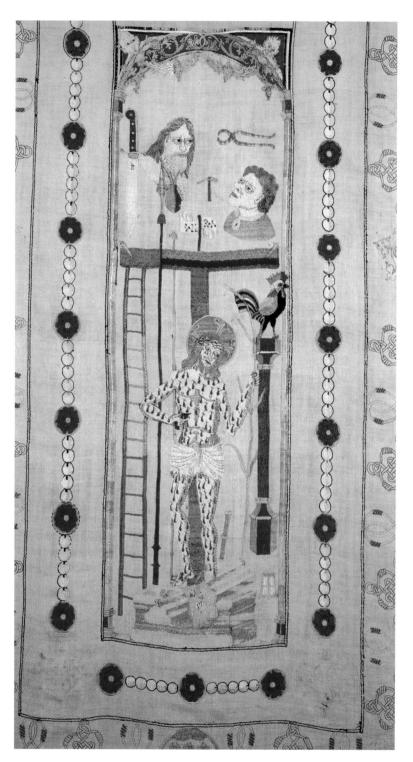

Plate 1
Central front panel of the Fetternear Banner, believed to have been embroidered
about 1520 for the Confraternity of the Holy Blood, St Giles'.
(© National Museums of Scotland. Licensor www.scran.ac.uk)

Plate 2
George IV at St Giles' by J. M. W. Turner. The King stands beneath the canopy of the Royal Seat, on the right. (© Tate, London 2008)

Plate 3
The St Giles' pulpit, designed by William Hay and carved by John Rhind in 1872–3.
(Photograph: Lars Strobel)

Plate 4
Memorial to William Hay, architect, died 1888, by John Rhind, in St Giles' Cathedral.
(Photograph: © Saul Gardiner)

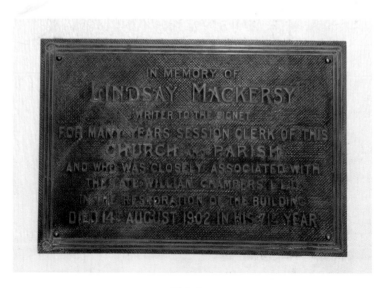

Plate 5
Memorial to Lindsay Mackersy WS, Session Clerk, died 1902, by an unknown carver,
in St Giles' Cathedral. (Photograph: © Saul Gardiner)

Plate 6
Robert Burns memorial window, 1985, by Leifur Breidfjord.
(Photograph: © Peter Backhouse)

Plate 7
The Rieger Organ in St Giles'. (Photograph: © Peter Backhouse)

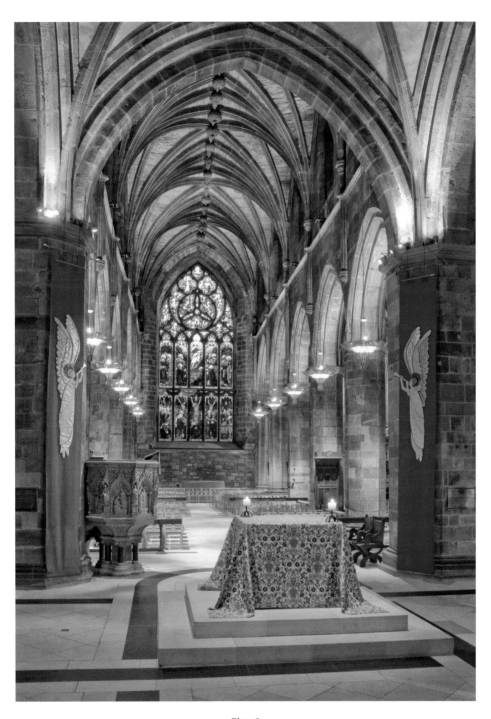

Plate 8
St Giles' interior, December 2008, looking east, showing the sanctuary and the new chandeliers.
(Photograph: © Peter Backhouse)

Plate 9
The crown steeple of St Giles', with gilded weathercock and finials.
(Photograph: © Peter Backhouse)

Articles of Perth, he died only two and a half months later. He was buried in the chancel of St Giles' and a handsome monument (no longer in existence) was erected on his grave, its long epitaph telling:

> Holy was his life without blemish or spot
> As was well known by God's servants most dear
> But alas, for pity! For such was his lot
> His days was few that he remained here.

By an unhappy coincidence, the first dean of the Cathedral, William Struthers, died only ten months after his own appointment. Both were swiftly replaced.

Less than a fortnight after his charter transforming St Giles' into a cathedral, Charles I ordered dramatic changes to be made to the building. The whole interior must be opened up again into one sacred space in keeping with the intention of its original founders, he told the town council. But what, they asked, were they to do about the two congregations who would be displaced? They could not possibly afford to build two new churches. The King was adamant. The partition walls must be demolished. Down they came and, back in London once more, Charles turned his attention to the arrangement of the newly revealed interior. In February 1636 the Cathedral Dean, James Hannay, was sent off to draw a plan of the chancel of Durham Cathedral, recently refurbished to the King's approval and including a marble holy table at the east end. By August 1637, John Mylne the master mason was busy in St Giles' overseeing repairs to the stonework of the great east window and purchasing wainscot, probably to line the chancel walls. Meanwhile, lengthy discussions were taking place about another, even more ominous matter.

Charles was not interested only in beautifying church buildings. As had become clear at his coronation and the subsequent St Giles' service, he was set on replacing the Book of Common Order. Some people have a need for austere church services with nothing that they would regard as a distraction, while others feel that beautiful music, words, windows and vestments facilitate worship and indeed speak to the soul. Charles was of the latter opinion. As early as 1629 he had sent for the discarded draft liturgy drawn up for his father, but when he saw it he and William Laud agreed that it was unnecessary. The English prayer book or something very similar should be adopted in Scotland. The Scottish bishops were opposed to the idea but Charles pressed ahead, telling them to draw up a liturgy as close to the English as possible and giving one of them a copy of the

English prayer book annotated with suggested amendments. While the text of the new book was being drafted and redrafted, a code of canons for Scotland was published on 23 May 1635 with royal approval. This repeated what had been said in the Five Articles of Perth, did not even mention the General Assembly, presbyteries or kirk sessions and insisted that churches must have a holy table (the expression used) at the east end. People were also ordered to accept the new prayer book, which they had not even seen, as it had yet to be published.

It was finally printed in the spring of 1637 (see Figure 4). The Scottish bishops had done their best to make it acceptable. The King James translation of the Bible, familiar to the Scots, was used and the word 'priest' had been changed to 'presbyter'. These alterations, however, were far outweighed by other aspects of the text insisted upon by Charles himself. He had inserted chapters from the Apocrypha, those scriptural books which were included in some Bibles but were not used in the Scottish Church because they were believed to be of doubtful authenticity. A calendar at the beginning of the prayer book included many saints' days, including that of St Giles. There were instructions that the holy table was to be placed, like an altar, against the east wall, and it was to be covered with a carpet, a fair white linen cloth and 'other decent furniture meet for the high mysteries there to be celebrated'. At communion, the minister would stand in front of it, with his back to the congregation, in a manner strongly reminiscent of a Roman Catholic priest celebrating mass.

Even those parishioners who could not read were liable to be infuriated by the very sight of the new prayer book, for it looked like a Roman Catholic missal with its illuminated capital letters and red print as well as black. The thought that an English book was being imposed on the Scots was equally if not more inflammatory and, to make matters worse, if that were possible, it had not been approved by the General Assembly as it ought to have been. Instead, the King had issued it on his own authority. It was obvious from the start that there was going to be trouble, and its introduction was postponed from Easter 1637 until the summer in the hope that people would become accustomed to the thought of it. Finally, on 16 July it was announced that it must be used in every Edinburgh church on the following Sunday.

On 23 July 1637 the congregation gathered in the Great Kirk of St Giles' because the chancel was still undergoing alterations. A large number had come, those who did not have seats of their own carrying the folding stools they would sit on. From the start, things went badly. Patrick Henderson,

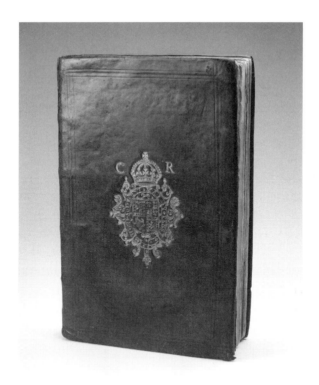

Figure 4
The controversial Book of Common Prayer, 1637, said to have
come from the Palace of Holyroodhouse.
(© National Museums of Scotland. Licensor www.scran.ac.uk)

the reader, refused to use the new prayer book and instead read the lessons
from the Book of Common Order. When he had finished, the Bishop of
Edinburgh went into the pulpit and Dean Hannay opened his new prayer
book. As soon as he started to read, 'all the common people, especially the
women, rose up with such a loud clamour and uproar so that nothing could
be heard; some cried, "Woe! Woe!", some cried, "Sorrow! Sorrow for this
doleful day, that they are bringing in popery amongst us!"' while others
hurled their stools at the Dean and rushed out of the church 'with a pitiful
lamentation'. According to tradition, Jenny Geddes was the woman who
threw the first stool, with a shout of 'Dinna say mass at my lug!' (Don't say
mass in my ear.)

In the uproar, Dean Hannay had to stop reading and when the Bishop
could make himself heard again, he preached a short sermon instead,

hoping to calm the remaining congregation. After the service was over and he went out into the street, people crowded round him, shouting and screaming their protests. In alarm, he hurried up the nearest outside stair to find refuge in the Earl of Wemyss's lodgings. Dean Hannay prudently stayed inside the Cathedral until the crowd had dispersed. That afternoon the Bishop tried again. This time magistrates were stationed at the church doors to keep out the troublemakers and afterwards the Bishop went home in Lord Roxburghe's coach, pelted with stones by the crowd.

Stools were undoubtedly thrown that day amidst agitated scenes, but did Jenny Geddes really exist? Sir Walter Scott wrote about her in his popular Scottish history book, *Tales of a Grandfather*, but none of the descriptions of the time mentions her name. In fact, a writer alive in 1705 claimed that in his day the woman in question was believed to be Barbara Mein, the wife of a leading opponent of Charles I's policies. There was a Jenny Geddes who sold fruit and vegetables in the High Street in the 1660s but there is no evidence that she had anything to do with the events of 1637. In spite of that, her name went down in history as a brave Presbyterian who was willing to battle against Episcopalian and Roman Catholic ways, a symbol of popular protest against authority, a Scottish heroine ready to stand up against the English, even a pioneering feminist. Some would say that her true identity is unimportant. What matters is that there was a riot in St Giles' that day and stools were thrown. Others feel that it is unfortunate when historical events are reinterpreted with a misleading modern slant.

At any rate, it is hardly surprising if descriptions of that confusing day were themselves confused. Rumours spread rapidly throughout the city and beyond, and the authorities tried to make sense of what had happened. The King blamed the Scottish privy council for mishandling the affair, as did William Laud, now Archbishop of Canterbury. The Scottish privy councillors tried to play down the whole unfortunate business and blamed the bishops. Some historians think that the riot in St Giles' had been deliberately orchestrated by aristocratic opponents of the prayer book and it has even been claimed that the protesting women were actually apprentices disguised in female clothing. That may have been true, but women were very often at the forefront of the Edinburgh mob.

Whoever was responsible for the debacle, church services in Edinburgh were suspended that week for fear of public disorder, and the town began to fill up with people eager to sign petitions against the changes. At first, the town council told the Scottish privy council that they were doing their best to maintain peace and quietness but by 22 September they had to admit that they feared an uprising. Sixty-eight petitions had been received as well as a lengthy plea signed by members of the nobility and the clergy. The King responded by ordering the petitioners to leave Edinburgh within twenty-four hours and moved the law courts to Linlithgow. There was another riot when his proclamation arrived, and on 4 October Robert Baillie, the principal of Glasgow University, wrote a letter to one of his regular correspondents, saying that he feared 'a bloody civil war'. These were prophetic words.

CHAPTER 7

Seventeenth-Century Turmoil

I n the early autumn of 1641, Charles I came back to St Giles' in circumstances very different from any that he could possibly have imagined. Instead of entering a magnificent cathedral with an altar at the east end and a bishop and dean officiating in fine surplices, he found himself sitting in a new royal loft in the East Kirk, which was partitioned off once more. His seat was against the south wall, facing northwards towards the pulpit. On one side of him were the town councillors in their loft and on the other was the loft belonging to Archibald, Earl of Angus, who was defying his own royalist father to support the King's enemies. Worse still, the Book of Common Order had been reinstated and not only did Charles have to listen to a lengthy sermon but he also had to join in the singing of the psalms. He had come north, after all, to try to win support and he dared not offend his fellow worshippers by seeming contemptuous of their services.

So what had happened since that day in 1637 when some woman had led a riot in St Giles' and petitions against his ecclesiastical innovations had come pouring in? On 28 February 1638, Charles I's leading opponents had met in Greyfriars' Church, not far from St Giles', to sign the lengthy document known as the National Covenant. Composed by Alexander Henderson, minister of the East Kirk and Archibald Johnston of Warriston, a leading lawyer and member of that same congregation, the Covenant proclaimed that Charles had violated a long list of parliamentary statutes favouring the Reformed Scottish Church. The signatories were therefore pledging themselves to defend the true religion, liberties and laws of the kingdom against any who tried to interfere with them. That meant the King, the implication being that no monarch could change the laws made by parliament. Only parliament could do that. Copies were to be sent to all the burghs and parishes, with orders that lists were to be made of those who refused to add their names. One such copy can be seen in St Giles', the gift of a much later benefactor.

When news of what was happening reached London and Charles realised the strength of feeling against him, he agreed to withdraw the prayer book, the code of canons and the Five Articles of Perth. He also gave permission for a General Assembly to meet in Glasgow in November, but his concessions came too late. In militant mood, the Assembly condemned all his innovations and deposed the archbishops and the bishops. The Covenanters, as the King's opponents were now known, raised an army and in the spring of 1639 Charles led his ill-equipped and demoralised forces north in an attempt to suppress them. During the two Bishops' Wars which followed, his campaigns were a failure, he was twice forced to negotiate a truce and by the Treaty of Ripon in August 1641 he agreed to go to Edinburgh to ratify all the Covenanting acts passed by the Scottish parliament during the past two years.

This was why Charles arrived back in the Scottish capital that autumn and on at least two Sundays attended services in St Giles'. During his three months in the town he engaged in complicated plotting with all those he hoped might help him, but he won little support. Indeed, when the English Civil War broke out the following year, the Covenanters allied themselves with his enemies in the vain hope that England would now adopt the presbyterian form of church government. That was one of the conditions of the agreement known as the Solemn League and Covenant, signed in London and then in the East Kirk on 13 October 1643. On that occasion the English commissioners sat in front of the reader's desk, the noblemen were opposite the minister, beside a table covered with a green cloth, and representatives of the Scottish parliament and the General Assembly were grouped at another table.

The proceedings began suitably with Robert Douglas, minister of the Tolbooth Kirk, preaching a sermon on the text 'And they entered into a covenant to seek the Lord God of their fathers with all their heart and with all their soul' (2 Chronicles 15:12). At first, prospects for the implementation of the Solemn League seemed promising. Henderson and Douglas were sent as delegates to the Westminster Assembly of Divines that year, an ecclesiastical gathering which produced a new confession of faith along with other documents laying down regulations for the uniform structure of church government throughout Scotland, England and Ireland. Nevertheless, it soon became clear that the English were not interested, while the Scottish General Assembly enthusiastically adopted the confession. Although modified in some respects in recent years, it has ever since been the subordinate standard of the Church of Scotland, the principal standard being the Word of God contained in the Scriptures of the Old and New Testaments, the supreme rule of faith and life.

The East Kirk was now accepted as being the finest of the churches in St Giles' and after the royal loft was sited there, leading parishioners abandoned the Great Kirk and migrated to it instead. Charles I had given permission for the General Assembly to meet in the East Kirk in future, but rather than disturb the expensive fittings, the 1643 Assembly used a

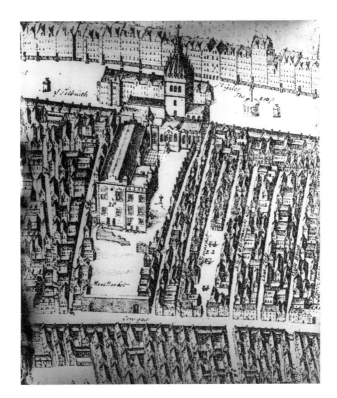

Figure 5
Detail of an anonymous engraving of Edinburgh showing St Giles', about 1645.
(© Edinburgh City Libraries. Licensor www.scran.ac.uk)

space close by, presumably the Preston Aisle. After the departure of its dignitaries, the Great Kirk lost its imposing name and was known as the Old Kirk or Mid Kirk or South Kirk, depending on who was mentioning it. In the spring of 1644, the armaments store above the north porch became a prison again when the captured royalist, Sir John Gordon of Haddo, was held there before his beheading by the newly sharpened blade of the Maiden guillotine. After that, the prison was known as Haddo's Hole. Meanwhile, the royalist army in England was suffering defeat after defeat.

By September 1648 the Civil War was entering its final phase. Charles I was held prisoner in England and Oliver Cromwell, commander of the New Model Army, marched into Scotland to root out any lingering support for the royalist cause. He was welcomed by the Covenanting Archibald, 1st Marquis of Argyll. Invited to Edinburgh, Cromwell stayed in the Countess of Moray's house in the Canongate and was entertained to supper in the Castle by a company which included Argyll and Johnston of Warriston. It was rumoured that, among other matters, they discussed what should be done with the King. Four months later, on a cold January day, Charles I was taken to his elegant banqueting house at Whitehall. He had been tried for treason and condemned to death. At two o'clock in the afternoon he stepped through an open window on to the scaffold which had been erected immediately outside. He made a short speech, saying that he died a Christian, according to the beliefs of the Church of England, and then he knelt down at the block. The watching crowds gave a loud groan as the axe fell and the executioner held up the King's severed head.

When they heard the news, the Scots were shocked. Much as they had hated Charles's ecclesiastical innovations, few had envisaged such a fatal outcome. The Edinburgh council immediately proclaimed that his eldest son was now King Charles II. The young monarch was in exile on the continent but, anticipating his return, the town council instructed John Scott the master wright to make a fine new carved loft for him. Perhaps to emphasise a fresh start, they decided to place it on the north side of the East Kirk, moving the pulpit to a pillar on the south side. At the same time, the existing lofts and seating were rearranged, a new great wainscot loft was put up immediately under the east window and two more great lofts were set against the partition wall dividing the East Kirk from the Old Kirk. The higher one was to be steeply raked so that people at the back could see the minister over the heads of those in front of them. The alterations involved considerable expense: it cost £12 Scots for moving Johnston of Warriston's seat alone. Finally, in May 1649, Scott put up a timber wall ten or eleven feet high between the East Kirk and the General Assembly's room.

While these modifications were being made, John Mylne, the town's master mason, was in 1648 overseeing important work on the roofs and the steeple. It was so difficult to find enough men to undertake the repairs that a slater named Gray had to be lured away from Glasgow with the promise of being made a free burgess of Edinburgh. Despite similar initiatives, the shortage of slaters persisted and in August 1649 the council was complaining of the extortionate rates they were charging, two and three times the normal amount. As to the steeple, Mylne not only repaired the crumbling masonry but replaced the stone obelisk at the top of the crown. Eight and a half feet high and three and a half feet square, in seven sections, its carved stone heads representing the four winds still look out over the city 350 years later. On top of the obelisk perched Alexander Honeyman's weathercock, above two copper globes. Not until 1651–2 do the dean of guild's accounts show a final payment of £1,621:11/- to John Mylne 'in perfecting the steeple', by which time it must have been finished.

While the masons toiled high above the rooftops, dramatic events were taking place below. Charles II could not return until careful negotiations to guarantee his safety had been made but, while these were going on, James Graham, Marquis of Montrose, led a rising in the Highlands aimed at bringing the young King back from exile. Montrose, a romantic figure passionately devoted to Charles I, had previously conducted highly successful campaigns against the Covenanters, but now he was defeated and captured. He was brought through Edinburgh to the Tolbooth in a cart and on the eve of his execution this soldier poet wrote the poignant lines which are inscribed on his nineteenth-century monument in St Giles':

Scatter my ashes, Strew them in the air
Lord, since thou knowest where all these atoms are
I'm hopeful Thou'lt recover once my dust
And confident Thou'lt raise me with the Just.

On 21 May 1650 Montrose mounted the scaffold at the market cross outside St Giles', wearing a scarlet cloak 'more beseeming a bridegroom nor [than] a criminal going to the gallows', a parishioner named John Nicoll wrote in his diary. Any condemned nobleman would normally have been beheaded, but the Covenanters hated Montrose and he was ignominiously hanged. His corpse was then dismembered, his head placed on a spike on the Old Tolbooth, his body buried on the Burgh Muir and his limbs sent

Figure 6
Memorial to James Graham, 1ˢᵗ Marquis of Montrose, who was executed in 1650.
This monument in St Giles' was erected in 1888. (Photograph: © Peter Backhouse)

to various Scottish towns to be displayed as a dreadful warning to all who had royalist sympathies.

A few weeks later, Charles II sailed back to Scotland, having finally agreed the terms for his return. On 9 July, as soon as they heard of his arrival, Edinburgh town council sent him their congratulations and invited him to visit his Scottish capital. However, even as they prepared an elaborate reception for him, ominous news reached them. Cromwell and his forces were marching north. Although Cromwell did not take the title of Lord Protector until 1653, he was now the most powerful man in England. Knowing that he was not coming this time to be entertained to supper, the council immediately ordered all able-bodied citizens, men and women alike, to go to Leith to work on its fortifications under the supervision of John Mylne. Edinburgh's town wall was repaired, provisions were gathered for the Scottish army and the current burgh registers were hastily moved for safety into the charter house in St Giles'.

When the King arrived in Leith, the council immediately sent a deputation to give him 20,000 merks 'in testimony of their humble respect and loyal affection'. However, they also advised him not to come to Edinburgh but to seek safety elsewhere. Charles did stay for long enough to visit the Castle and attend an entertainment in the Upper Exchequer House next to St Giles', before being persuaded that, for his own safety, he must withdraw northwards to Fife. Cromwell's army routed the Scots at the Battle of Dunbar on 3 September 1650 and marched on the capital. They took the town, captured the Castle and went on to conquer the rest of the country. Eluding him, Charles II was on 1 January 1651 crowned King of Scots at Scone by the Marquis of Argyll, who had changed sides. Charles then marched south at the head of the Scottish army, but he was defeated at the Battle of Worcester. After a series of narrow escapes, he managed to flee to the continent once more.

Scotland was forcibly united with England as a single Commonwealth. It was now an occupied country living under military rule, and relations between the townspeople and the army were tense. Major General John Lambert, Cromwell's second in command, established his headquarters in Edinburgh and took over the East Kirk for his men, 'being the special kirk and best in the town'. English chaplains and ministers began to preach there and so too did soldiers: captains, lieutenants and troopers, who entered the pulpit wearing their swords and even carrying pistols. Nicoll the diarist noted that General Lambert preached frequently in the East Kirk and so apparently did Oliver Cromwell himself on several occasions in 1651. Their presence must have been intimidating, to say the least. Cromwell's military record was only too well known, and that same summer Lambert had led a force which killed 2,000 Scots at Inverkeithing, and took 1,400 prisoner. Nicoll was willing to allow that some of the sermons he heard in St Giles' were delivered by gifted men, but in general people objected bitterly to lay preachers replacing their own ordained ministers.

The congregations also resented alterations to their services, for biblical readings and the singing of psalms were abolished in favour of very long sermons, and they complained frequently between 1648 and 1655 that their own ministers, in protest at current events, were refusing to celebrate communion. Then there were expensive but unnecessary changes to their church interiors. Not surprisingly, the King's loft was removed from the East Kirk in 1652, and over the years the intrusive English ministers insisted on the position of the pulpit of the East Kirk being changed twice, with consequent alterations to the placing of the lofts and seating. Similar alterations were made in the Tolbooth Kirk, now attended by the commissioners appointed by Cromwell to rule Scotland and the judges of the new Court of Exchequer set up to deal with forfeited estates. Finally, an innocuous improvement was made to the steeple clock, which in 1655 gained a third gilded face, 'for pointing out the hours to the neighbours on the south side of the town'. In those days a clock still had to be set from the time shown on a sundial, and two years later John Mylne erected on the south side of the Old Kirk a great vertical stone sundial which was then painted by Gavin Syme.

Oliver Cromwell's rule was by now drawing to a close and when he died in 1658 he was succeeded as Lord Protector of the Commonwealth by his ineffectual son, Richard. Modest and unassuming, Richard was unable to hold on to power and on 29 May 1659 the English army deposed him. For some time past there had been growing demands for the return of Charles II and the King finally sailed triumphantly back to England from the Netherlands in May 1660. Economically exhausted and ground down by Cromwell's military rule, the Scots were overjoyed at the news. Edinburgh's council sent off a humble letter to Charles, congratulating him on his restoration and four days before he had even landed they were considering where a new royal loft should be situated.

The magistrates made a tour of inspection, led by the ministers and it was decided that the East Kirk was the place for it. A month later, the council was emphasising that it should resemble the one used by the King's grandfather James VI, with similar carvings of the royal arms, the crown, sword, sceptre and thistle. Whatever the cost, they were anxious for it to be 'most fit, stately and beseeming to the grandeur of His Majesty'. Unfortunately, Charles II never did sit in his splendid new seat, nor did his successors, James VII, William and Mary, Queen Anne and the first three Georges, all of whom remained firmly in England during their various reigns. The days of the monarch attending services and taking a close personal interest in St Giles' had gone. However, the King always sent a Lord High Commissioner to represent him during sessions of the Scottish parliament and when the Duke of Rothes attended services in St Giles' in that capacity during the early 1660s, he occupied the royal loft with cushions, chairs, carpets, stools and other suitable furnishings brought from Holyrood, as if he were the King himself.

As well as restoring the royal loft, the council announced that 19 June would be kept as a day of public thanksgiving, with special services in St Giles' in the morning and bonfires in the evening, but there must definitely be no shooting of muskets, squibs or fireworks, lasciviousness or excessive drinking. In the early weeks of 1661, the Marquis of Montrose's head was taken down from the Tolbooth after almost eleven years and in March, Charles II's first parliament annulled all legislation passed since 1633. Montrose's body parts were reassembled and, on the King's orders, he was given an impressive state funeral in St Giles' on 11 May. A long procession led by black-clad members of the nobility accompanied his coffin from Holyrood to the Old Kirk, for burial in his grandfather's vault beneath the Chepman Aisle. On 27 May his great enemy, the Marquis of Argyll, was beheaded for treason by the Maiden guillotine.

On 21 June 1661, payments were granted to a series of royalist ministers or their surviving relatives. The list includes the sum of £100 to be given to the children of Mr James Hannay, Dean of Edinburgh. That same year, archbishops and bishops were restored, but Charles II was well aware of what had gone before and so the rights of presbyteries, kirk sessions and congregations were safeguarded. There would be no altars against east walls, no surplices, no kneeling at communion and no new liturgy. The new Bishop of Edinburgh, George Wishart, formerly chaplain to the Marquis of Montrose, was consecrated in St Andrews on 3 June 1662, watched by a small group of St Giles' parishioners who had travelled there with him, including Mylne the master mason. Robert Laurie, formerly minister of the Old Kirk, became the new dean, and minister of the East Kirk, which people took to calling 'the Dean's Kirk'. When Laurie's eldest daughter was married there in 1663, the town councillors were gratified to be invited to the wedding and presented her with a large gilded cup, out of respect for her father, 'who has been very long a faithful minister of God's word in this place'.

Thomas Garven and John Hamilton, ministers of the Old Kirk, Robert Douglas and David Dickson of the East Kirk and George Hutcheson of the Tolbooth Kirk were replaced because they opposed the reintroduction of bishops. Throughout the country in general, slightly more than a third of the ministers refused to conform. Deprived of their charges, they were forbidden to live or preach within twenty miles of their former parishes. More and more of their supporters began attending their outdoor services, known as field conventicles, and in the 1670s the Duke of Lauderdale, who was governing Scotland on behalf of Charles II, introduced severely repressive measures against them. Much of the trouble was in the west of Scotland but, during the 1666 Pentland Rising, Covenanters defeated at Rullion Green were brought to Edinburgh to be held before being released, deported or executed and Haddo's Hole was one of their prisons.

Eager to ingratiate themselves with Lauderdale, the Edinburgh town council in 1669 made him a gift of his own special 'desk, seat and pew' in the East Kirk, next to the Earl of Dunfermline's seat in that most prestigious position, immediately under the royal loft. Location was always an indication of status, and there were other ways, too, of showing a person's importance. The Lord Provost always had a special velvet cushion in front of him upon which he could rest his arms during services, and the loft which he and the councillors occupied was regularly decorated with flowers supplied by James Cuthbertson, gardener of the nearby Heriot's Hospital.

The population of Edinburgh was rising rapidly and would reach about 40,000 by the end of the seventeenth century. To deal with this increase, the town had been divided into six parishes in 1641, ten in 1656 and then reduced to six again in 1662, but the problem of overcrowding in the churches remained unsolved. In 1677, for instance, Bailie Riddell fell out with his brother-in-law Alexander Anderson about the pew that they shared in the East Kirk. The council, called upon to resolve the dispute, eventually declared that, as the pew held eight people, five of Bailie Riddell's family and three of Alexander Anderson's should occupy it. This was their final decision, they warned in some exasperation. Even the elders' and deacons' pew had to be enlarged in 1682 because it was 'too little and narrow and does not contain them fully'.

There was also the problem of seat rents. These had been introduced in 1640 in an attempt to raise additional revenue and so those seats which did not belong to a particular person were rented out to parishioners who were willing to pay a yearly fee in advance for the privilege of sitting there. Unfortunately, the response was disappointing. People were eager enough to apply for seats, but in 1664 it was reported that even 'the most able and considerable persons' were unwilling to pay, 'to the ill example of others'. This was all the more frustrating, because the rents were used to fund part of the ministers' stipends and so it was decided that the names of those who were in arrears should be read out before the whole congregation, in the hope of shaming them into paying.

Maintenance of the entire building remained, of course, the major part of the town's expenditure on St Giles' and in 1660 John Mylne's masons were busy pointing the stonework of the steeple, assisted by an anonymous water wife who was paid £12 Scots to carry no fewer than 240 tubs of water up to the roof for them. Seven years after that, Alexander Anderson, coppersmith (presumably Bailie Riddell's brother-in-law) charged £91:10 Scots for making a new weathercock for the steeple and Duncan Sandilands had the perilous task of taking down the old cock and putting up the new one. He was rewarded with £66:13:4 Scots. At ground level, Haddo's Hole was now being used as a store for the town's ammunition again.

When Charles II died in 1685, his loft was draped with black on the day of his funeral, as custom demanded. Since he left no legitimate children, he was succeeded, to the alarm of many, by his Roman Catholic brother James VII and II. James had spent two periods of time in Edinburgh as Charles II's Lord High Commissioner to the Scottish parliament and he had aroused angry opposition when he fitted out the nave of Holyrood Abbey as his Roman Catholic chapel. People feared that he might make similar alterations to St Giles', but in fact those who favoured presbyterian church government benefited unexpectedly in 1687 when, in his pursuit of toleration for his Roman Catholic subjects, he somewhat reluctantly extended freedom of worship to everyone. The following year he was deposed by his Protestant subjects and replaced by his daughter Mary and her husband, William of Orange, both Protestants.

In the Scottish settlement which followed their arrival, the events of the early 1660s were reversed. Bishops were abolished, ministers who supported them were ejected from their churches and the surviving ministers dismissed in 1660 were restored once more. Alexander Rose, last

Bishop of Edinburgh in the Church of Scotland, was deposed and William Annand, the much respected final dean, escaped deprivation only because he died in the summer of 1689 before action against him could be taken. All but one of the six ministers of St Giles' (two to each church) lost their charges. Finally, in 1690, the Scottish parliament passed an act establishing the presbyterian system of church government which in essence exists to this day.

Services remained largely unaltered and kirk sessions continued to do the work they had done both before and after the advent of bishops. The kirk session minutes of the period record matters of church discipline along with finance and, in so doing, they demonstrate the role of the elders as well as providing a wealth of colourful, circumstantial detail about the lives of the parishioners. Poor relief, for example, was an important concern, with the kirk session making regular payments to a variety of beggars, destitute widows and aged parishioners. There were some touching individual cases. In January 1704 a baby was found in Widow Allan's Close with a paper pinned to his wrappings, saying that his name was Thomas Campbell and that he had been baptised. The session gave him into the care of Jean Edgar, wife of a Canongate weaver, and paid her £4 Scots for nursing him for six weeks. Public order was another concern, and when Archibald Brownlee appeared before the session that summer, accused of allowing people to play cards and curse and swear in his Exchange Coffee House 'to the great dishonour of God and offence to hearers', they promptly referred him to the burgh magistrates because he had contravened a recent act of parliament.

Much of the elders' time, however, was spent chasing up members of the congregation suspected of having sexual relations outside marriage. Very often the people concerned simply vanished, the men going off to work elsewhere, the women seeking refuge with relatives in the country. However, in one long-running case which began in January 1704, both parties were present and eager to put forward their side of the story. Agnes Richardson, servant, accused her employer Master Thomas Dunlop, surgeon burgess, of being the father of her illegitimate child, a claim which he robustly denied. Agnes insisted that, the previous July, Thomas had sent his two apprentices out for the evening, tied her by the leg to his bedpost with the belt of his dressing gown and, ignoring her protests, forced himself upon her. Witness after witness gave evidence, the apprentices denied knowing anything about it, and the session referred the matter to the presbytery.

Equally unable to sort out what had really happened, the presbytery sent the case back to the kirk session, telling them to examine more witnesses. Agnes's brother-in-law then appeared and recounted how, when she went into labour at two in the morning, he ran to Thomas's house to ask to him to supply a midwife. 'Let her get a midwife to herself!' was the curt reply. When her brother reported this to Agnes, she sent him back again to Thomas, who callously threatened to kick him downstairs. Agnes's female friends then rallied round and the baby was delivered by the appropriately named Janet Charity, who was herself heavily pregnant. More and more depositions were taken and throughout the summer the surgeon continued to protest his innocence until, in the end, Agnes began to weaken, mixing up the dates in her story. This was important, because it turned out that she had a husband somewhere and so the child might really have been his.

Agnes was still determinedly insisting that she was telling the truth when the kirk session minutes come to an abrupt halt and do not resume again until four years later by which time, tantalisingly, her name has vanished from their pages. So why was Agnes willing to appear repeatedly before the kirk session in those circumstances? It may be that she was indeed the victim of Thomas Dunlop and wanted justice, but she also knew that she would not be able to have her baby baptised or claim maintenance for the child until she either proved her story or confessed before the congregation that she had lied and was duly absolved by her minister. The records show that, for their part, ministers and elders seem to have been genuinely trying to find out the truth in these difficult cases, rather than pursuing the unfortunate miscreants in a spirit of vengeance. Our feelings about such situations are very different today, but in the seventeenth century the whole purpose of these investigations was to reintegrate the accused into the congregation once more, welcoming them back to their place in the community once they had done their public penance.

While beadles searched for disappearing unmarried mothers and recalcitrant adulterers stood by pillars of repentance, only one significant change was made to the interior of St Giles'. That came in 1699 when the town council decided that the only way to solve the problem of overcrowding was to create a fourth church within its walls. The space at the north end of the Tolbooth Church still being used as a courtroom was therefore converted into what was at first called the New North Church. Later, it was known as Haddo's (and sometimes even Haddock's) Hole Church, because of its proximity to the room where Sir John Gordon had been imprisoned. Several members of its congregation – including three lawyers, a dyer and a merchant – presented their new church with communion plate: four silver cups, 'a large English flagon' and a pewter flagon.

In the same year that the new church was created, an unusual and pleasing addition was made when a set of musical bells was installed in the steeple. Edinburgh merchants trading with the Low Countries were familiar with carillons in continental churches and town halls and so, at the end of 1697, the town approached Deacon John Meikle, their official bell founder, to see if he would be willing to set up a similar chime in St Giles'. After he produced various sample bells, the provost and magistrates commissioned him to provide fifteen bronze bells of varying sizes and notes, with the date and the magistrates' names engraved on the largest one. Meikle went abroad to buy the metal and seek advice, then he went to work in his foundry at Castlehill. He had to cast several of the bells three or four times to get them right, not to mention supplying an extra six not specified in the contract, but by the end of August 1699 the bells were in place, the council decided that they were 'extraordinarily well done', and the nobility, gentry and all the townspeople were reported to be 'well pleased and satisfied'.

Meikle charged according to the weight of the bells, at twenty-two pence sterling a pound, and was paid a further £1,000 Scots when he cast another two bells producing the notes F and G sharp. Francis Toward, one of the teachers at the town's music school, was employed at 500 merks a year to play the bells for half an hour before and after noon every day but Sunday, and so everyone in the vicinity was entertained by traditional Scottish melodies and popular tunes. Daniel Defoe, visiting Edinburgh in 1706, described how these bells were not rung with ropes. Instead, there was a keyboard rather like that of a harpsichord, and the player had great strong wooden cases on his fingers, by which he was able to strike with more force. They were, Defoe thought, much better heard at a distance than near at hand. They remained in the steeple until they were finally sold singly by auction in 1890. One was presented to the Cathedral by an anonymous elder in 1955 and hangs on a specially made wooden stand, while several others may be seen in the Museum of Edinburgh in Huntly House.

By that time, William of Orange was dead, killed as a result of a fall from his horse in 1702, and his sister-in-law Queen Anne had inherited the British throne. She did not ever come north as Queen, but she had spent ten months in Scotland in 1681, when she was 17 and her father James VII and II was Lord High Commissioner. She may even have attended some services in St Giles', although she was a devout member of the Church of England with no great liking for Presbyterians. As monarch, national unity was her aim and she supported her statesmen who were working towards the union of the Scottish and English parliaments. When this was finally accomplished in 1707, a popular tune of the time, 'Why should I be sad on my wedding day?' rang out over Edinburgh from Meikle's carillon in the steeple of St Giles'.

CHAPTER 8

Four Churches in One

*T*he Act of Union came into force on 1 May 1707, bringing together Scotland and England as 'one kingdom by the name of Great Britain'. In future, there would be only one parliament, meeting in London. An accompanying act secured the Protestant religion and presbyterian church government in Scotland and an impressive thanksgiving service was held in St Giles'. No longer the scene of open ecclesiastical conflict, the four parish churches now within its walls would enjoy a long-lost tranquillity, undisturbed for the next seventy years by any major crisis or indeed by any major building works. Certainly, there was a brief moment of drama in 1745 when Bonnie Prince Charlie's Jacobite army advanced on the capital and the alarmed inhabitants met in the East Kirk to discuss what action to take. However, they quickly agreed to surrender, no damage was done and the following year when the Prince was defeated at Culloden the town council just as quickly ordered the musical bells to be rung in honour of the victorious Duke of Cumberland.

The Edinburgh council was now spending relatively small sums of money on its growing number of churches and indeed in some years the cost of the bread and wine for communion actually exceeded the expenditure on building repairs. New slates, blue and grey, and stone slabs were purchased from time to time for the roofs of St Giles' and in 1721 the clock mechanism was replaced by the firm of L. Bradley of London, much to the annoyance of the Edinburgh clockmakers. Inside, the favoured colour scheme of green and white was maintained in all four churches. James Norie the painter was busy whitewashing the interior of the East Kirk in

May 1736, painting the lower part of the walls olive green, varnishing the pillars to look like green marble and gilding the capitals of the pulpit. He also made the internal doors a novel chocolate colour.

Meanwhile his business partner, Roderick Chalmers the herald painter, worked on the painting of the British Royal Arms which to this day hangs high above the chancel on the west wall of the tower. He charged £5 for it, and a further £3 for drawing the Commandments, Lord's Prayer and Creed with black letters on a yellow ground. The Arms and Commandments were framed and put up together, while the Lord's Prayer and the Creed seem to have been hung on the east wall at either side of the pulpit, which was now immediately in front of the great east window. The windows all had plain lozenges of glass in them, and sash windows had been introduced by 1738, when there is mention of the top sash of the East Kirk Aisle window having been blown out by the wind.

In 1736 the royal loft was repaired, an unnamed carver making for it a new sword and sceptre and a new letter R (the abbreviation for Rex, the Latin word for king). Five years later, the loft was given a new cornice and door mouldings in the elegant egg and dart design. Various groups continued to have their own lofts – noblemen, judges, barons of the exchequer, Lord Provost and council, elders and soldiers too – and in 1758 the mistress and girls of the Trades Maidens' Hospital for some reason moved to the East Kirk from Greyfriars Church. They sat in newly painted, smart, bright green lofts which had red borders and brass nails, the seats covered with green cloth and the Incorporated Trades coat of arms displayed in front of them. The Lord High Commissioner to the General Assembly had his own throne in the Preston Aisle where the Assembly still met. Intriguingly, the person involved in taking down and putting up seats in the East Kirk almost twenty years later was a woman, 'Widow Cowan, wright'. Presumably she was running her husband's business, as many widows did, and employing men to do the work.

The East Kirk was the largest of the four churches and so it not surprisingly accommodated more people than the other three. When Alexander Boswell in 1750 painted numbers on the seats, it had 167, the Tolbooth Kirk had 137, Haddo's Hole 136 and the Old Kirk only 111. These would be the seats that were rented out, not the entire total. So how did people decide which of the four churches to attend? They should, of course, have gone to their own parish church but, as always, there were other considerations. Some fashionable members of society were eager to be seen in the East Kirk because, as one nineteenth-century historian observed, they did not care so much for the sermon as for the gratification of sitting in the same place as the high court judges and the magistrates. The services were dignified in manner and vaguely Episcopalian in style, he thought. The Old Kirk, he said, attracted people who were eager to hear 'a tough sufficient sermon of good divinity' of about three-quarters of an hour long and were willing to put up with the darkness and the draughts of 'that dungeon-like' place of worship.

Those attending the Tolbooth Kirk were rigid Calvinists who liked nothing better than an extempore evangelical sermon even if the 'social habits' of the minister, Alexander Webster, 'scandalised his devout and self-denying congregation'. He was too fond of claret, apparently. An amusing contemporary caricature by John Kay shows Dr Webster soberly preaching to his congregation, who are packed into their seats as tightly as

Figure 7
A Sleepy Congregation, showing Dr Alexander Webster (1707–84) preaching in
the Tolbooth Church, St Giles', by John Kay.
(© National Museums of Scotland. Licensor www.scran.ac.uk)

sardines. Not all services were as well attended, though, and one East Kirk minister complained ruefully that even were St Paul himself to preach in his church in the afternoon, no more than five of the judges would come to hear him.

The most famous preacher of the period was Hugh Blair, a stately man in a powdered wig with a long, aquiline nose and a neat mouth. Born in Edinburgh in 1718, he was the only child of John Blair, a clerk in the Excise Office. After John's early death, his widow Martha Ogston carried on her late father's business as a bookseller in Parliament Close, behind St Giles', and was able to send Hugh to Edinburgh University when he was 13. By the time he became minister of the East Kirk in 1758, he was a leading figure in the Church and counted among his close friends David Hume the sceptical philosopher nicknamed by James Boswell 'the Great Infidel' and William Robertson the historian, central figures in that period of great intellectual activity known as the Scottish Enlightenment.

As always, there were differing shades of opinion within the Church of Scotland and Blair was a distinguished member of the moderate as opposed to the evangelical party. The evangelicals were adamant that Calvinism must be strictly upheld and they were particularly strong supporters of the doctrine of predestination. The moderates, led by William Robertson, were more liberally minded. Francis Hutcheson, Professor of Moral Philosophy at Glasgow University in the 1730s and early 1740s, had said that goodness should be judged not by any biblical rules but by the promotion of the happiness of others, and he had argued that it was perfectly possible to have an awareness of good and evil without knowing anything about God. This appealed to people living in what was seen as an increasingly secular age. The moderates also held that church ministers should engage in cultural life and, to the horror of the evangelicals, moderate ministers saw nothing wrong with going to the theatre or playing cards.

Combining his ministry at St Giles' with his career as Professor of Rhetoric and Belles Lettres at Edinburgh University, Blair enjoyed an international reputation as a literary critic, but even greater was his fame as a preacher. He attracted crowds to his services, standing in his pulpit in his best black superfine cloth gown with its five dozen tasselled silk loops supplied by Margaret English and her sister Agnes. Some claimed that he and his followers delivered sermons which were no more than polished essays urging good works, kind thoughts and social order and, in certain quarters, they were even blamed for encouraging atheism. Others defended Blair, saying that he must not be blamed for the 'many

Figure 8
Parliament Close, Edinburgh attributed to John Kay and others; a view of the
south side of St Giles' in the late eighteenth century.
(© City Art Centre: City of Edinburgh Museums and Galleries)

wretched imitators who had his foibles without his virtues: for though
sufficiently enamoured of philosophers and philosophy, he never lost sight
of Christianity'. Whatever his critics said, the five published volumes of his
comforting, elegantly written and insightful sermons enjoyed enormous
popularity, not only in Britain but in America, and in translation elsewhere.
He earned over £2,000 for the first four volumes, a huge sum for any author
in those days, especially for a theologian and, by the time of his death, an
astonishing 33,500 copies of the first two volumes had been printed.

One of those who came to hear Blair preach was the poet Robert Burns,
who stayed in Edinburgh for six months in 1786–7. Burns was lionised
by polite society but he was sensitive and he resented the patronising
attitude of many of the people he encountered. Blair admired his work
and befriended him, but one unfortunate incident placed a strain on
their relationship. At a social event they were both attending, someone
asked the poet which public place had most impressed him. Burns replied
that St Giles' gave him the greatest gratification. He was then asked

who he thought was the best preacher. He was obviously expected to say 'Dr Blair', but instead he chose young William Greenfield, soon to be appointed Blair's colleague and successor. Burns's private opinion of Blair was not altogether flattering either. In one of his commonplace books he mentioned the minister's famous vanity and described him as being no more than an astonishing proof of what industry and application can do.

Another visitor to St Giles' at that period was Dr Samuel Johnson, the famous English lexicographer. Passing through Edinburgh with James Boswell in August 1773 on their way to the Hebrides, he did not go to a service but he was taken to look round St Giles' by William Robertson. As they went in, Johnson remarked teasingly, 'Come let me see what was once a church!' Sad to say, in spite of the efforts over the years by beadles wielding sow's head brushes, old man's head besoms and large pope's head besoms with shafts eighteen feet long for sweeping roof and walls, Johnson was more impressed by the general dirtiness of the East Kirk than by anything else. Perhaps it was fortunate that he made no comment on the pealing of the bells, for although George Begbie the smith regularly repaired 'Tinkling Tom' and the others, one of them was found to be cracked the following year and had to be broken up. Two years after that, a replacement was brought up on a sledge from Leith and hung in the steeple, along with two other new bells. Meanwhile, the mechanism of the music bells underwent constant repairs too and in the 1770s George Watt, bell-founder, made at least three new ones.

Far more dramatic improvements were already in the minds of the Lord Provost and council, however, and in the spring of 1777 James Craig the architect was commissioned to provide designs for a complete refurbishment of the interior of the East Kirk. Craig had found fame in 1766 when he had won a competition to design the New Town of Edinburgh. The Old Town had become impossibly overcrowded, and the fine new streets were duly laid out at a lower level to the north. With Craig's detailed drawings for the East Kirk before them, the town council now set up a committee to consider what should be done, King George III contributed a generous £500 although he had never seen St Giles', and Francis Braidwood the wright was contracted to undertake the alterations.

Braidwood was to replace all the lofts, seats, stairs and furnishings. The ceiling was to be painted a light French grey, probably to show up decorative plasterwork to the best advantage and the walls were to be whitewashed. The upper parts of the pillars would be painted in marble or stone colour, whichever the council decided. Braidwood would receive £1,000 sterling for the work and he was to have all the redundant fittings. Certain furnishings were, however, to be retained by St Giles': the globe lamps and their ironwork, the cushion belonging to the pulpit, the chairs of the barons of the exchequer and the paintings on the west wall. As well as the Ten Commandments and the Royal Arms, there were various others which are not identified.

There would be new lofts on the east, north and south sides of the Kirk, with the King's seat on the west side, opposite the pulpit, which would remain beneath the great east window, flanked by its two painted boards. Since the 1730s people had begun to take an interest in medieval architecture and so Hugh Blair's pulpit was to be in the latest 'Gothic' style, in keeping with the medieval building. He would enter it by one of two staircases of nine steps at either side, and below him, at ground level, was the seat for the precentor, who led the singing. The ledges in front of them were to be decorated with fringed crimson cloths. Braidwood was also to supply new communion tables, with seats. Communion was now being celebrated twice a year, in May and November, and the only change to the service had been that from 1757 onwards red port wine had replaced the claret used since the Reformation. The East Kirk's four silver communion cups were kept in a wainscot box lined with green and the silver flagons and the two silver plates for the bread, now termed 'sacrament loaves', had their own leather cases.

The King's new seat was quite different from any of its predecessors. Four columns in the Gothic style would support a circular dome, on top of which Craig visualised three angels representing Scotland, England and Ireland holding up an imperial crown. Britannia and Neptune would stand over the front columns and the ceiling beneath the dome would have the sun in the centre with a frieze of the months of the year along with figures representing the seasons, and the King's coat of arms. To the right of the pulpit, the loft for the Lord Provost and the principal town officials was faced with crimson velvet and tassels and the dean of guild's accounts reveal that the mahogany elbow chairs for the Lord Provost, the Lord President of the Court of Session and the Chief Baron of the Exchequer were made in 1781 by Francis Brodie, another leading wright. The backs and seats were stuffed and covered with Wilton carpet, and two dozen similar chairs without arms were supplied for the magistrates. Protective scarlet cotton slips were made for all twenty-seven chairs.

The new decorative scheme, begun in the summer of 1780, was inspired entirely by aesthetic considerations, not by any liturgical change, and whether all the ornate detail was actually achieved is not altogether certain. However, Joseph Farrington, the English landscape painter and diarist, was certainly impressed when he attended a service on 6 July 1788. Contrary to his expectation, he found that the church was decorated in rather an elegant manner, without any sign of the sour Presbyterianism he had expected to see. For much of the eighteenth century people had tended to refer to the East Kirk as 'the New Church', but about the time of Craig's repairs they evidently decided that this was now rather out of date and revived the old term, 'the High Church', briefly applied to the entire building in the reign of James VI. The change of designation was no doubt pleasing to the more status-conscious members of the congregation.

The other three churches in St Giles' retained their accustomed names but in the years that followed they gradually adopted such novelties as Olympian green passageways, brass chandeliers and coal and coke stoves, while the High Church acquired a gilded star on its ceiling and crimson coverings supplied by William Trotter for some of its seats and tables. In 1836, the entire building was enclosed in a set of iron railings about five feet high but the next really significant alteration did not take place for another forty years after Craig's refurbishment. When it came it was a major project, driven by a combination of practical necessity and architectural fashion. In the course of significant improvements to Parliament Close and its buildings, the council began demolishing the New and Old Tolbooths and all the shops known as luckenbooths built against the side of St Giles'. As they did so, it became painfully obvious that the church exterior was in an alarming state. Apart from the fact that the adjacent shops had damaged the stonework, the vertical walls were noticeably leaning outwards.

Repairs would have to be made as a matter of urgency and the council commissioned Archibald Elliot to find a solution. A well-known Edinburgh architect with his offices at Calton Hill, Elliot had put up various important buildings in the city and had just finished designing St Paul's and St George's Episcopal Church in York Place. The plan he now produced for St Giles' involved making safe the stonework, demolishing the Tolbooth Church with several medieval chapels to improve access to Parliament Close, creating a new main door on the west front and rearranging the interior into three great preaching halls.

As soon as the details were known, there was a public outcry, and *Blackwood's Magazine* published a highly critical report by the Society of Dilettanti condemning the 'extreme regularity' of the plan and making various alternative suggestions. Why not raise two bell-towers at the west front, paint the entire building with lime and preserve all the fading inscriptions on the exterior? The Society was particularly upset about the proposal to demolish the Tolbooth Church and the side chapels. Possibly because of the expense and maybe in part because of the controversy, nothing was done about Elliot's plans and he died in 1823. The following year a terrifying fire destroyed all the houses in Parliament Close, leading to further rebuilding by Robert Reid.

Meanwhile, an exciting event had taken place in St Giles' in 1822. The flamboyant King George IV decided to pay a visit to Scotland, the first time a monarch had come north since Charles II's stay in 1650–1. Famous as the former Prince Regent who had built Brighton Pavilion and was an extravagant patron of the arts, George took a good deal of trouble to please his Scottish subjects. He appeared at Holyrood, his large, stout figure arrayed in Highland dress, his legs modestly concealed by pink tights, and when his attendance at a service in the High Church was arranged, he carefully studied a plan of the interior and a detailed description of Presbyterian services as his coach jolted along the roads from Dalkeith Palace, where he was staying.

The King was not the only person involved in last-minute preparations. Dr David Lamont, the elderly Moderator of the General Assembly, was to take the service that day and, according to one favourite anecdote, while he was making his way to the High Church he was intercepted by his friend Dr Inglis, the minister of Greyfriars Kirk, who asked him anxiously if he was remembering that the King would expect to hear the Lord's Prayer recited. This, of course, had not been done in the Scottish Church for many years, and Dr Lamont was dismayed. Perhaps he would get the words wrong, for he was unused to saying the prayer in public. His friend helpfully drew him into a neighbouring close and made him repeat it over and over until he was word-perfect.

Arriving at St Giles', George IV handed over for the offering a sealed packet inscribed 'One Hundred Pounds from the King', and was escorted to the Royal Seat. Dr Lamont preached a lively sermon on the sins of fornication and the duty of husbands to love their wives. This was embarrassing to say the least, in view of George IV's marital record – a secret, illegal marriage to a Roman Catholic, followed by energetic attempts to divorce his official wife, Queen Caroline – but the King tactfully avoided any mention of the sermon afterwards and instead cheerfully praised the singing of the choir. Among those who had come north with him was the famous artist J. M. W. Turner, who was present at the service that day. His painting, *George IV at St Giles'*, which the King disliked, clearly shows both Craig's pulpit and the Royal Seat (see Plate 2).

However diverting such occasions might be, the dangerous state of the walls could not be forgotten and on 20 January 1826, the Lord Provost of Edinburgh's request for financial assistance towards restoring the stonework was passed on to the barons of the Exchequer. In March, William Burn the architect was asked for his ideas about restoring St Giles' for a sum not exceeding £10,000 sterling. Burn had trained with his Edinburgh architect father before moving to the office of the famous Sir Robert Smirke in London, where he became site architect at Covent Garden Theatre. On his return to Scotland his design for North Leith Parish Church made his reputation and he embarked on a long career as a church and country house architect.

Comfort with modern amenities was one of his main concerns, and his ingenious adaptations of historic houses such as the Castle of Mey brought him a significant number of commissions. T. L. Donaldson, a fellow architect, would later describe him as being frank, plain spoken and no flatterer but, although he was rather impulsive, he possessed great shrewdness and commonsense. In short, Donaldson regarded him as being a man of the highest integrity. The council decided that he would be the ideal person to solve the problems of St Giles' while at the same time modernising it, both inside and out.

By late 1826 Burn had produced his plans, which were firmly based on Elliot's designs. They were, he told the Lord Provost, 'intended to preserve with the most scrupulous care the whole external features of the building worthy of preservation and every portion of the interior'. Because any repairs to the stonework would result in a very patched and imperfect appearance, he was convinced that the entire exterior would have to be faced with ashlar. Apart from anything else, this would make St Giles' blend in with the recently constructed neoclassical freestone buildings of Parliament Square, as the Close was now called. His estimate exceeded the financial limit by £2,210, but he helpfully pointed out where reductions might be made and it was accepted by the council. In the end, the cost was £20,000, with the government supplying £12,600 and the town council paying the rest. The presbytery was consulted since Burn intended having only two congregations in St Giles' instead of four, and parliament gave the necessary approval in its Improvement Act of 1827.

The plans had also been sent to Robert Reid, architect of the new Parliament Square buildings, and when he gave his opinion of them he stressed the necessity of improving access to Parliament Square. The barons of the Exchequer were adamant that this must be done, not least because the government was about to put up new courts of justice there, at great expense. Commenting that in its present state the masonry of St Giles' was very rugged, decayed and 'in many respects very unseemly', Reid warned that its general appearance would be considerably changed by the intended alterations. Burn himself was well aware that by adopting Archibald Elliot's scheme to demolish the south-west corner of the building he had aroused much anxiety among 'many of the principal inhabitants' of Edinburgh. However, his reply to the critics was that, at the moment, the space between the Signet Library and St Giles' was only six feet eight inches, terminating in a long lane. His alterations would increase it to between nine and ten feet, leading to a large open area. 'I beg leave only to add that no one can feel more solicitous than I do for the preservation of every characteristic feature and peculiarity of our ecclesiastical structures', he told the town council earnestly.

In May 1829 the councillors were at last ready to enter into contracts and the Lord Provost and council bound themselves to complete the project within four years at most. Work finally began, and the congregations of the High Church and the Old Kirk moved out into the High School Hall. This was not without its problems, for the Old Kirk ministers complained bitterly about their fears of being permanently ejected while the High Church congregation were unhappy when they were told that they could not drive over the High School playground in their carriages for fear of damaging the surface. It was far too dangerous, they protested, for 'infirm and delicate' members to walk across it on wet Sundays. Meanwhile, the congregation of Haddo's Hole Kirk met in the Methodist Chapel, Nicolson Square, while the Tolbooth Kirk members assembled in the Albany Street Chapel during the renovation work.

So what did Burn actually do? Discovering that in some places the rough stone walls were leaning outwards by as much as one and a half feet, he inserted iron cramps (tie bars) two feet long and enclosed the masonry of everything but the tower in a casing of Cullalo polished ashlar sandstone which varied in thickness from eight inches at the foot to four or five inches at the top. This stone veneer was not only in keeping with the buildings in Parliament Square but it acted as an effective buttressing agent. In order to emphasise the original cruciform shape of St Giles', the roofs of the transepts and the centre aisle of the nave were raised, the latter by sixteen feet, to match that of the choir, and the entire building was re-roofed, many of the old stone slabs being replaced with slates. The tower was later given a coat of light-coloured paint to preserve the stonework from the weather, hence its somewhat ghostly appearance in the painting of Parliament Close attributed to John Kay and others (see Figure 8).

At the south-west corner of the church, two of the five side chapels built in 1387 were demolished as Archibald Elliot had intended, as was the west bay of the Holy Blood Aisle. This not only gave the desired improved access to Parliament Square but allowed Burn to create a symmetrical west front with a fairly plain central door. The east bay of the Moray Aisle and the south transept were then added to the Preston Aisle to form a larger Assembly Aisle. On the north side of the building, two small projecting bays and a stair turret were taken down to give the appearance of a longer north transept and some fairly minor alterations were made to the vestry (now the Chambers Aisle). The east front was already symmetrical, so little needed to be done there.

Since most of the windows had lost their medieval tracery, Burn recreated traceried Gothic window openings and in January 1830 the High Church kirk session decided to think about putting stained glass in the great east window. There had been no stained glass in St Giles' since 1560 because of the Reformers' disapproval of anything resembling images and it was only with the Gothic Revival in architecture that High Church Episcopalians began to introduce stained glass into their buildings again. Stained glass windows for the chancel of St John's Episcopal Church in Princes Street, Edinburgh, were commissioned from the English firm of W. Raphael Edginton in 1815. Evangelical Presbyterians, however, had a lingering prejudice against stained glass and in September 1830 the High Church kirk session were regretfully noting that the town council had refused their proposal, ostensibly on the grounds of expense.

Inside, St Giles' underwent a fairly dramatic alteration, for it lost its east/west axis. Instead, the main door was now on the north side, on the High Street. Entering that way, visitors found themselves in a long vestibule, with doors neatly going off on either side to the High Church on their left and the enlarged Tolbooth Church on their right. The Old Kirk had vanished, and so had the town police office which for some time had occupied the north aisle of the nave. Ahead of those who entered was a door leading to the improved Assembly Aisle. Turning right into the Tolbooth Church, now to be known as the West Church, they would find that the former nave of St Giles' had undergone a transformation.

The walls were plastered and painted as they had always been, but not only had the roof been raised. There was now a lath and plaster ceiling, which had been painted light blue and the original row of clerestory windows had been filled up and plastered over. Marks on the west side of the tower still show the line of the former roof. Moreover, the solid medieval pillars lining the nave had been replaced by much thinner, elegantly fluted ones based on the design of the pillar in the Albany Aisle and there were large new lofts. The very occasional burial inside St Giles' had taken place as late as 1752, but throughout the building all the memorials, many of them dating from before the Reformation, had been broken up and removed, along with cartloads of ornamental stones. Even the much respected Regent Moray's tomb was demolished, only the brass plate with the inscription surviving, and several of the side aisles became storage areas.

The High Church congregation was able to return to St Giles' on 13 March 1831. A roll of seventy-three male heads of households, compiled three years later, shows that some lived nearby, like Dr Robert Burt who was in Bank Street or Archibald Tait in Fleshmarket Close, a sprinkling came from the south side of the city, but the majority were now living in the New Town. Of the sixty-six who gave their occupations, twenty-five were lawyers, six were doctors and two were ministers. Others included W. H. Lizars the engraver, a tailor, a baker, a fishmonger and a hatter. No households headed by women were recorded. The Tolbooth congregation returned to the new West Church in May 1832 and members of Haddo's Hole joined them when they came back in 1843. That was the year of the Disruption, the major upheaval which divided the Church of Scotland as a result of a longstanding quarrel over church patronage. A third of the ministers, including Dr James Buchanan of the High Church, and many members left to join the newly formed Free Church. Old Kirk members were temporarily allowed to occupy the new Assembly Aisle and members of the Tolbooth Kirk were in the end provided with a new church built on Castlehill in 1839–44.

At the time, people were well satisfied with William Burn's work, declaring it to be 'extraordinary fine' and admiring the way that St Giles' now blended in with its surroundings as well as appreciating the improved appearance inside. Burn himself continued his very successful career, working on many more churches and country houses until his death in 1870. However, as time went by, there was more and more criticism of what he had done at St Giles', with particular regrets that the exterior stonework had been concealed and the south-west chapels lost. 'Nothing can excuse this wanton and heedless destruction', a later minister of St Giles', would write. 'Surely never was money more senselessly wasted.' Burn could hardly be blamed for the demolition of the chapels, since that was the only way to satisfy the barons of the Exchequer, and time has vindicated his work on the exterior of the building. While the smooth stonework and the vanished chapels may be regretted on historical grounds, there are now many who believe that Burn's restoration saved St Giles' from at least partial collapse.

For the next forty years there were few changes to St Giles'. The enlarged Assembly Aisle, refitted by Burn at a cost of £3,000, proved inadequate and the assembly met there only once. During the period 1837–42 there were plans to convert part of the West Church into a completely new Assembly Aisle, with a room for the Moderator and a suite for the Lord High Commissioner, but in the end the Assembly moved to the new Tolbooth Church on Castlehill. More ominously, in 1860 the Annuity Tax Act transferred responsibility for the administration of all the city churches, including those of St Giles', to the newly appointed Edinburgh Ecclesiastical Commission. The town council retained its centuries-old position as proprietor of the building but the Commission would now receive the seat rents and would be responsible for repairs. All too soon the High Church kirk session was locked in combat with the commissioners over the collection and expenditure of the seat rents, for the money was being put to the use of other city churches and it seemed that any future improvements to St Giles' were out of the question. However, within a few years, an astonishing transformation was to take place, thanks to the energy and inspiration of one determined man.

CHAPTER 9

William Chambers

Sitting in his loft in the High Church of St Giles' one Sunday in 1867, William Chambers, Lord Provost of Edinburgh, looked around him critically. A slender man with thick white hair and a beaky nose, he was reserved in manner but his alert gaze always took in every detail of what he saw. To his right was the King's Pillar with the coats of arms of James II, Mary of Gueldres and Prince James. To his left he could see the huge pulpit, its lofty sounding board shutting out the light from the great east window. Opposite him the judges occupied their large, dark loft and to his right was the ramshackle royal seat resembling nothing so much, he thought, as a four-poster bed with a shabby blue canopy. Everywhere else old-fashioned, plain wooden pews were crammed in from floor to ceiling and, as always, he was aware of a distressing mustiness pervading the atmosphere. Deploring the dark and dingy appearance of his surroundings, he was suddenly seized with an idea. Why not renovate St Giles' – not just the High Church but the entire building? If all the partition walls were demolished, it would become once more the original sacred space intended by its founders.

The past thirty years had seen an enthusiastic revival of interest in medieval church architecture and ritual in England, with church interiors being restored to something resembling their pre-Reformation appearance. Now the chancel of Glasgow Cathedral had undergone just such a restoration, with notable success. Surely St Giles' could be similarly transformed? Many objections immediately sprang to mind. Apart from the tremendous cost of such a scheme, the evangelicals in the Church of

Figure 9
William Chambers (1800–83), publisher, Lord Provost
of Edinburgh and restorer of St Giles'.
(© Edinburgh City Libraries)

Scotland would be bitterly opposed to any hint of Roman Catholicism in the internal arrangements. Everyone knew what had happened when Charles I tried to return St Giles' to its pre-Reformation state. However, Chambers said to himself firmly, 'What good thing is ever done without trouble?' and he left St Giles' that morning determined to make his exciting idea a reality.

If anyone possessed the necessary tenacity for the task, it was William Chambers. The eldest of six children of an energetic mother and a feckless father, he was born in Peebles, in the Scottish Borders, in 1800. At first the family's circumstances were comfortable, for his mother had money, but there was soon to be a dramatic change in his lifestyle. His father's drapery business failed, they were reduced to poverty and his parents decided to move close to Edinburgh. There William was apprenticed to a bookseller, which pleased him, because he and his brother Robert were great readers, with a particular love of Scottish history and literature. William took lodgings with a poor widow and had to live on three pence halfpenny a day. It was, he observed afterwards, semi-starvation.

When his only friend, another apprentice, emigrated a few years later, William told himself sternly, 'Isolation is independence', and in summer he rose at dawn to read such books as Adam Smith's *Wealth of Nations*, John Locke's *Essay Concerning Human Understanding* and Hugh Blair's *Lectures on Rhetoric and Belles Lettres*. One day, he made the acquaintance of a baker who loved stories but never had time to read. The baker employed William to come to the bakehouse each morning at five o'clock to read to him and his two sons as they went about their work. They did not mind what they heard, as long as it was 'comic and laughable', and so William would sit for two and a half hours on a folded sack on their windowsill, a book in one hand and a candle stuck in a bottle in the other, reading to them. His reward was a hot roll straight from the oven, a welcome addition to his frugal diet.

When his apprenticeship ended, William was determined to set up in business on his own, but he had only five shillings of capital. However, a London bookseller who had come up for a trade sale allowed him some books on credit and he spent his five shillings on wood to make a stall which he set up on Leith Walk, a busy thoroughfare. In no time the books were sold. He then bought a small printing press and he and Robert began to publish their own writings on Scottish history and tradition. This was the era of self-improvement, and William quickly saw the possibilities of 'cheap literature' – instructive magazines and books produced at a price that anyone could afford. In 1832 he founded *Chambers's Journal*. Its success exceeded even his expectations and he and Robert established the firm of W. & R. Chambers, publishing school books, popular versions of the classics, dictionaries and an encyclopaedia with the subtitle *A Dictionary of Universal Knowledge*. They always paid cash, he would later recall, lost no time in 'financial scheming', avoided all controversial subjects such as politics and religion and soon their publications were famous throughout the English-speaking world. William was presented at Buckingham Palace, entertained by the President of the United States at the White House and even earned fresh fame as the man who rescued Greyfriars Bobby from certain death by taking official responsibility for the little dog after his master died.

Although reluctant to enter public life, Chambers agreed in 1865 to become Lord Provost of Edinburgh. He was a vigorous advocate of improved housing for workers and their families, and he took on his new role so that he could put into practice the latest methods of town planning. Many properties in the Old Town were overcrowded slums, with people living in dreadful conditions and, as his friend Dr Henry Littlejohn the public-health pioneer pointed out, disease was rife. Chambers visited all the old tenements and closes around St Giles' and was instrumental in having the City Improvement Act passed by parliament in 1867. By the time he retired from office, no fewer than 2,800 properties had been demolished, new streets had been laid out and the annual death rate had been reduced from 26 to 20 per cent. The restoration of St Giles' would be a natural sequel to his revival of the Old Town.

His new scheme began very well. At a meeting in the City Chambers on 1 November 1867 he made an eloquent speech to an invited audience of councillors and other leading citizens, describing how he would begin with the High Church and then move on to the other parts of the building, removing partition walls and the lofts and inserting about thirty stained glass windows with 'a general harmony of style and colouring ... unimpeachable in point of taste and drawing'. Queen Victoria might even be invited to put in the great east window in memory of her husband, Prince Albert. When everything had been done, St Giles' would become the Westminster Abbey of Scotland. Services would take place in the former High Church, once more the chancel, and the nave and aisles would form a flexible space, empty for the most part but with memorials to famous Scots on the walls. This would enhance the reverent atmosphere as people gazed at them and felt not only national pride but the desire to follow the example of these eminent forebears. Again like Westminster Abbey, St Giles' would be the setting for great national services, and on those occasions chairs would be placed in the nave and aisles to accommodate the large numbers who would attend.

It was not yet time to divulge all these ideas, and for the moment Chambers circulated preliminary plans drawn by Robert Matheson, the board of works architect who had been in charge of the Glasgow Cathedral refurbishment. He also warned his listeners that permission would have to be given by the government, the presbytery, the town council and probably the ecclesiastical commissioners. Funding would have to come from public subscriptions, though he hoped that the government might be persuaded to contribute. Throughout his speech there were loud bursts of applause and afterwards various members of the audience spoke, all expressing enthusiasm. The meeting closed with a restoration committee being set up with Chambers as chairman.

Everything looked very promising, but the difficulties soon became all too apparent. Money was disappointingly slow to come in, not all the official bodies involved gave their permission and Chambers suffered a spell of poor health. It looked as though the whole scheme were going to founder, but he bided his time. He resigned as Lord Provost in 1869 and the following year he turned to St Giles' once more. This time he would begin cautiously. There would be no high-profile meetings. Some people had been put off by the enormity of what he was proposing and, more to the point, the ecclesiastical commissioners were against him. Because their revenues for paying the city ministers and repairing the churches came from seat rents, they were strongly opposed to the idea of St Giles' being emptied of many of its pews.

In order to avoid an immediate confrontation with them, Chambers decided to try a different approach. Instead of dealing with them direct, he would work through the kirk session of the High Church. Dr David Arnot, the minister since 1843, an able painter and sculptor in private life, was very sympathetic to Chambers's proposals. He was nearing retirement, but the recently appointed session clerk, Lindsay Mackersy, was a dynamic young lawyer who now became secretary of the Restoration Committee. No picture of him seems to have survived, but we know that he was small and devoted himself to St Giles' with 'unwearied energy'.

On 10 March 1870, Mackersy wrote a long letter to the ecclesiastical commissioners pointing out that the High Church was badly in need of repair. 'In winter the cold is so intense the congregation complain of draughts in every part of the church. In the afternoon, in consequence of the imperfect lighting ... it is impossible to use either Bibles or hymn books and even in the summer time the atmosphere ... reminds one more of a vault than a place of worship.' People had put up with these unpleasant conditions patiently, in 'the hope that Provost Chambers' scheme for the renovation of the church would have been carried out', but it seemed clear that this was not going to happen. Something would have to be done, and if the commissioners would obtain plans for improvements, then the kirk session was willing to raise the necessary funds.

No reply to this letter was forthcoming but Mackersy persisted and in the end the commissioners sent David Cousin, the city architect, to inspect the building. He announced that obviously nothing could be done until the existing lofts were removed. Not to be deterred, the kirk session promptly commissioned an architect named William Hay to prepare a sketch of what they termed 'temporary improvements' and with that the third key figure in the great restoration scheme was in place. Hay, a native of Peterhead, was 52 years old, sturdy, with a broad face and a short, bushy beard. Calm and efficient, he had all the experience necessary for his latest task. Not only had he been assistant to that eminent restorer of English cathedrals, Sir George Gilbert Scott, but also he had enjoyed a highly successful career in Canada.

Scott had sent him to Newfoundland in 1847 to oversee the erection of the new Anglican cathedral in St John's. After that, he had worked in Bermuda before settling in Toronto, where he designed an impressive number of Neo-Gothic churches and public buildings. He would probably have spent the rest of his life there but after his wife died in 1860 he handed his lucrative practice over to his assistant and by 1864 he was back in Scotland. He settled at the quaintly named Rabbit Hall, Joppa, on the outskirts of Edinburgh, with his second wife Joanna Huddleston, an English lady from the Isle of Wight, and their small daughter Fanny.

At the end of March 1871 the presbytery gave their consent to Hay's plans for what they called 'the cathedralizing of the High Church' and, when the town council, the court of session and even the reluctant ecclesiastical commissioners followed suit, Chambers decided that the time had come to involve the public once again. On 13 November 1871 he told a crowded meeting that he still intended to restore the entire building. Stressing the national importance of the project, he emphasised that there were no sectarian motives for going ahead, and he hoped for the support of all religious denominations, Presbyterian, Episcopalian, Roman Catholic or any other. Although he was 71 now, he promised to work with 'whatever ardour and enthusiasm he could muster at his age.'

Once more his remarks were received with loud applause, and although Bailie Lewis was against giving the St Giles' scheme any financial support, declaring sourly, 'Let those who worship in it put their hands into their own pockets', Bailie Miller emphasised that they were dealing with 'a national and historical church, separated from all sects'. After that, subscriptions flowed in. A donation of £200 from Queen Victoria was received with much excitement and the town council granted £250 as the cost of their own new stalls. The High Church congregation arranged to hold their services in St John's Church, Victoria Street during the restoration and work began at last on Monday, 10 June 1872.

From then onwards, William Hay divided his time between his office in Hill Street and St Giles', where he went every day to supervise what was happening. Although Mackersy was taken up with his own business as a solicitor and his growing family of young teenagers, he proved just as attentive, hurrying up the Mound from his Queen Street chambers to keep an equally close eye on what was going on. He was always worried that Hay would start to introduce unauthorised innovations of his own, while Hay no doubt thought him tiresomely interfering. The two men were members of the same masonic lodge, but the social divide between them in status-conscious Victorian Edinburgh meant that although the lawyer was always referred to respectfully as 'Mr Mackersy', the experienced architect about fourteen years his senior was merely 'Hay'. For his part, William Chambers appreciated both of them, for each played a vital role in carrying through his restoration.

While government officials removed the canopy and the furniture of the royal seat, which they said were crown property, the heavy lofts were dismantled. The pillars to which they had been fixed were left with many unsightly holes which had to be repaired but, before that could be done, layer upon layer of paint and dirt had to be scraped off. The holes were then patched with what happily turned out to be exactly matching stone from Mary of Gueldres' Trinity College Church. The great pillars supporting the tower still bore the marks of flames dating from 1385 when the English set fire to the church, although despite the passage of time there had not been any settlement and they stood as firmly as ever on their foundations.

The walls and vaulted roofs were washed down, repaired and re-plastered and the floor was lifted. Much of the paving still consisted of old gravestones carved with the insignia of the craft associations, and these were given to the Incorporated Trades. Beneath the floor were found the many bones of long-dead medieval churchmen and parishioners. This was exactly the sort of insanitary arrangement which Chambers deplored and so he had them placed in five large black boxes. Hay and several other gentlemen solemnly escorted the hearse which took them to Greyfriars churchyard for burial. The floors were then relaid with fashionable encaustic tiles. Decorated with the Scottish lion rampant 'and other national emblems', they were supplied by Minton, Hollins & Co, the Stoke-on-Trent firm often used by Sir George Gilbert Scott.

That done, the furnishings could be installed. William Hay designed a fine new hexagonal pulpit which was carved by John Rhind the sculptor, son of a Banff master mason (see Plate 3). Still in use today, it is made of

Caen stone and rests on dark-green marble columns. Deep Gothic panels display carved scenes depicting the acts of grace such as visiting the sick, clothing the poor and feeding the hungry. The pulpit was placed at the far end of the chancel, against the south pillar nearest the east wall. A new Caen stone font, in the form of a kneeling angel holding out a large shell which forms the basin, was set up temporarily in the nearby Preston Aisle. Also carved by John Rhind, it is a replica of a font in Copenhagen by the famous Danish neoclassical sculptor, Bertel Thorvaldsen. Later it was moved to the south-west corner of the Cathedral, where it was enclosed by a brass railing.

Hay had also planned a reading desk, but Chambers vetoed the suggestion as 'a departure from the plain and simple service of the Scottish Church, and one likely to give rise to controversy and offence'. However, at a later date, a lectern of Caen stone was introduced, presumably designed by Hay, who was also responsible for the new royal pew. Carved in oak in the Gothic style by Messrs Taylor & Son of Princes Street, this had ornate, canopied stalls. The imposing central stall was for Queen Victoria, and it bore the royal coat of arms on the front of its canopy. It was placed against the partition wall at the west end of the High Church, where its predecessor had stood, looking towards the great east window. Because the pulpit had been moved further forward, the east wall was left looking very bare. Hay therefore decided to create beneath the east window a modest arcade of Caen stone. Ten and a half feet high, it consisted of a row of Gothic arches resting on pillars of green marble, and it was decorated with carved stone angels in low relief (see Figure 10).

Staring at it in dismay, people feared the worst. Surely this was 'a horrid idolatrous reredos', the sort of screen to be found behind altars in Roman Catholic churches? When its niches were filled with small statues representing prophets and the evangelists, it was viewed with even greater suspicion. Were these saints? Because the high altar had once stood in this part of the church, the floor there had always been raised, and Chambers had decided to retain the different level because it was an original feature of the medieval St Giles'. This, of course, only seemed to bear out rumours that an altar was about to be put there. Hay had to write to the papers denying any such intention and explaining that nothing more sinister than seats would be placed in front of his arcade. Large stalls for the six royal chaplains in Scotland and the Dean of the Thistle and Chapel Royal were then positioned there, while heavy oak pews for the judges and other notabilities faced each other across the central aisle of the chancel.

Determined to combine modern comfort with medieval authenticity, Chambers introduced a system of hot-water pipes to supply the heating instead of the old coal stoves, and lighting would come from a series of brass standards, each with several gas burners. These were ornamented with carved thistles and judged to be 'very beautiful specimens of hammered metal work'. By the beginning of March 1873 everything was ready and Chambers chaired another public meeting, attended not only by the usual gentlemen but by Mrs Chambers and 'a number of other ladies'. 'The object aimed at is one truly national', he told them. 'It is alone as an historical and aesthetical monument that I, with others, have attempted the recovery of this ancient building.'

Once again, he was trying to deflect any hint of criticism on sectarian grounds, but of course he was not devoid of spiritual intentions. His speeches often included biblical allusions and a hymn that he had written would be sung at a programme of sacred music in the High Church later that year. Nor was his ecumenical outlook based on mere pragmatism. He had a mature view of the world, his marriage to his English wife, Harriet Clark, may well have led him to attend Episcopalian services from time to time and his personal faith had certainly been tested in his younger days by the death of all three of their children within hours of birth.

Not everyone was happy with what he was doing, of course. When he had finished speaking on that March evening in 1873, a member of the audience read out a long protest against 'the restoration to a Popish aspect of the interior of the High Church'. Chambers explained that this was not what was happening and Thomas Knox, Master of the Merchant Company, supported him, declaring that the scheme was 'worthy of the new spirit of enlarged and enlarging Christian sympathy and toleration among all denominations'. Knox proposed that the Restoration Committee should be re-elected to pursue the work of renovating the entire building and his motion was carried unanimously. Five days later, the High Church reopened with Dr Arnot preaching from the text, 'The Lord is in his holy temple: let all the earth keep silence before him'.

The total cost of restoring the chancel had been £4,490, but subscriptions totalled only £3,840. In the end, William Chambers and several other members of the committee supplied the shortfall. That was all very well, but could enough money be raised for the next phase of the restoration, and could an annoying legal obstacle be overcome? The Old Kirk had been officially abolished by an act of parliament in 1860 and had since then lain empty, apart from a temporary occupation by the congregation of Trinity

College Kirk. However, members of the former Old Kirk congregation had not accepted what they saw as their expulsion from the building and subsequent legislation seemed to provide them with a loophole. Some of them were now petitioning the Teind Court, which dealt with such matters, asking for their part of St Giles' to be retained as a separate church. If that came about, it would ruin the plan to open up the whole interior. Eventually, the court of session rejected the applicants' request but the financial and legal problems had caused a long and frustrating delay.

During those anxious months, one aspect of the work did go ahead. On 24 April 1873, the town council and the ecclesiastical commissioners approved the setting-up of a committee to take charge of inserting stained glass windows in St Giles'. For more than 250 years after the Reformation no stained glass had been made in Scotland but in 1837 James Ballantine, a former house painter, founded a stained glass studio in Edinburgh, having spent some years training, probably in the north of England. His firm would supply the windows which Chambers was encouraging friends to donate. Chambers did not, of course, want a miscellany of themes and so it was decided that they must form a sequence illustrating the life of Christ. Robert Herdman, himself the son of a church minister and famous for his paintings of scenes from Scottish history, supervised the designs for all the windows in the series, along with Sir Joseph Noel Paton, who regarded himself as a religious painter but is perhaps best known for his incredibly detailed fairy paintings which hang in the National Gallery of Scotland.

The first window, inserted in October 1874 on the north side of the chancel, was given by Duncan Monteith in memory of his brother James, a merchant in Calcutta. Others commemorated include George Lorimer and Robert Stevenson. Lorimer, a former dean of guild, had died trying to save people in a disastrous fire at the Theatre Royal in 1865, while Stevenson, engineer to the Northern Lighthouses, is even better known as the grandfather of Robert Louis Stevenson the writer. The notion of a great east window commemorating Prince Albert had been allowed to lapse and it proved difficult to fill that particular space because of its size. However, Lord Provost Sir James Falshaw, a long-term supporter of Chambers, came to the rescue. The focal point of the chancel, the window he gave shows the Crucifixion in the lower panels with the Resurrection above. At a ceremony marking its insertion in 1877, Chambers made a speech thanking him and remarked that people were beginning to feel that churches should be embellished by art and made as beautiful as possible. Who knew how many this window 'might yet comfort and lead to higher and better things.'

That same year, Dr Arnot died and was replaced by James Cameron Lees, son of a Lewis minister. For the past eighteen years, he had been minister of Paisley Abbey, where he had initiated a highly successful restoration scheme. He was reluctant at first to leave there and when he did finally arrive in Edinburgh he despaired at the sight of his new High Church. It had been carefully restored, it was true, but the adjoining area was a shambles of debris, and when he first met Dr Chambers he found him frail and depressed. However, their conversations encouraged both of them and they became firm friends. An excellent preacher of strongly ecumenical views, Dr Lees was soon attracting large numbers to his services and the High Church congregation increased rapidly.

The following summer, the ecclesiastical commissioners and the town council at last sanctioned the plans for what had been the Old Kirk – on condition that William Chambers take responsibility for the entire cost, which he had already offered to do. While tenders for the new work were submitted, an exciting innovation was introduced. Not since the Middle Ages had there been any organ in St Giles', but in recent years Presbyterians had relaxed their opposition to musical instruments and in 1872 Dr Arnot had persuaded the kirk session to take on trial an oak Alexander's First Class Harmonium with twenty-two stops and two sets of keys. This was hired from James Curle, music seller, 52 Hanover Street, Edinburgh at the rate of £5 a month. There were one or two objections, but the kirk session agreed to keep it after the trial period was over and now they were prepared to go further. They purchased a two-manual organ at a cost of about a thousand pounds from Messrs Harrison & Harrison, the well-known Durham organ builders.

The second phase of the Chambers restoration finally began on 27 January 1879. The side chapels on the south side of the building would be stripped and as far as possible restored to their medieval condition. In the Preston Aisle, heavy layers of whitewash were removed from walls and ceiling to reveal the beautiful stone vaulting and carvings which included Sir William Preston's coat of arms with its three unicorn heads. The partition wall separating that aisle from the High Church was demolished and then the workmen moved on to the Chepman Aisle. It was in a particularly bad state because at the time of the Burn restoration fifty years earlier it had been divided into three floors, with a coal cellar at ground level, a big iron stove for the heating system on the middle floor, a room with a fireplace on the top floor and a chimney right through the keystone of the archway leading into it.

During preliminary excavations, Chambers hoped to find the Marquis of Montrose's coffin in a burial vault beneath the floor, but Burn's work had disturbed the vault and only a few fragments of bone were discovered and carefully reinterred. Lath and plaster were then scraped off walls to expose the stonework and dirt and layers of whitewash were removed from the ceiling. As that was being done, the workmen uncovered not only a finely carved boss with the arms of Walter Chepman and his first wife Mariota Kerkettill, but a carving of an eagle, the emblem of St John the Evangelist to whom his altar had been dedicated. Chambers erected to Chepman's memory the brass tablet on the west wall of the Aisle. It was produced by the well-known firm of Skidmore Art Manufacturers of Coventry. Francis Skidmore, one of the best metalworkers in England, frequently undertook commissions for Sir George Gilbert Scott and created the famous screen (now in the Victoria & Albert Museum) which Scott designed for Hereford Cathedral. Skidmore also supplied the decorative railings for the Chepman Aisle and the other side aisles in St Giles' (see Figure 6).

When excavations began in the adjoining Moray Aisle, they too proved initially disappointing. Chambers was convinced that the coffin of the Regent Moray would be found in the vault beneath but, once again, the area had been disturbed by Burn's alterations. Three coffins were discovered, one of them containing the remains of a middle-aged, red-haired woman who may well have been the Regent's wife, Lady Agnes Keith, but of his coffin there was no sign. However, some scattered bones were dug up along with an unusually large skull which Chambers decided was probably Moray's because of its impressive cranial capacity. All the remains were interred again and George, 14th Earl of Moray generously agreed to put up a replica of his famous ancestor's destroyed monument, incorporating the surviving brass plate. He also inserted the stained glass window in the adjacent wall, which shows the Regent's assassination and Knox preaching at his funeral. Beneath this window, Hay repositioned a medieval monument or shrine carved with symbols of the Passion. Found nearby, it had probably belonged to the Confraternity of the Holy Blood.

The most ambitious plan Chambers had for the south side of St Giles' related to the south transept. It was well known that the Knights of the Thistle, Scotland's senior order of chivalry, had no chapel of their own. The Scottish equivalent of the Knights of the Garter in England, there are sixteen of them, all prominent Scots personally chosen by the monarch. Probably founded during the reign of James III, their Order had been revived in 1687 by James VII and II, who intended the Knights to have stalls in Holyrood Abbey. However, after he was deposed the following year, the Abbey was ransacked by an anti-Catholic mob and no accommodation had since been available to them. It seemed to Chambers that St Giles', with all its historical associations, would be the very place for their chapel, and so he offered them the south transept for the purpose. Disappointingly, they did not take him up on this, but the idea was not forgotten and in 1882 Lindsay Mackersy commented that if Lees could be made Dean of the Thistle, that would be 'the first step towards securing the Knights for St Giles'. Four years later, Lees did indeed become Dean, but nothing happened about the chapel at that time.

When the refurbishment of the south aisles had been completed, work on the second phase of the restoration came to an abrupt halt. Nothing more could be done until the nave was available, but it was still being used by the congregation of the West Church, and they could not move out until they were supplied with new premises. On 30 April 1879 Edinburgh Presbytery assured Chambers that neither they nor the congregation would make any unnecessary objection to his plans, and so, to speed matters up, he offered to pay for the restoration of the rest of the building as well, on condition that the keys of the West Church must be handed over to him by Whitsunday 1880.

An act of parliament was needed to sanction the new arrangements but that too ran into difficulties when various MPs objected to its title, 'The St Giles' Cathedral Bill', saying that there could be no such thing as a cathedral without a bishop. In the end, the name was changed to 'St Giles' Ancient Church Bill' but even then the problems were not over, for when Mackersy scrutinised the text of the Bill he realised that the town council would have to give permission whenever a service was to be held in what had been the West Church. That was entirely unacceptable, and so, after much lobbying, several additional clauses were inserted to safeguard the rights of the minister and kirk session over what would once more become the nave of St Giles'.

That autumn, Chambers was also thinking about the bells in the steeple. In 1865 a letter had been printed in *The Scotsman* drawing attention to their sorry state. The wires of the musical bells were so twisted and rusted that the tunes they produced were completely unrecognisable. Catherine Macleod still played them, as her father had done before her and although she was an elderly lady now, she gamely climbed up the stairs and ladders in the darkness to perform her daily task. However, it was lucky, said the anonymous correspondent to the newspaper, that she was so deaf that she could not hear the results. A peal of steel bells which had been purchased that same year from Messrs Naylor, Vickers & Co of Sheffield at an estimated cost of £371:12:6 was no help, for it had fallen into disuse after a brief trial. Chambers now announced that he would have both sets of bells repaired as soon as the restoration work was finished.

No-one, of course, knew when that would be. By the St Giles' Ancient Church Act, the town council was required to raise £10,500 to pay for a new church for the congregation of West St Giles', but they had not begun collecting the money quickly enough and only about £5,200 had been raised by Chambers's 1880 deadline. A few weeks later he warned in a letter to *The Scotsman* that 'at my advanced age [he was 80] the thing must be done soon or not at all, as far as I am concerned'. However, he was not about to give up. Visitors were flocking to St Giles' to see what was being done, and 'the crowding of Americans in particular at this season is very considerable', *The Scotsman* reported, with the Montrose vault 'eagerly sought after by the higher class of visitor'.

In June 1880 Chambers announced that he was willing to extend his deadline by another year. With that, donations poured in, a site for a new West Kirk was purchased at Meadow Place and Chambers bought one of the popular corrugated-iron churches for the displaced congregation to use until their building was ready. Towards the end of April, Hay sent his specifications for the next phase of the renovation to Chambers, who amended them with a very shaky hand in his favourite purple ink. Finally, on 17 May 1881, the town council formally accepted his offer to restore the rest of St Giles'.

CHAPTER 10

Scotland's Westminster Abbey

Work on the final phase of the Chambers restoration scheme began on 11 July 1881. As a result of William Burn's alterations, the nave's central aisle was lined with slender, fluted pillars quite unlike those in the chancel and tiers of pews rose up towards the heavy lofts. Even the floor posed a problem, for it was at a lower level than the crossing. However, William Hay knew what to do. The furnishings were dismantled, the lofts taken down and instead of attempting the major task of demolishing the pillars, he cleverly encased them in sturdy replicas of their medieval predecessors. When the plaster was being removed from the walls, a double range of clerestory windows was discovered above the arches. Burn had filled them in with rubble, which was now removed, and research identified their mouldings as being identical to those of the clerestories in the medieval cathedrals at Fortrose, in the north of Scotland and at Chester. As the pale-blue ceiling was in good condition, Hay retained it but had it painted a rich dark blue with gold stars. The glass in many of the windows had been accidentally cracked by workmen and broken by boys firing catapults, so it was replaced with plain, tinted Cathedral Glass until more stained glass windows could be donated.

The floor of the nave would be repaved after hot-water pipes were laid beneath it. There was no plan to make it the same height as the floor of the crossing, which in its turn was lower than that of the chancel. Instead, Chambers decided to insert marble steps linking the different levels. He wanted marble similar to a black and white marble fireplace in his country

Figure 10
The High Church of St Giles' after the Chambers Restoration, 1882, showing
the reredos designed by William Hay, beneath the great east window.
(© Edinburgh City Libraries. Licensor www.scran.ac.uk)

house at Glenormiston. Hay had considerable difficulty in finding any to
match, but in the end he settled for a polished Italian Burdello marble from
the George Street warehouse of the Edinburgh firm of Field & Allan. He
ordered a total of 243 feet six inches at a cost of ten shillings a foot, and the
steps were installed in the early autumn of 1882. They no longer exist, but
a similar arrangement may be seen in St Mary's Episcopal Cathedral in
Edinburgh, which was being built at the same period.

Meanwhile, the north side chapels of St Giles' were receiving attention.
The floor of the Albany Aisle was laid with Minton tiles and Irish marble.
Three tiled medallions showed the royal arms of Scotland along with the
coats of arms of the Duke of Albany and the Earl of Douglas. These had
been carefully copied from seals on documents in the Register House (now
the National Archives of Scotland). The Aisle was then separated from the

nave by a fine ironwork screen designed by Skidmore and gilded by his son. St Eloi's Aisle required even more work. During the Burn restoration its vaulted ceiling had been removed, the central boss had been given to the Society of Antiquaries' Museum, a mezzanine floor had been inserted and a circular stair leading to the tower had been put in. Now the extra floor was removed and the stair was rebuilt in an adjoining wall six feet thick. The vaulted roof was reinstated, the boss was retrieved from the Museum and fixed in its original position, a Skidmore screen with two enamelled roundels was set up and a Minton mosaic and marble floor completed the effect.

The north door leading in from the High Street would no longer be the main entrance to St Giles', but it was improved by the creation of an inner porch when a screen of Craiksland stone was put up in an effort to keep out the draughts. On the side of it facing into the church, John Rhind carved the figures of the patron saints of ten of the Incorporated Trades who once had altars in the church and everyone was delighted when a fifteenth-century fragment of stone panelling was dug up, suggesting that there had been a medieval screen on that very spot. Chambers's coat of arms also features on Rhind's screen, with his Latin motto, *Facta non Verba* (Deeds not words). Mackersy felt that this was an inadequate tribute to their great benefactor, and he suggested that the old vestry next to the north entrance could be converted into a side chapel called 'The Chambers Aisle'. Chambers replied austerely that this would have to wait until everything else was done.

Everyone had assumed that work on the chancel was well and truly over until Mackersy noticed that its plasterwork looked grotesque when viewed in conjunction with the attractively bare stonework of the Preston Aisle. Chambers agreed, and gave orders for the plaster to be stripped off the walls and ceiling. The chancel pillars also needed attention. Huge monuments had been attached to some of them, including David Bryce junior's excessively heavy white marble memorial to Dean of Guild Lorimer, the Theatre Royal fire hero. They were taken down and temporarily stored in a disused coach house belonging to one of the contractors until they could be re-erected in the north porch. As they were removed it was found that the pillars had been badly damaged by the insertion of the iron beams which had supported them. Moreover, the paint on six of the pillars proved particularly hard to shift, because of the 'centuries old' layers of green, red and blue paint. They also bore marks of severe damage which Hay could only think must have been caused by sledgehammers during the struggle between the supporters of Mary, Queen of Scots and her opponents during the early 1570s.

In spite of these difficulties, the work was going well. When John, 6th Earl of Aberdeen was Lord High Commissioner to the General Assembly in May 1882, he brought 'a distinguished party' to view progress and everyone in his group was much impressed. 'The Ladies particularly took a most intelligent interest in the building and they all insisted on going into the Montrose vault, to which Dr Lees conducted them', Mackersy told Chambers. Hay himself was surprised at the amount of public interest in what was going on, remarking that 'People whom I fancy I have never seen before stop me in the streets to praise the work and ask questions'.

It was all very encouraging, and the most exciting moment came at the end of July when Mackersy was able to report, 'I have my first look at the building from end to end – the royal pew is down, and from the west end you can see the lower lights of the great east window ... The effect even now is remarkably fine'. The rest of the old stone partition blocking the archway between the chancel and the crossing was taken down, and for the first time in more than 300 years there was an uninterrupted vista 196 feet long from the west door right through to the great east window. St Giles' might still be full of noise, workmen and dust, but the effect was breathtaking and it was not surprising that great numbers of visitors flocked in, 'strangers from England and America daily visiting the church' in spite of the dismantled state of the chancel.

Not everything went smoothly, of course, and there was a crisis over the position of the royal pew. It had to be taken down before the partition wall was demolished, and Hay meant it to stand against the east wall, but the government board of works objected and when they insisted on it being placed on a platform three feet high in its new location in the Preston Aisle, Mr Mackersy realised that it would block one of the recently erected stained glass windows. After a great deal of fuss, a new carved royal stall was made which could stand between the windows, and the redundant royal pew later found a home at the west door, its back forming the wall of a new inner porch. In future, the west door was to be the main entrance to St Giles', in keeping with the practice at other cathedrals, and it would be much more elaborate than Burn's plain doorway. Hay ornamented the west front, adding a carved panel showing St Giles' and his hind above the door, with niches containing statues of medieval Scottish monarchs and significant churchmen at either side. John Rhind and his assistants did the carving and Skidmore supplied the ornamental hinges and locks for the two oak doors, which are separated by a central stone pillar.

Apart from the royal pew drama, there were other problems too. There were delays in getting enough matching paving stones for the floor from a quarry in Arbroath, there was a frustrating shortage of masons, which Hay attributed to current emigration to western Canada, and despite all precautions the organ pipes filled up with dust. 'Mr Skidmore is not the most punctual of men', complained Mackersy when the new gas chandeliers were slow in coming and when the mosaic tiles failed to appear on time, Minton's Edinburgh agent, William Hawley blamed his employers and they blamed him. Throughout the summer and autumn there were also lengthy discussions about a proposed octagonal chapterhouse where the kirk session would meet.

When Mackersy called at Hay's office one day and found an assistant gravely preparing a scheme for it which would encroach on Parliament Square by fourteen feet, he was horrified. As he hastened to report to Chambers, 'I told him he might as well prepare a plan for a Chapter House in the moon ... I don't profess to know anything of an architect's business but looking at Mr Henderson's design through commonsense spectacles I showed him how he could have it all there without encroaching an inch ...' Despite this helpful intervention, a lengthy wrangle with Hay ensued and the chapterhouse was never built. Instead, at Mackersy's suggestion, what was now called the session house was constructed on the north side of St Giles', in a vacant recess between the Albany Aisle and St Eloi's Aisle. At the same time, there were arguments about the location of a new vestry on the south side, and Mackersy decided that Hay was 'the most quietly obstinate architect I ever came across'.

The High Church had been closed since the end of July but the kirk session had announced that services would be resumed on 1 October 1882 and this deadline was causing a good deal of tension. Because the chancel would not be ready in time, services would have to be held in the unfurnished nave. Dr Lees would not have access to his vestry so what could he use as a robing room? St Eloi's Aisle was curtained off for him instead. The old precentor's oak desk from the West Church was found to make 'a capital temporary pulpit', and a new musical instrument called a Vocalion, a form of reed organ, was lent by its inventor, James Baillie-Hamilton, to supply the lack of an organ. Even more alarming was the panic over chairs. There was, of course, no seating yet in the nave. Chairs were the responsibility of the kirk session and Mackersy had been down to

Henley-on-Thames to order 360 of them from Messrs West & Collier. They did not arrive and he had to send a series of frantic telegrams before they slowly appeared in small batches. 'Mr Mackersy is nearly distracted', Hay noted with some satisfaction as he quietly arranged to move pews from the chancel to supply the lack.

William Chambers had become increasingly frail and was spending most of his time at Glenormiston to try to improve his health, while his wife remained at their Chester Street house in Edinburgh with their small dog, Charley. Mackersy and Hay were now sending him increasingly frequent reports. 'The month of August seems to have been very much wasted', Mackersy would announce indignantly, while Hay would retaliate with 'Mr Mackersy, who has no knowledge of work of this kind, has been saying, I understand, that no progress appeared to have been made for a month … but he was quite mistaken, as our weekly returns and the amount of work done amply shows'. In the end, the gasoliers arrived in time. Skidmore had copied their design from a medieval lamp in St Mary's Church, Redcliffe, Bristol, and they were much admired when they were hung from the arches of the nave. The Minton flooring of St Eloi's Aisle likewise proved highly effective.

The new heating system was turned on a week before the opening service on 1 October, when everything passed off successfully. William Hay did not stay for it, for he was complaining of a bout of rheumatism brought on by long hours spent standing on the cold paving in the Cathedral. However, he instructed his assistants to sit at the very back of the nave and they were able to assure him afterwards that they had heard every word that Dr Lees said. The following Sunday so many people came for the evening service that several hundred had to be turned away.

A fresh controversy then arose about hanging military flags in St Giles'. There are those who see flags in churches as a proud tribute to the men who have fought for their country, but others regard them as symbols of violence, utterly inappropriate in a place of peace. It seems that Chambers was against their introduction, but there was powerful lobbying by a committee of influential supporters and he gave way. By 10 January 1883, fifteen sets of colours had been sent in, with the promise of five more. The great restoration scheme was almost complete. One day, in the early spring, a very frail William Chambers was carried into St Giles' and placed carefully on a chair in the nave. Gazing around him, he remarked with deep satisfaction, 'I never could have believed that the interior was so fine.'

Plans were now in hand for the grand reopening service in St Giles' on 23 May and everyone hoped that Queen Victoria might honour it with her presence. However, she sent word that she was unable to be there. Instead, she would be represented by the Earl of Aberdeen, and she stressed that the ceremonial must be exactly as if she herself were present. The Queen also conferred a baronetcy on William Chambers. Two years earlier he had declined the offer of a knighthood from William Gladstone the Prime Minister, but this was something which he could not refuse. At the beginning of May he thought that he felt a little better. He was kept closely in touch with all the arrangements for the service and until the last moment there were hopes that he would be in St Giles' that day. However, he suffered a sudden relapse and he died in his Edinburgh house on 20 May, just three days before St Giles' was solemnly reopened.

On 23 May 1883, as planned, the Earl of Aberdeen arrived in procession at the Cathedral to a fanfare of trumpets. A large awning draped with crimson and decorated with flags had been erected outside the main door, over which was a wreath of everlasting flowers with the words 'In loving memory', a touching tribute to William Chambers. Waiting beneath the awning was an official party which included the Lord Provost in court dress, the magistrates in their robes, Dr Lees in cap and gown, Chambers's nephew Robert and Mr Lindsay Mackersy WS. Robert Chambers read out a short speech composed for the occasion by his late uncle and, making a suitable reply, Lord Aberdeen symbolically placed the key in the lock of the new west door before handing it to Dr Lees. Inside were almost 3,000 people: the general public in the nave, clergy and representatives of public bodies in the chancel and transepts. In a gallery above the north porch were the workmen who had toiled on the restoration, with their relatives and friends (see Figure 11). As soon as Lord Aberdeen entered, 200 choristers sang the national anthem and at three o'clock the service began with the singing of Psalm 100.

Lees preached on the text 'What mean these stones?' (Joshua 4:21) describing the stirring history of St Giles' and outlining the great hope for the future, 'to make this place for Scotsmen what Westminster Abbey, for similar reasons, has been called: the temple of silence and reconciliation'. These stones signified the relationship of beauty to religion and worship, he said, and although attempts had been made in the past to extinguish beauty from Presbyterian services, 'we can retain our evangelical character even though the music of our praise be sweeter'. He went on to speak

Figure 11
The tradesmen employed on the Chambers restoration of St Giles', photographed at the
west door, 24 May 1883. (Original photograph with St Giles' Cathedral.
Photograph: © Peter Backhouse)

affectionately of his old friend Dr Chambers, who had believed that the
restored St Giles' 'might teach great historic lessons – that it might inspire
men with the feeling of reverence – that it might be a source of good and
sweetening influence in this city ...'. Two days later, Lees officiated in the
Cathedral at the funeral service for William Chambers, who was then
buried in Peebles, beside his mother.

So what were the reactions to the restored St Giles'? *The Scotsman*
newspaper was enthusiastic in its praise, admiring the rugged stonework
of the now bare walls, praising the newly opened vistas as 'marvellously
fine' and aligning itself firmly with the ecumenical spirit which had
inspired it. 'The Minister now uses it in much the same form in which it
was used by the Roman prelate and priest', the journalist reported proudly,
for this meant, or so he thought, that 'the age of unreasoning prejudice is
passing away'. Presbyterians had at last realised their mistake in allowing
their rivals to enjoy a monopoly of beauty of worship, and Edinburgh
people need no longer blush to take strangers and foreigners to see their

Cathedral, for it had been 'set in order, beautified and dedicated afresh as a national temple of the national religion'.

Even so, in 1887 what became known as 'the images controversy' erupted when the Reverend Jacob Primmer of Dunfermline saw the statues of the Scottish monarchs and ecclesiastics at the west door and thought that they were 'Popish Images'. He was even more affronted when he attended a Christmas Day service and observed a procession of clergy led by a man (the beadle) in a red and black gown carrying a small mace with a carved burning bush at the top. Worse still, one military memorial took the form of a large brass cross, the font was in the shape of an angel and then there was that 'popish reredos' at the east end. Nearly 600 parishioners signed a petition to Edinburgh Presbytery complaining about these features, although it emerged that the signatures had been gathered under false pretences by someone saying he was checking the population and needed the names of everyone over 16. The matter was subsequently brought before the General Assembly, but in the end the petition was withdrawn and in 1899 Primmer was admonished by the Moderator, Dr John Pagan.

As Primmer had noted, with the 'cathedralization' of the building, the form of worship had changed too, as of course it had to do, in part because of the greatly enlarged space now available, but more significantly because of developments in liturgical thinking. Some praised Lees's services as simple and dignified, but others sneered that St Giles' people were 'ritualistic' and he was frequently accused of 'aping Episcopacy'. The journal *The Christian Leader* was particularly scathing. Its columnist (probably Primmer) objected not only to the furnishings but to processions of choir and clergy, the sight of ministers wearing academic gowns and hoods, the congregation kneeling on the new hassocks to pray, and people saying the Lord's Prayer out loud, not to mention the sound of the organ and choral music.

Declaring that what it termed mimicry and mongrelism of this kind filled the author and his friends with the most supreme contempt, the article went on to ask whether this was the kind of thing to strengthen the faith and rejoice the hearts of poor sinners. Obviously not. Norman Maclean, official biographer of Lees, would take a different view. Discussing Primmer and the images controversy, he declared that it was St Giles' with its ordered and beautiful worship which stemmed the current drift from Presbyterianism, adding that whatever strengthened Presbyterianism also strengthened a bulwark against Rome.

Sectarian comments apart, services certainly were more elaborate now, and the form of the communion service had changed significantly. Until the 1870s, trestle-tables and benches were still being set up for communicants but now they seem to have been replaced by a plain wooden communion table on a dais at the east end. The elders brought in the bread and wine before the service began, placing them on the table and then, at the appropriate moment, passing them along the pews. In the early 1880s some of the congregation suggested that there was no need for a sermon on a communion Sunday, but the kirk session pointed out that this would be contrary to the practice of the Presbyterian Church. After all, those who did not wish to hear the sermon could come in for communion during the short interlude at the end of the first service.

Music had now become a significant part of services. When a Christmas Day service (itself a novelty) was held in St Giles' in 1879, the recently formed choir of two sopranos, two altos, two tenors and two basses was augmented by eight more voices for the singing of Handel's *Hallelujah Chorus*. After the entire building was opened up, the choir had to be permanently enlarged, with at least eight sopranos, four contraltos, four tenors and six basses. A St Giles' Choral Society was formed to give performances and encourage the development of the Cathedral music. The existing two-manual organ was inadequate now and Messrs Harrison & Harrison were employed to reconstruct it as a four-manual instrument. Sited in the south transept, it had a chamber for its gas engine and bellows built just outside. Subscriptions towards the cost were regrettably slow to come in, however, and it was not ready until 1891, by which time Harrison & Harrison had refused to have any more to do with it and it had been completed by Ingram & Co.

Lees also introduced additional services. At half past nine on a Sunday morning, a military service was held for the garrison of Edinburgh Castle, with their chaplain officiating. An evening service was established for the first time and the daily service, suspended since Cromwell's rule, was revived. Held each afternoon at half past three in the Moray Aisle, it would, Lees believed, benefit the many lonely and sorrowful persons who were always to be found in a great city. John Findlay, proprietor of *The Scotsman*, funded the daily services anonymously and, to mark the occasion, presented for the Moray Aisle a delicately carved wooden pulpit designed by Robert Rowand Anderson. For a time there were also Gaelic services every third Sunday, with preachers from different denominations.

The Christmas Day service became a regular feature, a popular watch-night service was established on New Year's Eve, and there were the services for civic and national occasions. On 14 November 1883, the regimental colours, now hanging from the pillars of the nave and the crossing, were dedicated in the presence of Prince George, Duke of Cambridge, commander-in-chief of the forces. The following year Edinburgh University marked its tercentenary with a service in St Giles' and Queen Victoria's Jubilee was celebrated in 1887. The long-established kirking of the town council continued to be an annual event, and there were numerous memorial services for members of the royal family and other public figures. Such occasions require meticulous planning, and the elders along with forty-four other men of the congregation were appointed to act as stewards.

Dr Lees's inspirational preaching always attracted large numbers, his dignified services were perfect for state occasions and although he was essentially a shy man, he could be both forthright in expressing his opinions and genial and kindly in his manner towards his assistants and parishioners. When one of his assistants complained of insomnia, Lees said sympathetically, 'I'll tell you a cure'. 'What is it?' asked the young minister eagerly. 'Read one of your old sermons', came the jovial reply. With Lees's encouragement, there were plenty of lively congregational activities. His programme for Parishioners' Entertainment in 1891–2 began with a lecture by himself on 'Yankee Humour', progressed to 'Drawing Room Entertainment' with songs and conjuring tricks and later included illustrated talks by members of the congregation about their holidays. Events were held in a hall the Cathedral rented in the Lawnmarket and admission cost a penny a time. Another of his assistants remembered how Dr Lees always took a great interest in the parishioners, attending the entertainments organised for the poor people in the High Street, sometimes singing them a song and telling them many stories. They loved to see him.

There were more serious occasions too. The St Giles' Lectures which Lees established on Sunday afternoons were given from 1880–6 by a series of eminent preachers and then published, and by 1904 the Guild of St Giles' was holding talks on Buddhism, Hinduism and 'Mohammedanism' as well as organising a series of fortnightly concerts. Most of these activities were held to raise money for charitable purposes, with the congregation doing what they could to help the poorer parishioners living in the High Street and its narrow closes. A Cathedral Penny Savings Bank was open on Monday evenings, the Working Boys' Club met on Saturday evenings and the Bible Class for Working Lads was on Sunday evenings. The Boys' Brigade, formed 'with a view to elevating the moral and physical tone of the boys in the parish', held its meetings every Friday and had its own Bible Class on Sunday mornings. At the associated Junior Boys' Club, Sergeant Major Dalby instructed the Gymnastics Class and from time to time put on Indian club and dumbbell displays.

The women of the congregation were equally active. Lees set up the St Giles' branch of the Woman's Guild in 1904, with the help of Lady Victoria Campbell, who worked energetically for the Church of Scotland despite being severely disabled by poliomyelitis since childhood. There was a Mothers' Meeting, Guild members taught in the Sunday School, sewed for the Cathedral's annual sale of work, visited the poor, distributed cast-off clothing and collected donations for the Fortnight Holiday Fund. Girls under the age of 14 were taught sewing and those who were over 14 could learn useful vocational skills by attending the classes in cooking, dressmaking and millinery. A few years later there was a St Giles' Literary Society, and the monthly parish magazine listed the meetings of the various Cathedral organisations, printed obituaries of prominent members, reviewed religious books and serialised improving novels such as *Life in the Coal Country* by Jane C. Hunter.

While all this was going on, the enhancement of St Giles' continued, for there were frequent applications from those who wanted to insert stained glass windows or put up memorial plaques. William Chambers might be gone now, with his breadth of vision and meticulous attention to detail, but his high standards had to be maintained. Another familiar figure was missing too, for William Hay's work was done. He went on to plan an addition to the Holy Trinity Cathedral in Hamilton, Bermuda, which he had designed almost forty years earlier, and created a hopefully uncontroversial reredos for St John's Cathedral, Newfoundland. Early in 1888 he fell ill, and died at home in Rabbit Hall on 30 May, at the age of 69. Two years later, the kirk session put up a bronze memorial plaque to him, with his portrait carved in low relief by John Rhind. It was said to be a good likeness (see Plate 4).

Lindsay Mackersy, in his mid-fifties, was as actively involved as ever, and apart from his role as session clerk he was now secretary to the managing board which oversaw the insertion of the new windows and memorials. The other members of the board included Dr Lees, John Inglis the Lord Justice General, Robert Chambers and an artist who was a member of the Royal Scottish Academy, initially Robert Herdman. They were extremely particular and scrutinised all proposed designs with great care. They decided exactly where each window and memorial should be placed and they were never slow to point out an inappropriate feature or an infelicitous inscription.

Even Dr Lees did not always have his own way with his colleagues on the board. In 1887 he suffered great sorrow when his wife Rhoda died prematurely, leaving him with a young family. She had not only worked tirelessly for the poor of the parish but she had joined in the battle to have deaconesses introduced into the Church of Scotland in order to give women of the congregation a formal role. Bereft, Lees tried to console himself by compiling a comprehensive history of the Cathedral which he dedicated to her. It was published in 1889 and, although old-fashioned today, remains a classic work. He and some of his wife's friends also thought that they would like to put up a window in her memory and, perhaps remembering her deaconess struggles with the kirk session and others, they chose Daniel of Lions' Den fame for the theme.

The board replied sharply that they disapproved of the subject, and proposed female figures representing the Church's virtues. Daniel Cottier, the prominent stained glass artist, produced a new set of designs, but the board criticised them too, asking for more refinement in the drawing. They were perfectly right, of course for, even after subsequent modification, the sturdy figures of Faith, Hope and Charity, Truth, Justice and Mercy have a decidedly muscular look as they gaze down on the congregation from their place in the north wall of the nave.

Edward Burne-Jones the famous artist fared no better when he was commissioned to design a window in memory of Lord Curriehill, a high court judge who had been an energetic supporter of the Chambers restoration. Burne-Jones noted in his account book in February 1886, 'If I were to make a charge ... for the trouble and annoyance I experienced in a long correspondence with the clergy of Scotland at the outset of this work ... I should treble the laughable trifle which I set down as compensation for my toil.' Made in the studio of William Morris & Company, his window is arguably the most beautiful in St Giles' and when Morris visited the Cathedral in September of that year he congratulated himself on its appearance: 'Our window is fine & looks a queer contrast with its glittering jewel-like colour to the daubs about it.'

The managing board did not charge a fee for the insertion of windows, because these beautified the Cathedral, but they did have a scale of charges for memorials. William Chambers had meant to establish a Poets' Corner like the one in Westminster Abbey by donating a monument in honour of James I of Scotland, who had written a long autobiographical poem. However, he died before that could be arranged and instead the first memorial in the transformed St Giles' was to a much more controversial figure, Dean Hannay, the clergyman who had started to read from Charles I's service book in 1637. When a descendant was allowed to place a decorative brass plaque on one of the great pillars, there was a storm of protest from enraged Presbyterians. John Stuart Blackie, the eccentric Professor of Greek at Edinburgh University, led the charge, demanding that 'Jenny Geddes' should have her memorial too.

A donor came forward in the person of Robert Halliday Gunning, a successful Scottish doctor living in Rio de Janeiro who would subsequently endow the famous Victoria Jubilee prizes and lectureships in his native land. Whatever Lees may have thought of the questionable Jenny Geddes, a memorial to her as well as to Hannay accorded with his vision of St Giles' as a temple of reconciliation and so the offer was accepted. The managing board objected to the first design, which incorporated an allegorical drawing, presumably showing the 1637 riot, and instead John Inglis composed a carefully worded inscription. Fixed to the floor not far from the Hannay plaque, the new memorial attracted the attention of no less a personage than Queen Victoria when she visited St Giles' on 21 August 1886. She was shown round by Dr Lees and he observed that, although she particularly admired the regimental colours, the object that seemed to interest her most was the Jenny Geddes plaque.

The Queen was knowledgeable about Scottish history and she also expressed astonishment that there was no monument to the Marquis of Montrose. Funds were hastily raised by an appeal committee led by the Duke of Montrose and Robert Rowand Anderson designed a fine monument in seventeenth-century style, with a white marble effigy of Montrose lying on a black marble bier, columns of black and gold marble at either side. The figure was based on the well-known portrait of Montrose by Honthorst and on armour in the collection of Sir Joseph Noel Paton. Next to it, in the Chepman Aisle, where Montrose was buried, is a memorial window with the coats of arms of his supporters. The monument cost £1,250:8:3, the managing board charged thirty guineas for its erection and £300 was paid for the window. Five years later Dr Gunning gave a similar monument in memory of Montrose's great enemy, the Covenanting Marquis of Argyll.

By then, William Chambers had his own memorial. Lindsay Mackersy had revived his idea of a Chambers Aisle and, after considerable delays, the kirk session in 1890 approved plans submitted by David MacGibbon and Thomas Ross, now the Cathedral architects. The wall dividing the vestry from the north aisle was demolished and the new aisle was created, with a handsome memorial plaque and a stained glass window which appropriately depicts the rebuilding of the biblical temple by Solomon. A second window to Chambers' nephew Robert was added in 1892. William Chambers's notion of a Poet's Corner was also to an extent realised, when part of the Moray Aisle became the home to plaques in memory of a number of literary figures. These would eventually include Margaret Oliphant, an almost forgotten nineteenth-century novelist whose books were extremely popular at the time, John Stuart Blackie and, most notably, Robert Louis Stevenson, who is represented by a large, low-relief memorial by the American sculptor, Augustus Saint-Gaudens.

This was all very satisfactory, but there still remained what many felt to be a notable omission. There was nothing to commemorate John Knox. For years people had been arguing about where and how the reformer should be remembered. Discussions had reached a climax in 1872, the three hundredth anniversary of his death. A special meeting held to consider the matter got off to a bad start when Robert Andrew Macfie, MP for Leith, was invited to take the chair and immediately refused. The whole idea seemed to him to be incongruous, he said bluntly, adding that he had actually come along to protest against it. Many shared his view that Knox, that hater of images, would not have wanted a statue of himself to be placed anywhere, least of all in his own church, and nothing was done. However, Lees had always wanted to commemorate Knox, and in 1902 the managing board finally agreed to a statue being commissioned for the Cathedral.

The sculptor chosen was Pittendrigh Macgillivray, and an appeal fund was set up to raise the £1,250 required. Money poured in from all over the British Empire and the USA, ranging from a modest shilling to £350 given to Lees for such a purpose during a visit to Australia nearly twenty years earlier. The statue was placed in the Albany Aisle and unveiled by Lord Balfour of Burleigh on 21 November 1906, in the presence of a large and fashionable company of ladies and gentlemen. A little over six feet high and cast in bronze, it stood in a Gothic stone niche with polished columns and a carved canopy. Wearing a sixteenth-century cap and gown and a severe expression, Knox points energetically to the Bible that he holds, as if engaging in lively debate.

Lindsay Mackersy was still alive when the Knox statue was commissioned. A newspaper article of 1893 had described him as being 'well on in years, small and somewhat phlegmatic in movement, with a deliberate way of talking ... In the Cathedral itself he is popularly supposed to be the ruler of the congregation and he is generally known as "the Pope of St Giles'".' He was not at the unveiling, however, for he died on 14 August 1902, after a short illness, aged 70. The kirk session noted somewhat ambiguously, 'They cannot forget his presence with which they were so familiar ...' and the following year they erected a bronze plaque to him. Smaller and without a portrait, it is next to William Hay's (see Plate 5).

CHAPTER 11

The Twentieth Century

*I*n March 1909 James Cameron Lees, on the verge of retirement, received an exciting letter from King Edward VII's private secretary, Lord Knollys. Would the Cathedral authorities look favourably upon a plan to accommodate the Knights of the Thistle in St Giles'? The kirk session received the news with 'much gratification' and 'a high sense of honour'. This was what William Chambers had always wanted, so how was it that his great ambition was about to be achieved at last? Some years earlier, after decades of speculation about the possible location of a chapel for the Order, Ronald, 11th Earl of Leven and Melville, one of the Knights, had offered a handsome sum of money to restore Holyrood Abbey for the purpose. Its ruinous condition made this impossibly expensive but, after his death in 1906, his son the 12th Earl said that he would give £24,000 to establish a chapel in St Giles'.

Edward VII was enthusiastic and royal trustees were appointed to oversee the project. They drew up a draft memorandum of agreement between themselves and the other bodies involved: the managing board, the Edinburgh ecclesiastical commissioners, the kirk session, Edinburgh presbytery, the commissioners of works and public buildings and the Lord Provost and town council. The Chapel would be an integral part of the Cathedral, linked to it by an antechapel, and £2,000 would be given to the managing board to invest as a capital fund for its upkeep. None of the existing aisles was suitable and so an entirely new chapel would be built at the south-east corner of the Cathedral, on the space once occupied by James III's mint. The chosen style would be Gothic, in keeping with the rest of the building and Robert Lorimer was appointed architect. He had trained in the office of Robert Rowand Anderson and had made his name with the sympathetic restoration of large Scottish country houses.

Needless to say, there were complications. The new building might block out the light from some of the chancel windows, one of the stained glass windows did indeed have to be relocated, and there was the question of the Chapel encroaching on Parliament Square. However, royal approval smoothed the way and the work speeded ahead. The antechapel, a low-ceilinged, dimly lit room was constructed, its heavy stone roof weighing about seventy tons and ornamented with fifty-seven carved bosses. The names of all the Knights from 1687 until 1909 were carved on wall panels, along with the arms of the Earl of Leven and Melville. A doorway in the south wall would lead into the Chapel itself, which would be a small, astonishingly ornate space measuring only 8.5 metres long by 12.8 metres high and 5.5 metres wide, yet giving the impression of being much larger because of its height.

Lorimer's assistant, John Matthew, provided day-to-day supervision and James Grieve was clerk of works. Joseph Hayes undertook the elaborate stone carving of the vaulted ceiling, which has almost a hundred bosses with coats of arms, angels and ecclesiastical symbols. Douglas Strachan, the leading Scottish stained glass artist, designed the east window with St Andrew and the Scottish lion rampant while Louis David, a London friend of Lorimer, was responsible for the other windows with their coats of arms of King Edward VII and the various knights. Louis Deuchars devised the models for the medieval and heraldic plants, animals and angels which decorate the nineteen oak stalls carved by William Clow and his brother Alexander. The monarch's stall, most impressive of all, has the royal arms immediately in front of it, and it is flanked by two stalls for members of the royal family (see Figure 12).

The Clow brothers also carved the dean's chair and kneeler and the lectern with its figures of the four evangelists. The crest of each of the sixteen Knights was placed on the pinnacle of his stall, while a special stall plate with his coat of arms was fixed to the back of the stall, facing into the Chapel. The crests were made by Whytock & Reid, the Edinburgh furnishings firm, while the shimmering enamelled stall plates were the work of the well-known Arts and Crafts artist Phoebe Traquair, an Irishwoman who had settled in Edinburgh. Each knight had his own colourful banner and although it was intended that these should hang

Figure 12
The Thistle Chapel, interior, showing the royal stall. (© Royal Commission on the Ancient
and Historical Monuments of Scotland. Licensor www.scran.ac.uk)

above the stalls, there was no room for them and so they were displayed
in the nearby Preston Aisle instead.

The Chapel was completed in 1911, three months ahead of schedule
and just under its budget of £24,000. King Edward VII had died by then,

149

but his son George V and Queen Mary came to the opening service on 17 July 1911, he in his Thistle robe, she in a turquoise satin gown and a white hat trimmed with white barley ears and pink carnations. With them were two of their children, the Prince of Wales and Princess Mary, along with the Duke of Connaught, one of Queen Victoria's sons. The Knights were clad in their dark-green velvet mantles with their black velvet caps trimmed with ostrich feathers, the Royal Company of Archers (the King's bodyguard in Scotland) stood to attention with their long bows, peers and peeresses and a host of other dignitaries filled the Cathedral and Dr Lees was proudly back in his capacity as Dean of the Order of the Thistle. It was an historic occasion, and ever since then the Knights and nowadays Ladies of the Thistle have attended services in their chapel, with the monarch coming to install each new member of the Order.

Almost two years later, on 26 June 1913, Dr Lees died of cardiac disease in his house in Kingussie, which he had named 'St Giles''. His funeral was held in the Cathedral and *The Scotsman*, in its lengthy appreciation, noted that his life 'was proof that the friend of every denomination need not be unfaithful to his own ... He mapped out a line for himself and, serene and dignified, he followed it to the end, faithfully and without pause or deviation'. Lees left orders that all his sermons and manuscripts were to be burned, but he bequeathed to St Giles' a generous sum of money to help in the parish work of the High Street, along with a silver bowl given to him by Dr Chambers and a silver tankard. These were to be, and indeed still are, used at those baptisms which do not take place at the font.

Lees was succeeded at St Giles' by Andrew Wallace Williamson, 53 years old and at the height of his powers. One of six children of a Dumfriesshire tailor, he had studied at Edinburgh University, where he was the most distinguished divinity student of his year. Since 1883 he had been the colleague of Dr James Macgregor at St Cuthbert's, Edinburgh. The two men got on famously, but from the start Williamson had shown that he had a mind of his own. Twelve days after his appointment, he had insisted on marrying a young woman considered by some to be socially unacceptable. Agnes Blackstone might be well-educated and refined, they said, but her father was a mere janitor and she worked for her living, in *The Scotsman* office.

Williamson ignored all criticisms, for he loved her, but sad to say she faded away and died of heart trouble less than two years after their wedding. By the time he came to St Giles' he had married again. His second wife, Elizabeth Croall, was the daughter of Robert Croall, Esquire, of Craigcrook

Castle. Williamson's biographer noted that 'both in public and in private life in the Church and in society, she well maintained the great tradition of "the minister's wife", of whom so much is expected and who often gets but scant recognition of her services'. She and her husband called the eldest of their three children Agnes, after Williamson's first wife, but the little girl died of whooping cough when she was only three.

Dr Lees had approved of his successor, who shared many of the same liberal opinions. Williamson loved beautiful services, liturgy, symbolism and fine music, and he had strongly ecumenical views. In 1900 he had preached before the synod of Lothian and Tweeddale a stirring sermon welcoming the reunion of the Free Church of Scotland with the United Presbyterian Church, and now he would work hard and successfully for the joining together of the United Free Church with the Church of Scotland, not least as Moderator of the General Assembly in 1913. On his arrival at St Giles', the congregation totalled 1,152 and, over the next ten years, membership rose to 1,657. Among the lawyers, doctors, businessmen and occupants of the crowded High Street closes were W. Birnie Rhind the sculptor and his family, 'Edinburgh Mary' who sold fruit, flowers and vegetables from her barrow and Tertia Liebenthal the concert promoter.

St Giles' had eighteen elders in 1906 and the kirk session included various prominent men. The handsome Colonel James Sconce of the Indian army had taken part in the Relief of Lucknow. Lord Salvesen the judge and his brother Theodore, head of the famous shipping firm of Christian Salvesen & Company, were both generous benefactors to the Cathedral. Sir Robert Inches, former Lord Provost of Edinburgh and co-founder of Hamilton & Inches, the well-known jewellers, always took a particular interest in the music. Thomas Ross, the eminent architect, compiled scrapbooks of press cuttings relating to St Giles', and William Chambers's friend Sir Henry Littlejohn, the public health pioneer, kept a watchful eye on the hygiene of the common cups at communion.

Williamson made few changes to the form of service established by his predecessor, but he did introduce the saying of the Creed by the congregation and, the year after he came, the choir were provided with gowns in violet-coloured cord. He also had the font moved from the south-west corner of the Cathedral to the large, semicircular recess in the Albany Aisle which had once been the entrance to Haddo's Hole Kirk and, for the next thirty years and more, babies were christened under the stern gaze of John Knox's statue. In 1911, an anonymous member of the congregation gave a new communion table designed by Robert Lorimer and elaborately carved and painted with angels and the Lamb of God. Its severely plain predecessor was presented to the West Parish Church in Stirling. Williamson was anxious to have more frequent communion services, and in 1913, he announced to his kirk session that he would like those to take place on the last Sunday of every month. The elders were doubtful. However, when they investigated they found that this would in no way contravene Church of Scotland practice, and so they agreed. Subsequently, new silver communion cups, some of them regularly in use today, were presented by several of the elders including Robert Inches and Lord Salvesen and his brother.

As time went by, more and more organisations sought the public recognition of an annual service in St Giles'. Some of them were very much establishment groups, but others were not. This was the period when there was a growing demand for votes for women, and a service for the Church League for Women's Suffrage was held in the Cathedral on 14 November 1910. Three years later, a memorial tablet by Robert Lorimer was put up to Sophia Jex Blake, reputedly the first woman to be heard in St Giles' since the riots of 1637 when she spoke at a crowded meeting there in 1871 in favour of women being allowed to train as doctors. The tablet was erected at the request of her brother, Dr T. W. Jex Blake, former Dean of Wells, but relationships with suffragettes were not always so harmonious. When Williamson declined to pray for imprisoned suffragettes, there was a short series of protests in late 1913 and early 1914, with their supporters interrupting services by chanting the women's names. The disturbances ended, however, with the outbreak of the First World War.

The first Edinburgh casualty of the war was John Maxwell, 18-year-old son of the St Giles' church officer. He was killed on 10 August 1914 when his ship, HMS *Amphion*, was blown up by a mine. Members of the congregation were by then hastening to enlist and William Howarth, principal tenor in the choir, joined the Sportsman's Battalion of the Royal Fusiliers. He went with a gift from his colleagues, the good wishes of the kirk session and the promise that his post would be kept open for him. He did indeed return, for the kirk session minutes of 17 December 1933 record that, on his resignation from the choir after twenty-nine years, he was presented with a crystal table-lamp and box. However, ninety-nine members of the congregation were killed, as was Matthew Marshall, the promising young assistant minister.

Hardly a month went by without Dr Williamson taking special services of intercession and memorial services. On 29 November 1917, for instance, he preached eloquently at the funeral of one of his own congregation, Dr Elsie Inglis, founder of the Scottish Women's Hospitals for Home and Foreign Service. The funeral took place with full military honours. Dr Inglis had set up hospitals in Serbia, becoming a passionate advocate for that country and so her coffin was draped not only with the Union Jack but with the Serbian flag. An impressive contingent of leading Serbians attended, along with many representatives from her medical and suffragette interests. At the end, the Royal Scots buglers sounded the *Last Post*, the organist played the *Hallelujah Chorus* and her coffin was borne away to the Dean Cemetery on a gun carriage drawn by six horses. Several years later, an elegant stone wall memorial to her designed by Frank Mears the architect was unveiled in the Holy Cross Aisle.

St Giles' organised collections for the Belgian Relief Fund, the Red Cross and the French hospitals for wounded soldiers. Marie Thomson, the choir's principal soprano, was given leave of absence to sing at concerts for the troops in France and in May 1915 and September 1917 Dr Williamson visited the headquarters of the British Army in Flanders, calling on many of the Scottish regiments and preaching before Field Marshal Haig. When the conflict finally ended, King George V, Queen Mary and the Prince of Wales attended a service of thanksgiving in St Giles'. In the years that followed there was a whole series of services of dedication as memorials were unveiled to the fallen of Scottish regiments, particularly the Royal Scots, members of the congregation, the Royal Army Medical Corps and Scottish military nurses and chaplains. These monuments have long lists of the dead and a few commemorate individuals, including the sons of Lord Rosebery and Lord Salvesen.

Several commemorative stained glass windows were also inserted during Williamson's ministry, notably the one above the north door given by Captain Charles Taylor of Stonehaven. A naval man himself, he stipulated that it must show Christ stilling the waters and walking on the waves. Douglas Strachan was commissioned to design and produce it at a cost of £2,650. There were lengthy delays occasioned by his ill-health and by the war, but it was finally inserted in 1922 and ever since has been one of the most admired windows in the Cathedral, with its striking shades of blue and green. The cost of Strachan's materials had gone up considerably since his original estimate. In recognition of his fine work, the kirk session therefore paid him £3,349:7:3, the full amount of interest available from Captain Taylor's bequest. His daughter Elma evidently inherited Strachan's love of colour, for when she was married in St Giles' in 1939 wearing a dress of parchment satin with a long train, her five bridesmaids were arrayed in 'striking dresses of flamingo pink velvet ... over underskirts of silver lamé veiled with matching net'.

Another unexpected gift to the Cathedral came in the form of a new clock for the tower. The existing clock was nearly 200 years old and entirely worn out. In 1911 James Ritchie, the Edinburgh watchmaker and clockmaker, therefore presented an entirely new clock with a pendulum thirteen feet long. The hours and quarters are struck on the three bells still in the steeple: the great bell, recast at Whitechapel Foundry in 1846 but believed to contain metal from the its medieval predecessor, and two small bells dating from 1706 and 1728. Because Ritchie was of the opinion that the clock-faces spoiled the look of the tower, he did not replace them. The old clock was given to what is now the Museum of Edinburgh in Huntly House, where its mechanism can still be seen.

Modern technology made possible another two innovations designed to improve the comfort of the congregation. In 1911, after almost fifteen years of argument between the kirk session and the managing board, electric lighting was installed. Special chandeliers were designed by Lorimer, who oversaw the work. They were in a graceful vine branch pattern, with six lights above and four below, giving what was described as a cascade effect. Two particularly elaborate chandeliers were hung above the communion table. Thirteen years later, a new heating system was put in. Its installation was not without its problems. Not only did the kirk session have to pay £100 in compensation to Miss Pearson, a visitor from the USA who was unlucky enough to fall into one of the workmen's trenches, but angry protests in the correspondence columns in *The Scotsman* condemning the unsightly pipes ('Vandalism in St Giles") turned into a furious argument between Lorimer and the session clerk as to whether Lorimer ever had been the official Cathedral architect. He had in fact been appointed to that position by the managing board in 1910.

By the early 1920s, Dr Williamson was suffering from serious heart trouble. Various periods of rest abroad saw no improvement in his condition and in 1925 he had to resign. When he died at his house in Palmerston Place on 10 July 1926, the kirk session lamented his loss, praising his 'unbounded love and human sympathy, and his genuine goodness'. He was succeeded by Charles Warr, son of a prominent Church of Scotland minister. Warr had served in the army and been seriously wounded at the second Battle of Ypres in 1915, leaving his left arm permanently bent at the elbow. As he lay in the dressing station waiting for attention, he was suddenly seized with the conviction that he must enter the ministry and, when he had recovered, he studied divinity, becoming minister of St Paul's Parish Church in Greenock. A few weeks later he married Christian Tatlock, an accomplished musician, always known as Ruby, from her red hair.

People thought that Warr was very young to be minister of St Giles' Cathedral – he was 33 – but he had been elected with a majority of 330 to 26 and, to celebrate his induction, the kirk session entertained him to a lavish dinner in the North British Hotel. Tickets cost eight shillings and six pence (without wines) and the menu included sole, lamb and pheasant followed by what sounds like a very indigestible *bombe plombière* (which translates literally as 'leaden bomb'). Since there was no manse and Warr was having difficulty finding a house, the kirk session lent him money to help him to buy 63 Northumberland Street in the New Town of Edinburgh. Five years later, at his suggestion, they purchased it from him to be the official manse. Dr Warr proved to be well-suited to St Giles'. In his very first sermon he emphasised that the Cathedral had a special mission in fostering the spirit of Christian unity and healing the divisions in the Scottish Church. Its national role as the sister to Westminster Abbey would not be forgotten, he promised, nor would he overlook his duties towards the welfare of his parishioners.

Later, he would often speak about the importance of beauty in architecture and symbolism in worship, pointing out that human nature needs encouragement in the form of furnishings which point towards spiritual truth but which always retain simplicity and dignity. He even argued in favour of prayers for the dead, telling an Edinburgh conference that these were in no way related to the Roman Catholic doctrine of purgatory but merely implied that the dead as well as the living were capable of progress. That was a step too far for many, and he commented wryly that he found himself ostracised when he went on holiday that year to the Kyle of Lochalsh. Be that as it may, he was usually much appreciated, he was a devoted visitor of his congregation and Dean Matthews of London's St Paul's Cathedral once told him that his normal Sunday services were a most impressive combination of the Catholic and Evangelical traditions.

An important change in the administration of St Giles' came about at the beginning of Warr's ministry, with the 1925 Church of Scotland (Property and Endowments) Act. This legislation transferred responsibility for the city churches from the Edinburgh ecclesiastical commissioners to the Church of Scotland's general trustees. At the same time, the managing board was expanded and in 1931 the Pilgrim Trust granted it £1,000 for the upkeep and improvement of the fabric, having in mind the rich historical associations of the church and the reverence and affection with which it was regarded by Scotsmen of all creeds and classes throughout the world.

Congregational numbers continued to rise, from 1,860 members on Dr Warr's arrival to 2,592 ten years later and Edinburgh presbytery's visitation committee in 1932 praised his success in combining his role as a spokesman of the nation with his activities as minister of a parish which had its own difficulties, meaning the unemployment and poverty resulting from the Depression. Members of St Giles' did what they could to help, distributing bread, oatmeal and coal to the most needy and taking cooked meals to people who were ill or disabled. Dr Warr was also anxious to engage the interest of the families of the congregation and he was very much taken when Dr Williamson's daughter Verona, who was deeply involved with the Guides, suggested that a place in St Giles' could be set aside for the banners of the various youth organisations, giving them a spiritual home.

Warr agreed enthusiastically and his thoughts turned to the Chambers Aisle, which for some time had been used as a lumber room. He decided to transform it into a Chapel of Youth, and in 1928 Robert Lorimer was asked to prepare drawings for its conversion. He duly designed a new screen, stalls and a small communion table and, although he died before the work was finished, his colleague John Matthew completed his plans. Lorimer had employed Alice Meredith Williams the sculptor at the National War Memorial which he had designed for Edinburgh Castle, and he commissioned her and her artist husband Morris to produce a carved oak reredos with a painted nativity scene for the Chapel of Youth, while Douglas Strachan and his wife donated a stained glass lantern to be suspended from the roof. A Banner of the Grand Cross of the Bath was then hung on the west wall of the Chapel. It had belonged to Earl Haig, the First World War commander-in-chief. When his body had lain in state in the Cathedral in February 1928, almost a hundred thousand people had filed past the coffin and to commemorate that occasion, his widow now presented the banner.

Two years later, there were alterations to the seating in the chancel. Warr, a small, slight man, had always disliked the heavy, cumbersome stalls behind the communion table for himself and the other royal chaplains. He never used his and when three new chaplains were added in the autumn of 1929 he took the opportunity of effecting a change. Ten stalls were needed and so he had the existing stalls removed. The base of William Hay's reredos was now revealed and the communion table was moved back towards it. Warr had hoped that it could be elevated on a marble pedestal five inches high but, after agreeing, the kirk session took fright when they saw it experimentally raised on wooden blocks. They feared that this made the table look like an altar and so it was left standing on the floor. The new, more modest seats for the royal chaplains were arranged in two rows facing each other in front of the communion table and Warr himself was supplied with a handsome oak stall in the Gothic style with elaborate carvings. The Moray Aisle was also improved at this time, with John Matthew designing a fine new carved oak reredos and screen put up in 1931 at its east end. These were the gift of Jane Findlay and her sisters, in memory of their brother, John Ritchie Findlay, founder of the Scottish National Portrait Gallery.

In the midst of these pleasing improvements, the Cathedral music was giving cause for concern. The congregation seemed most unwilling to join in the hymn singing, preferring to sit silent, as if at a concert. The kirk session were of the opinion that this was because of the position of the choir. Its members sat on a sloping platform immediately in front of the large organ, which occupied the whole of the south transept. When it played loudly enough to be audible in the more distant parts of the Cathedral, the choir could not hear themselves sing, and in any case they were too far away from the congregation. The session's music committee had already fallen out with John Hartley, the organist, who had been appointed to St Giles' in 1878 at the surprisingly early age of 15. He had always attracted a good deal of admiring attention, but thirty years on, the committee members were irritated by his habit of introducing unauthorised improvisations on a Sunday morning and his dismissal of the unoffending chief contralto was the last straw. Forced to resign in 1923, he emigrated to Canada.

His successor was the accomplished Dr Wilfrid Greenhouse Allt, who found that he had to struggle with an organ which was rapidly wearing out. There were still recitals by celebrities such as Signor Fernando Germani of St Peter's, Rome, Marcel Dupré of Notre Dame, Paris and Dr Albert Schweitzer, who performed Bach and Mendelssohn in aid of his African hospital at Lambaréné. However, there was no denying that the organ was becoming an embarrassment and, said the committee wistfully, 'cannot be compared for a moment with the instrument in Glasgow Cathedral'. In 1928 the kirk session decided to have it reconstructed by Henry Willis & Sons Ltd at an estimated cost of £8,070 and Lorimer prepared to design the organ case. Unfortunately, the congregation were reluctant to contribute towards the work, and after ten more years the instrument had completely collapsed and was pronounced to be beyond repair. Something would have to be done. A public appeal for £12,000 to rebuild it was launched on 23 February 1939 and Henry Willis & Sons began to work on it. However, on 3 September 1939, in the middle of the morning service, a messenger arrived in St Giles' from police headquarters with the ominous news that war with Germany had been declared.

Precautions were immediately taken to protect the Cathedral. The city fire-master gave advice about minimising damage by fire-bombs and a water tank was installed at the top of the tower. The stained glass window above the west door showing two rows of prophets and the Burne-Jones window next to it were boarded up, and the window behind the organ was bricked up. Chain-link curtains were hung up inside other windows, while the regimental colours were put into store in the basement of the Office of Works building in Parliament Square. If there was an air-raid warning during the services, the congregation had permission to use the air-raid shelters in the nearby Parliament House Buildings and the City Chambers.

Many of the elders thought that work on the organ should be stopped and the finished parts stored for safety somewhere in the Scottish countryside until peace returned. However, the organ builder pointed out that these would be much safer in St Giles' itself and the rebuilding continued. Esmé Gordon the architect designed the organ case and Elizabeth Dempster the sculptor was given leave from her VAD nursing to carve its large figures of two angels and Jubal, biblical ancestor of all who played the lyre and pipe. The reconstructed organ, using most of the former pipes, occupied a third less floor space than before but it had a more varied specification and two consoles, one above the north door for major services and a smaller one opposite, in the present Holy Blood Aisle, for the daily services. The choir was moved to a much better position beneath the tower and the organ was dedicated by Warr at a short evening service on 15 March 1940.

Meanwhile, Warr was very active raising funds for huts and canteens for Scottish soldiers abroad and he would write afterwards of the multiplicity of services he led: days of civic dedication, national intercession, intercession for the Poles, French, Yugoslavs, prisoners of war ... the list seemed endless. Victory in Europe Day was finally celebrated on 8 May 1945 and a week later King George VI, Queen Elizabeth and their daughters, Princess Elizabeth and Princess Margaret, attended a crowded service of thanksgiving in St Giles'. The war ended on 15 August 1945 and

Warr hoped that a large ten-ton victory bell might be hung in the steeple to celebrate but, when this proved to be impractical because of its size, his thoughts turned to the recent casualties.

He and the kirk session had hoped that Ian Macaulay would come to be deputy minister at St Giles' when peace returned, but he was killed while serving as chaplain to the Fife and Forfar Yeomanry and thirty-nine members of the congregation were among the fallen. Warr therefore decided to convert the Albany Aisle into a special war memorial chapel. Esmé Gordon, by now Cathedral architect as well as being an elder, produced the design. The statue of John Knox and the font were moved to the south-west corner of the nave, several other monuments were moved out and the 1914–18 congregational war memorial was moved in, to stand impressively against the west wall beneath the Burne-Jones window. The now unfashionable Minton floor tiles were replaced with Leoch paving stones from Dundee, but Chambers's grey-green marble bands with the inset coats of arms were left in place.

A small but heavy, carved oak communion table was placed against the east wall. Bronze vases and a lectern were provided for it and four ladies of the congregation, Isobel, Jean and Alice Gracie and Hilda Nimmo Smith embroidered four covers for it, for the different liturgical seasons. Elizabeth Dempster carved the large cross above it, with the symbols of fire, air, earth and water and a wrought-iron lamp of remembrance with a glowing red light was suspended from the roof. The new memorial for casualties of Second World War was slow in coming, because of the usual lack of funds and arguments over design, but by 1951 the names of the dead had been carved on the wall in the semicircular recess and on 2 December Viscount Cunningham was present at the Chapel's dedication.

In 1951 Warr celebrated his twenty-fifth anniversary as minister of St Giles' and, at a special meeting before the service of thanksgiving on 11 February 1957, the kirk session paid him a warm tribute, praising him as an inspired preacher and adding, 'No minister could be more approachable or a better pastor'. Two years later, on 24 June 1953, there was an even more exciting occasion when Queen Elizabeth II attended a large national service in the Cathedral to mark her first visit to Scotland after her coronation. Special preparations were made for the occasion. William Hay's controversial reredos was dismantled and removed, to be replaced by a handsome new gold textile reredos presented by the Edinburgh Merchant Company and designed by Esmé Gordon. Gordon also converted the huge and uncomfortable royal pew into a simpler but dignified new seat and desk. Early on the morning of the 24 June the Honours of Scotland (the Scottish crown jewels) were brought from Edinburgh Castle and placed on the communion table, cleverly extended for the purpose. Not only was the service televised but, at Warr's request, Stanley Cursiter the artist was allowed to paint the scene, showing the 14th Duke of Hamilton kneeling before the Queen with the Scottish crown. The painting hangs in the Palace of Holyroodhouse.

Later that year, Warr fell ill and on medical advice wrote to Edinburgh Presbytery asking them to allow him to have a colleague and successor. The two ministers would share their duties, with the colleague taking on more of the responsibilities and receiving a salary of £1,300 to Warr's £900. The colleague would also have the manse, but there was no difficulty about that because the Queen now granted Warr the only grace and favour residence in Scotland, a spacious flat in Edinburgh's elegant Moray Place. This had recently been presented to her by the Lord Provosts of Edinburgh, Perth, Glasgow, Dundee and Aberdeen with this sort of purpose in mind. Warr proudly took up residence there with his wife, and in the autumn of 1954 he warmly welcomed the appointment of Dr Harry Whitley as his new colleague.

Unlike his three predecessors Whitley was an Edinburgh man, but most of his career had been spent in the west of Scotland. He had entered the ministry after becoming deeply interested in social work in deprived areas, and served as an assistant to George (later Lord) MacLeod in Govan. During the Second World War he was an army chaplain and was wounded, then with the return of peace he became minister of Partick Parish Church in Glasgow. Now in his late 40s, he was elected to St Giles' by 542 votes to 6 and he was, Warr told the congregation at his induction, very experienced, robust, fearless, merry and compassionate, with transparent selflessness and sincerity.

Whitley, his journalist wife Elizabeth and their children moved happily to Edinburgh, but the position of colleague and successor was notoriously difficult. As Dr MacGregor of St Cuthbert's had once remarked, this type of relationship was either heaven or hell, usually the latter, and so it proved to be for Dr Warr and Dr Whitley. They were very different in personality and the trouble began when Warr unexpectedly made a complete recovery from his illness and returned to St Giles' expecting to take up all his previous duties. Whitley was understandably eager to carry out his own ideas for the Cathedral. The ensuing power struggle, very painful for both men, threatened to divide the congregation. Five years later, in 1959, they finally

Figure 13
Dr Charles Warr (*left*) and Dr Harry Whitley (*right*) after the latter's induction in 1954.
(© The Scotsman Publications Ltd. Licensor www.scran.ac.uk)

signed an agreement specifying their different responsibilities in minute detail. Whitley, for instance, would be in charge of the pastoral oversight of the parish while Warr would be responsible for services attended by the Queen. Even so, the difficulties really only ended with Warr's retirement in 1962, marked by a managing board dinner in his honour. There was no *bombe plombière* this time, but the table centrepiece was in the form of the crown steeple of St Giles', made of spun sugar.

Warr died in 1969, and if he had particularly enjoyed St Giles' dignified services as Scotland's national church, Whitley was more concerned with its parish church aspect. Because of the migration of population from the Old Town to new housing estates on the edge of the city, attendance at services was falling, with a significant number of people coming only for communion. He succeeded in abolishing seat rents after more than 300 years because he felt that people were deterred from coming by the thought that they might sit in someone's rented seat by mistake.

Anxious to encourage members' activities, he was instrumental in purchasing premises on George IV Bridge to act as a permanent church hall and provide space for the various flourishing youth organisations such as the famous 75th St Giles' Rangers and the Youth Fellowship, whose participants still remember them with affection. He was eager to support musical events and in 1963 had Sax Shaw, Lecturer in Colour at Edinburgh College of Art, design cheerful scarlet gowns for the choir to replace their more restrained purple ones. To make visiting the scattered congregation easier, a scooter was acquired for his assistant ministers in 1960 and the following year the kirk session approved the purchase of a second-hand Ford Zephyr car for Whitley himself. The number of elders had likewise been increased in 1942 from twenty-seven to sixty-four, to facilitate visiting, and during Whitley's ministry there were nearly 100.

Dr Whitley could also never resist engaging in public controversy, and the newspapers liked nothing better than to report his views on everything from a Scottish parliament (which he supported) to women elders (whom he abhorred). Their introduction had been discussed by the Church of Scotland as long before as 1946, when 557 members of the St Giles' congregation voted in favour but 1,026 were against it. The Church went on to ordain the first women elders in 1963, but Dr Whitley's opposition meant that his elders were men. He had once allowed the Cathedral's lady missionary in Northern India, Alexa Scott, to attend a kirk session meeting, but he believed that women elders were an affliction to the congregation, commenting that women who insisted on taking over had never been admired for it, least of all by him. That apart, during one particularly traumatic episode he came into conflict with the Episcopal Churches of both California and Scotland when he tried to allow his American Episcopalian assistant, John Tirrell, to officiate at a communion service without obtaining their permission. Some people were delighted to see him so ready to stand up for his convictions, but others felt sad that St Giles' was being dragged into these all too public arguments.

At this period, continuing postwar austerity meant that there was little in the way of money to fund anything other than very necessary repairs to the building and in 1958 the fall of a small piece of masonry inside St Giles' resulted in a detailed survey of the stonework being undertaken by John Wilson Paterson who, as Office of Works architect, had inspected it thirty years earlier. At first Paterson was inclined to attribute the trouble to vibration from the passing traffic, but further inspection revealed that some of William Burn's iron tie bars were the cause of the problem. No-one had realised that they were there, but they were discovered and found to have rusted, expanding and fracturing the stone, which then fell off. This was alarming and the firm of Bell & Rose, builders, was hastily employed to cut out the damaged stones and remove the ties, replacing them with steel.

In 1959 the last available window space, in the Albany Aisle, was filled with stained glass designed by Francis Spears on the theme of St John the Divine. Six years after that, Whitley decided to move the statue of John Knox from the Cathedral interior, thinking it more appropriate to place it prominently on a plain plinth in Parliament Square, overlooking Knox's burial place. The plaque beneath it was unveiled by one of Knox's descendants, 5-year-old John Macfie. Meanwhile, tastes in interior design were changing, and heavy Victorian ornamentation was now much disliked. When new lighting had to be installed in 1958, it was decided to do away with Lorimer's decorative electric chandeliers and replace them with what was considered to be an unobtrusive system of concealed lighting, the bulbs hidden by metal boxes set high on the walls and painted to blend in with the stonework. Some of the old chandeliers were given away to St John's Kirk in Perth and others found a home in Cleish Church.

There was more to this change, of course, than mere aesthetic fashion. Whitley and the kirk session felt that simplicity suited the Church of Scotland better than elaborate ecclesiastical furnishings and in 1967 attention began to focus on the east end of St Giles'. The fabric of the Merchant Company reredos had become tarnished and a discussion of what to do about it led to a general consideration of the area around the communion table. There were those who felt that not only was the whole arrangement inappropriate but it was difficult to see the communion table from the nave, in part because it was so far away but also because the chancel stalls and their book rests were in the way. By 1970 the kirk session was engaged in detailed discussions, but before anything could be done, Dr Whitley announced that he would have to retire in July 1971 because of ill-health caused by his war wounds. He had been minister of St Giles' for eighteen years, and the kirk session paid him a warm tribute, praising his sincerity of purpose, his abilities as a preacher and his determination to speak his mind. Obviously a vacancy was not the right time to go ahead with alterations to the Cathedral, and so the question of the east end was deferred until a new minister could be appointed.

CHAPTER 12

The Renewal

O n 21 January 1973, Gilleasbuig Macmillan preached in St Giles'
as sole nominee for the vacancy. A son of the manse, he spent
his earliest years in Mull until the family moved to Argyll. He
graduated in philosophy and divinity from Edinburgh University before
becoming assistant to the Reverend David Steel at another historic church,
St Michael's in Linlithgow, and was now minister of Portree, on the Isle
of Skye. Eyebrows were raised in some Edinburgh circles when his name
was mentioned. How could a man from a small island parish be suitable
for prestigious St Giles', Scotland's national cathedral, internationally
recognised as the Mother Church of Presbyterianism? More worrying
still, he was only 30 years old, younger even than Dr Warr had been when
he began his ministry. The congregation, however, were impressed when
they heard him preach, he was elected that day by an overwhelming
majority and the members soon found that he was a profound and
imaginative thinker who already had in mind far-reaching ideas for St
Giles'.

Ninety years had passed since the Chambers Restoration and the
interior of the Cathedral had become depressingly dark and gloomy. The
increasing volume of traffic on the busy street outside meant that fumes
and pollution had covered the windows with a layer of dirt, keeping out a lot
of the light. The heavy stalls in the chancel were dated and unfashionable
and row upon row of ageing chairs in the nave added nothing to the
general effect. Tastes had changed. Ornate Victorian furnishings were
now seen as ugly and cumbersome and, most importantly, thinking about

worship had altered too. Nineteenth-century research into early Christian texts had aroused dissatisfaction with the current form of services across the denominations and there was a growing desire to return to the purity of those vanished times when mass or communion was simpler and the congregation were more actively involved in it. This was all the more essential because the general drift away from churchgoing was continuing, more people had moved away from the city centre and the roll of members contained the names of a significant number who were never seen in St Giles'. Something would have to be done, not only to improve the building but to revitalise services, making them truly meaningful for the late twentieth century.

Many Roman Catholics had come to regret the fact that worshippers sat in rows, like an audience at a play, watching the actions of a priest who stood with his back to them at a distant altar. The Second Vatican Council of 1962 to 1965 had discussed a wide range of ideas, deciding for example that in future its services should no longer be in Latin and that the priest should face the congregation as he stood at the altar, fostering a sense of community and participation. This meant that church interiors would have to be rearranged, because altars usually stood against the east wall, with no room for priests to stand behind them. As a result, the altars were moved forward, some right to the centre of the church. Episcopalians possessed of large cathedrals had been very conscious of the same problem, and they adopted a similar solution, in small churches as well as large. In Edinburgh in the 1950s the near neighbour of St Giles', the Scottish Episcopal church of St Columba-by-the-Castle, had removed its chancel screen and much of its furniture, bringing the altar forward. The rector had then been able to remark with satisfaction that what they had lost at St Columba's was the feeling that the priest was away up at the front doing something for them. Instead, they had gained an understanding that the people of God are one priesthood. Could it be that these new developments showed the way forward for St Giles too?

The situation in the Church of Scotland was very different, of course, because the elders and ministers usually sat in a row facing the congregation at communion and it was the elders who took round the bread and the wine, not the minister. However, there was an equal desire for active congregational participation in services and so the notion of a central communion table had its attractions. There were also other important implications in all of this. Previous ecumenical initiatives within the Reformed community had met with varying success but now, with the different churches looking to their common, pre-Reformation past and adopting similar forms of service, they might naturally grow closer, the Church of Scotland and the Church of England eventually coming together within a reforming Catholic Church. Gilleasbuig Macmillan was already deeply committed to ecumenism and he was eager to initiate a programme of renewal for both the congregation and the building. Perhaps the time had come to look again at the plans for alterations to the interior discussed by Whitley and the kirk session towards the end of his ministry.

The firm of Ian G. Lindsay & Partners, architects, had given advice and in 1971 John Reid, the senior partner, had presented three alternative plans, all of which envisaged bringing the communion table further forward into the Cathedral and clearing some of the seating from the chancel. 'Radical Plan One' proposed that it be placed at the crossing, that the entire floor be repaved, the roof vaults whitened and the regimental colours removed. There had also been discussions about exploring the possibility of excavating a new space below the floor level of the Cathedral. All this would involve great expense, the kirk session had been wary of such drastic change and in the end they settled for moving the communion table away from the east wall by just one foot, to make room for the minister's chair behind it. They believed that 'a simple background to the communion table is more appropriate to a Presbyterian church', and so, after explanations to the Queen and to the Merchant Company about the tarnished state of the fabric reredos, it was removed and the wall behind it was refaced with suitable stone, creating the plain effect they desired.

In spite of the minimal nature of these alterations, there remained at St Giles' a real desire for change, although the difficulties ahead were formidable, not least because any building work would be very costly and there were already serious financial problems. For some years past the congregation had been unable to meet its commitment to the mission and service fund of the Church of Scotland, much to the indignation of the presbytery. That regrettable situation must be addressed urgently, and there were other complications too. The purchase of St Giles' House might have solved the perennial problem that the Cathedral had no hall, but it meant that congregational activities took place there and that was also where the minister had his office. Now it was true that St Giles' House was just round the corner but, at times when there was no service taking place in the Cathedral, the many tourists and other visitors could see no sign that it was a living church.

This would have to be remedied as well and there would inevitably be a good deal of resistance to change from many of the congregation. That had been the experience both in England and abroad when parishioners saw their cherished buildings altered, their seats moved, memorials to their ancestors relocated, the reassuringly familiar ruined, in their view, as the place they had loved from childhood was transformed into something very unfamiliar. These worrying thoughts were outweighed, however, by the need for renewal for, as one kirk session paper put it, 'Much might be done with the building; and much requires to be done, if St Giles' speaks not the romantic gloom of Victorianism plus neglect, but the beauty and stimulation of a holy place of vital worship'.

As a first step, William Hay's session house next to the Albany Aisle was converted into a room for the minister and an office for his secretary. In 1971, Mrs Marguerite Ninian Hill had generously bequeathed the Tower House in Bruntsfield as a manse for St Giles', but it proved expensive to heat and its huge garden was difficult to maintain. When a house in Northumberland Street came on the market in 1978 the kirk session sold the Tower House, bought it instead and the minister moved there with his wife Maureen, a former hospital theatre sister who would later become Senior Lecturer in Nursing at Napier University, and their small daughter Mary Jane.

Church architecture, it has been said, is the art of shaping space around ritual, and the design for church interiors must always grow out of the liturgy and not the other way round. Aware of this truth, Macmillan began his ministry by altering the pattern of services and their content, gradually at first but working determinedly towards his vision for the future. When he came, the principal service each Sunday was at eleven o'clock and took the form established by Dr Lees in the 1880s, with sermon, prayers, readings, hymns and psalms. After that, led by the minister, a long procession of elders in morning suits walked slowly in from the Moray Aisle, carrying the silver plates of bread, cups of wine and flagons, while the congregation sang a paraphrase.

The elders took their places beside the communion table and, after the Lord's Prayer, they passed the elements along the pews to the seated congregation. Further prayers, the Doxology and the benediction followed, before the congregation sang a final psalm and the procession made its way out again. It was truly impressive, but Macmillan felt that it could be more meaningful if it was a separate service in its own right and, by the spring of 1974, the kirk session had agreed that a separate communion service should take place at 9am, on an experimental basis. By the autumn they said that this would be the permanent arrangement.

In the summer of 1974, the opportunity came to move the communion table away from the east end of the chancel. Reginald Barrett-Ayres, head of music at Aberdeen University, had written a new two-act opera about Hugh Miller the geologist and evangelical writer. It was to be given its first performance in St Giles' during the Edinburgh Festival and it had been decided that it should be staged underneath the great east window. To make this possible, the heavy stalls in the chancel would have to be moved away and so too would the communion table. It was brought forward to a position between the third pair of pillars from the east end, to the place where the high altar had probably stood in the Middle Ages.

People liked its new situation, and there it remained when the Festival was over. This allowed the way the 9am service was conducted to change too. The elders still carried in the elements, but they did not pass the bread and wine along the pews. Instead, the eighty or so communicants were invited to come forward and stand in a circle round the communion table. Although at first this startled many, it echoed both the medieval mass, when the St Giles' parishioners came forward to receive the Host, and Reformed services from 1560 until the Chambers Restoration, with communicants moving to the long tables where they would sit. During a transitional period, the congregation were still served in their pews at the late morning and afternoon communion services, but these were eventually discontinued, as was the communion for elders which had been held by Whitley before kirk session meetings.

The liturgy of the communion service was evolving too. Macmillan wanted to create a service which would be closer to those held in Anglican and Roman Catholic churches. Pointing out in a later interview that pre-Reformation mass in St Giles' was just as much part of our heritage as the Reformed tradition, he added that he was always pleased when visitors asked him after the service, 'What denomination is this?' preferring the question to a comment of 'That was a real Presbyterian service!' By 1976, he had introduced into the 11am service a new sequence entitled 'Confession and Pardon', which began with a short prayer of confession and moved on to the singing in Latin of *Kyrie Eleison* (Lord, have mercy) by the choir. After that, the minister pronounced the declaration that God pardons our sin, and the choir sang the Latin *Gloria* (Praise to the Lord). This part of the service ended with a short silence, for meditation and prayer.

Soon afterwards, the new sequence was quietly transferred to the 9am communion service, as was the saying of the Creed. To some church members, a service which included Latin words and followed so closely the pattern of the mass seemed shockingly popish, but in fact it was and is distinctly Calvinist too. No priest acts as intermediary between God and the people. The communicants serve each other, passing the bread and wine round the circle which, by its very formation, emphasises the equality of all in the sight of God, with high court judges and young backpackers standing anonymously next to each other. In short, it is, as Dean Matthews had once said of Dr Warr's Sunday services, a most impressive combination of the Catholic and Evangelical traditions.

By this time, another significant change had come about with the ordination of the first women elders in St Giles' on 4 February 1979. Twenty-six new elders were ordained that day, seventeen of them women. Two years earlier Nancy Norman, an American with degrees in theology from Richmond, USA and Edinburgh University, was employed as secretary to the minister, with special duties as coordinator of congregational meetings, and in 1980 the first woman assistant minister, the Reverend Helen Alexander, was appointed. Formerly a medical social worker, she was ordained the following year.

St Giles' had a long tradition of welcoming a series of preachers from other Protestant denominations, and in September 1975 Macmillan took this further by inviting Dr Edward Daly, Roman Catholic Bishop of Derry, to preach at the evening service. The occasion was disturbed by rowdy scenes and shouts of 'No popery' from sectarian demonstrators, but the minister and kirk session were undeterred, and well-known Roman Catholics including Father Anthony Ross and Father Jock Dalrymple subsequently came to speak at the 6pm Sunday services, which now included dialogues and addresses as well as music. In 1981 Cardinal Gordon Gray was principal guest at the annual elders' dinner.

By this time, plans for alterations to the building were well under way. Everyone knew, of course, that before anything could be done funds would have to be raised. The routine upkeep of a large Grade A listed building, let alone any intended alterations, was far beyond the means of the congregation. Money would be needed for a variety of projects, such as cleaning the stonework, and installing improved lighting and sound systems, as well as for pastoral work and financial support for the choir. On 3 February 1975 Macmillan, Eric Ivory and A. M. Dawson, managing director of Craigmyle & Co (Scotland) Ltd, fundraising consultants, held an informal meeting to discuss the possibilities of establishing a major appeal and a few weeks later it was decided that a detailed report on the entire building was necessary before any priorities could be established. The Ivory Family Trust generously offered to pay for the survey, and it was agreed that if possible Dr (later Sir) Bernard Feilden, the eminent architect should be commissioned to undertake the task.

An expert in the conservation of historic buildings, Feilden was at one time and another architectural consultant to Norwich Cathedral, York Minster and St Paul's Cathedral. Macmillan went to Norwich to meet him, an encounter which had far-reaching consequences for the future of St Giles'. The two men struck up an immediate rapport and the Feilden Report of June 1976 grew out of their discussions. Having addressed the state of the fabric, which was generally sound, and advised careful future maintenance, the report continued 'A great church, however, must not stand still. Our forefathers contributed in their days to the enhancement of St Giles' … If the contemporary church is to live and grow, we too must express our faith and our worship in contemporary terms.' St Giles' had many different roles: congregational, ecumenical, civic, national and upon occasion regal. Indeed it was like Westminster Abbey, St Paul's Cathedral and St George's Chapel, Windsor combined in one building. More than that, the fabric should be the agent by which casual visitors were transformed into worshippers, if only at the most basic level, by making them think about why they came and where they might be going.

The next part of the report was the most controversial. Discussing the arrangement of the interior, it said that a new, central sanctuary should be created beneath the crossing, symbolising the fact that the Eucharist was at the centre of the faith. The holy table would stand in the middle, with fixed, raked seating arranged on three sides, so that as many people as possible could see the communion service from close quarters. A step or two away was the pulpit, reminding people of the Reformed Church's emphasis on preaching the Word of God. There should be wide aisles for processional purposes and for large services, when extra seating was required, there would be light chairs, stackable but able to be linked together. Music was a vital part of services and so the failing organ must be rebuilt, its pipes put in the north transept to allow light to flood in towards the sanctuary from the south window, which it presently blocked.

Because good sightlines were vital, the choir must not be located in such a way as to intervene between the congregation and the sanctuary, a problem in many churches. The choir stalls would therefore be placed between the pillars in front of the south transept. New lighting was needed, to shine upwards to the shadowy carvings on the roof as well as downwards on to people's hymn books and it was even more necessary that everyone should be able to hear what was being said. The obsolete and trying sound system would have to be replaced. Further to foster a close sense of community, the congregation, now scattered across the city, would need premises inside St Giles' for their meetings and social events. There was no space to build on extensions, and so an area under the cathedral floor should be excavated and made into suitable rooms.

At first sight these recommendations seemed to many to be over-whelming, and astronomically expensive, but the report was confident that with careful planning and a major appeal for funding, everything was achievable. Feilden came to speak to the kirk session and the congregation about the report, and on 3 October 1976 Gilleasbuig Macmillan preached an eloquent sermon, emphasising that what was planned was not merely a series of alterations to the building. Intertwined with those would be the renewal of the congregation and there were wider aspirations too. Looking around him, he said that St Giles' had not been built merely to cover the heads of worshippers when it was raining and stop the cold Edinburgh winds from blowing through them. No, it was not merely a utilitarian box. 'It is a creation of mystery in response to the mysterious Creator, a sanctuary consecrated and set apart for the strengthening of the children of men with the comfort and nourishment of the Spirit of God, a meeting place where the things of daily life could be set within the atmosphere of eternity.' They must make this great building fulfil its purpose so that it was in truth the temple of reconciliation envisaged by Dr Lees, in our own day healing the divisions of the Christian Church.

This was a challenging vision, and naturally not everyone liked it. A marathon series of congregational meetings was therefore held to explain the implications of the Feilden Report. Some members of the congregation, deeply attached to the church they had attended for many years, could not bear to contemplate the prospect of their familiar spiritual home being altered, and left. Others were alarmed at the likely cost of all that was to be done. However, the Renewal already had its own impetus and Macmillan was determined that the Feilden Report recommendations would be carried through. With permission to proceed from the general trustees of the Church of Scotland and the presbytery, a general committee of the kirk session was appointed to supervise the scheme and in November 1976 trial holes were dug at the east end to determine the practicality of excavating there. In December, Craigmyle & Co (Scotland) were appointed as fundraisers and the following January the presbytery decided to take no action against St Giles' because of the shortfalls in their mission and service fund contribution. In view of the Renewal plans, they said, they would await developments and indeed in due course the money was paid.

Fundraising would obviously have to take priority over everything else, and the St Giles' Renewal Appeal Fund was set up with Lord Clydesmuir as chairman. The appeal got off to a slow start, but in September 1977 Jo Penney became appeal director. One of the elders, he was also the Cathedral factor and he had an intimate knowledge of the building as well as many useful contacts. Four months later, trustees for the fund were appointed under the chairmanship of Lord Emslie, the Lord Justice General, and the following year the Appeal brochure was launched. At the same time, great energy was put into organising the congregational aspect of the Renewal. The elders' districts were reduced in number and reorganised, as a means of improving pastoral care and encouraging contact among the members. Volunteers were enlisted to engage in community service, welcome visitors to St Giles' on Sundays, guide tourists round on weekdays, clean and polish the cathedral interior to make it look cared for instead of neglected, staff the small shop and arrange flowers.

At the same time, working groups considered relations with other churches, publicity, and the running of the various youth groups. A surprisingly large number of the congregation lived well beyond the outskirts of Edinburgh and rarely if ever attended services. Indeed in 1977, out of a roll of 1,393, only 499 members took communion at least once a year. In keeping with Church of Scotland policy, those who never came at all were subsequently encouraged to move to their own parish churches in an effort to ensure that people were not members of the congregation in name only but were active, committed and concerned not only for each other but for all who came to St Giles'.

Creating the new communal space under the Cathedral would obviously have to take place before the interior could be rearranged. The foundations of St Giles' are surprisingly shallow at the west end and so it was decided to create a large area to be called the East Hall underneath the four eastern bays of the chancel and its aisles, underpinning the pillars and linking it to existing rooms and cellars below the Thistle Chapel. The east end would have to be partitioned off while this was being done, and work would start as soon as funds were available. By August 1979 the appeal fund stood at over £686,350. This was a substantial sum, but it was £500,000 short of the total needed. An American fundraising firm had been appointed, but its returns were disappointingly poor and in Britain inflation was dramatically putting up building costs. On 23 October the general committee met to discuss the financial situation. Satisfactory tenders for the first phase of the East Hall project had come in, but the committee could only recommend that the work must not go ahead until more funds were available.

Soon afterwards, expensive repairs to the stonework suddenly became necessary when, during a gale on 4 December 1979, people in the High Street looked up and saw with alarm that the weathercock on the steeple was rocking perilously from side to side. The police hastily closed the street and when the top of the steeple was inspected it was discovered that not only was the cock loose. The top eight feet of stonework were rocking too and would obviously have to be rebuilt. The estimated cost of the repairs was £40,000. During the course of the work, Alexander Anderson's 300-year old weathercock was brought down and examined. The bronze pole on which it stood was bent, one of its eyes was missing and its gold leaf had almost completely worn away. It was carefully repaired and put on view in the Cathedral before finally being returned to its perch, on a new stainless steel pole (see Figure 14). After that, a lengthy programme of fabric maintenance and repair began. Burn's rusting iron tie bars on the West Front were giving trouble and would have to be replaced with stainless steel ones, while extensive lead roof repairs and the re-leading of various windows would also have to be undertaken.

In August 1980, Dr Feilden came to discuss the situation with the kirk session. His availability had decreased since his appointment as Director of the International Centre for Conservation in Rome, but he remained keenly interested and actively involved as a consultant to both his own firm and the recently established Edinburgh architects, Simpson and Brown, who specialised in the conservation of historic buildings. Seeing the doubtful expressions on the faces of some of the elders, he stressed that excavating the east end was the only possible way of finding extra space. The chancel should be screened off and the old floor lifted. A concrete roof would be put over the excavated area, forming a new chancel floor. He foresaw the cost as being within £1 million, and suggested that there could then be a pause until a further million was raised to complete, heat and furnish the new space. Persuasive as he was, the elders were not convinced.

Figure 14
Ian Fraser re-gilding the St Giles' weathercock, 1980.
(© The Scotsman Publications Ltd. Licensor www.scran.ac.uk)

A month later, the general committee said that they could not recommend the continuance of the East Hall project as planned, but were willing to investigate more limited ways of proceeding. Accepting this view, the kirk session reaffirmed their commitment to the Feilden Report in the long term. By November 1980 the actual and promised income of the appeal fund stood at over £1,106,000, most of it coming from companies and trusts, but with £100,000 from the City of Edinburgh District Council and £182,135 from the congregation. More than £6,000 of this had been raised by the first of a series of annual St Giles' Fairs held in Parliament Square West that summer, when members of the congregation arrayed in medieval dress sold baking, food, plants, books and handicrafts at temporarily erected stalls. The atmosphere of carefree fun was still remembered fondly by participants nearly thirty years later.

Also in November 1980, David Mawson of the architects Feilden & Mawson presented a detailed report analysing progress, pointing out that inflation had increased building costs by about 100 per cent so far and outlining the possible way ahead. There could be three main areas of activity. The first would be the transformation of the existing cellars at the south-east end of St Giles' into a coffee house and meeting room, with a stair leading to the main level. This would be followed by the rearrangement of the interior, as Macmillan and Feilden had planned, and thirdly a rolling programme of repair and maintenance ought to be drawn up. Each of the three proposals was of equal importance, he said, but the new accommodation at the lower level would be by far the most expensive. The kirk session decided to press on with this amended plan, expressing the hope that the new sanctuary at the crossing would be created as soon as was practicable. Preliminary work began in the summer of 1981 and when the Queen and Prince Philip came to see what was being done, they stayed for twice the expected time. This was encouraging, progress was good, and it was decided that the converted space should be known as the Lower Aisle.

The structural work was complete by the end of August 1982 and the stair linking the new rooms to the main part of the Cathedral was being built from a pinkish Lazonby stone which sparkled with quartz grains and blended well with the sandstone interior. The steps would be constructed of limestone to match the new parts of the cathedral floor and Macmillan suggested the biblical quotation which was then carved on the archway leading to the new rooms: 'That they all may be one.' This comes from John 17:21, and he chose it not only because the unity of the church and indeed of all life is a central theme of the faith but because, as we have seen, it was John Knox's favourite chapter and might serve as a corrective to the Reformer's misleading reputation for being extremely divisive.

In order to enhance the association with Knox, it was decided that his statue ought to be brought back in from Parliament Square to a position where it would be more prominent as well as being sheltered from rain and pollution. With the permission of the presbytery and the General Assembly's committee on artistic questions, this was done in 1983. The intention was to place it near the stair to the Lower Aisle, but in the end it was put beside a pillar at the west end of the nave, not far from its original position in the Albany Aisle. When it had first stood there, people had thought it inappropriate that Knox, who hated images, was on a pedestal beneath an elaborate Gothic canopy, rather like a saint, and so he now stands firmly on the floor, without plinth or canopy, at the eye-level of all who pass his way.

By now the Lower Aisle was finished, complete with restaurant, which would generate income for St Giles' as well as providing a meeting place for the congregation after services. One of the two seating areas would act as the room for kirk session meetings, and Christian Shaw, son of Sax Shaw who had designed the choir's red gowns twenty years earlier, made a series of tiny stained glass windows on the theme of the Creation. These were set into the thick walls.

Attention had also turned to the rearrangement of the Cathedral interior. Even though people had accepted the holy table's altered position in the middle of the chancel, they would probably be horrified at the thought of moving it to the very centre of St Giles', beneath the crossing. There were always those who were ready to pounce on anything which they thought smacked of Episcopalian or Roman Catholic practices. The alterations would have to be undertaken gradually, to assess the visual effect, a good deal of experimentation might be needed, and various bodies had to be asked for their permission before any alterations could be made. The Edinburgh ecclesiastical commissioners who had plagued William Chambers no longer existed but the managing board had been saved from extinction by Macmillan's arguments in its favour in 1979, and the presbytery of Edinburgh and the committee on artistic questions would also have to give their agreement.

This they did, and the trial arrangements began in the autumn of 1981. The holy table would be placed beneath the crossing and seating was arranged around it. Lorimer's heavy oak table with its carved figures did not look right in its new position and it was put at the east end of the Preston Aisle instead. A temporary holy table in the form of a square wooden framework covered with a heavy cloth was placed beneath the centre of the crossing so that the effect could be properly gauged. The creation of the sanctuary brought with it other changes too. The east end dais would have to be taken away and, to improve sightlines, it was decided to remove the Moray Aisle screen and the Skidmore railings which divided that aisle from the nave. The small shop which had recently occupied the Moray Aisle was transferred to the south-west corner of the nave, the railings were used to enclose a chapel in the north-east corner of the Cathedral which Macmillan suggested should be known by its pre-Reformation name of the Holy Cross Aisle and the Moray Aisle screen was later sold to the National Museums of Scotland.

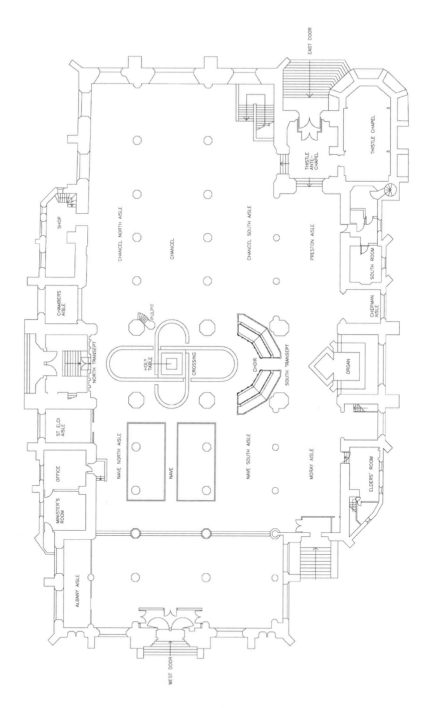

Figure 15
Plan of St Giles' interior, 2008, showing the central Sanctuary.
(© Campbell & Arnott Ltd, architects.)

Sitting on the floor by itself at the crossing, the holy table was certainly beneath the lowest ceiling in the cathedral but it was nevertheless dwarfed by the great octagonal pillars and it could easily be overlooked, particularly as people familiar with churches automatically expected to find it at the east end, the traditional location of altars and communion tables. Its new position would somehow have to be emphasised and Macmillan urged the imaginative use of colour, light and textiles in the sanctuary. In the spring of 1982, however, several pieces of masonry fell from the exterior of the building and it was realised that alarmingly extensive repairs to the stonework could be necessary. Once more William Burn's tie bars were rusting, and it was feared that the cost of the repairs might run into millions of pounds. Could the plans for the Renewal really continue under these circumstances? Would the ambitious ideas in the Feilden Report ever be fully achieved?

CHAPTER 13

Colour, Music and Light

At the beginning of 1983, the kirk session met to consider a new report on the current state and future development of St Giles'. Fortunately, the worst fears about the stonework had not been realised. The Renewal Appeal committee had set itself the target of raising at least £300,000 by 1985 and a new pattern of services proposed by the minister would begin on the first Sunday of Lent in 1983. In future, there would be two communion services every Sunday morning, at 8am and 10am, followed by the services at 11:30am, 6pm and 8pm. This proved highly successful and has become the established sequence. In August 1984, Thomas Hunter Thomson retired as session clerk after thirty-six years, having given loyal service to three consecutive ministers and been much appreciated for his dignity, his scrupulous fairness and his kindly manner. His respect for the past in no way inhibited his appreciation of the need for Renewal, and he was an enthusiastic supporter of the Feilden Plan.

Meanwhile, a single project partnership, Bernard Feilden, Simpson & Brown, had been established to act as the Cathedral architects, with James Simpson as the partner responsible for St Giles'. Having trained with Ian Lindsay in Edinburgh and with Bernard Feilden on St Paul's and Norwich Cathedrals, Simpson was very experienced in conservation and indeed had worked on the Cathedral since 1977. He produced a detailed report on likely maintenance costs and devised a major plan for improving facilities by building an eight-foot-high partition wall across the west end of the nave. There would be seating for up to 200 people in a loft above, and stores, a shop and a meeting room below. With the close involvement of Gilleasbuig Macmillan, the report also envisaged a greatly enhanced sanctuary with painted roof vaults, colourful banners and a canopy of lights above the holy table, like the one over the tomb of St Thomas Cantilupe in Hereford Cathedral.

These were bold and imaginative ideas, but they also proved controversial. Some of the elders were enthusiastic, but others were highly critical. Roof and stonework repairs were liable to run to £40,000 a year, the west end scheme would require between £100,000 and £150,000, while the improvements to the sanctuary and the seating were estimated at £175,000. One elder said that the reaction of members in his district to the ongoing innovations already ranged from the sad to the hostile, while a number of his colleagues were concerned about what they regarded as aesthetic rather than practical considerations being given priority. An effective heating system was far more necessary than a nimbus of light above the holy table, they said, and they particularly disliked the notion of the west end being blocked off by a partition. If the west door were to be kept closed instead of being left invitingly open, as it was at present, the whole effect of the west front would be spoiled and fewer people would come in.

On 10 February, the kirk session approved the repairs and maintenance expenditure but withheld permission to develop the west end design until they had considered further. Six days later they decided to allow the design work to go ahead, but in June the west end scheme was abandoned, partly because of financial constraints, partly because of continuing opposition. There would be no partition or loft at the west end. Instead, there would be a more limited set of objectives, some concerned with new seating and an improved heating system, some with the enhancement of the sanctuary which the minister was so anxious to achieve, but none of them affecting the west door. In the months that followed, the sanctuary floor was paved with Cadeby magnesium limestone, incorporating an inlaid pattern of dark-grey Cumbrian slate. This took the form of a type of Celtic knot, and it came to be the line on which the circle of communicants stood to receive the bread and the wine.

A new temporary dais for a new holy table was made, and the vaulted roof above it was cleaned and plastered. In the centre of the crossing roof was the bell hole through which the medieval bell ropes used to hang. This was now closed with a board designed and painted by Don Pottinger, the herald painter. It shows a gold crown of glory in a starry firmament, against a background of dark blue. A brass lectern given by Sir Henry Littlejohn in 1886, which had stood in the Moray Aisle, was refurbished for the sanctuary, replacing the Caen stone one. Something was also done about the endlessly frustrating sound system which had been installed in 1959 and ever since had been the subject of constant complaints. Dr Robert Craik of Heriot-Watt University and his advisers now designed an entirely new system.

The regimental colours hanging from the nave pillars were also in need of attention. Always fragile, they had gathered dust over the years and in 1982 the Scottish Command of the army had offered to take them down, list them and store them until the kirk session decided what to do with them. Threadbare flags are notoriously difficult, time-consuming and therefore expensive to conserve and, the following year, army headquarters advised that only twenty-nine of them were in a fit state to be hung up again. It was decided to display these in the Moray Aisle, send back to their regiments any requested by them and store the rest.

On 14 May 1984 Whytock and Reid delivered the new choir stalls. Placed in a semicircular position opposite the pulpit and in front of the organ, they were left unpainted so that a decision about their colour could be made once they were in place. After much discussion and some changes to their construction, it was finally agreed that a pale green would set off the pinkish sandstone of the great pillars. The following year, it was decided to have eighteenth-century-style box pews made for the nave, with underfloor heating. Not everything was going well, however, and two important projects had run into serious difficulties. Dr Greenhouse Allt had left St Giles' in 1944, to take up the position of principal of Trinity College of Music in London, and he had been succeeded in 1946 by Herrick Bunney, who had been serving as a major in the Royal Corps of Signals. Ever since his appointment, Bunney had been enhancing the reputation of the Cathedral music, not least with his performances of the works of Bach. Increasingly, however, he was having to struggle with the worn-out organ which Dr Warr had optimistically believed would last for several hundred years.

An expert committee was set up to advise on the acquisition of a replacement. It consisted of four leading organists, Bunney himself, Francis Jackson of York Minster, George McPhee of Paisley Abbey and Noel Rawsthorne of Liverpool Anglican Cathedral. They were later joined by Peter Williams of Edinburgh University. Having considered a wide range of possibilities, they agreed unanimously on 5 June 1980 that the commission for an entirely new organ should go to Messrs C. B. Fisk Inc. of Gloucester, Massachusetts. Charles Fisk, a former Harvard physicist and now a renowned organ builder, would design an organ of about fifty stops, three or four manuals and his famous suspended tracker action, at a cost of around £400,000 to £500,000. It should be ready approximately five years after the contract was signed, and it would be placed in the south transept. This was all very satisfactory and Fisk had impressed everyone as 'a most interesting and genuine person'. Fundraising for the new organ was launched and Fisk began work on the design, but in November 1982 concern was being expressed about his health and he died the following year. The Fisk organ project died with him.

Another exciting plan was also giving trouble. For many years the various Burns Clubs had been agitating for a memorial to Robert Burns to be placed in St Giles' but their requests were always refused by the managing board, on the grounds that, with his fondness for 'the lasses', the poet was not a suitable person to be commemorated in a cathedral. Late in 1979, they decided to try again and the Burns Federation approached Macmillan, who immediately thought of the great west window. Entitled 'The Prophets', it had been erected in 1886 by Robert Hamilton-Bruce, a prosperous flour merchant, in memory of his wife Fanny who had died of septicaemia following childbirth at the age of only 24. The prominent stained glass artist Daniel Cottier had designed it, but by now it had deteriorated so badly that it was beyond repair. Perhaps the Federation might consider inserting a replacement? The Federation members were surprised and delighted. They had probably resigned themselves to another rebuff and they had certainly never expected the opportunity to put up something so prestigious. They quickly agreed and launched a worldwide appeal for £25,000.

News of the plans provoked further argument. No one seemed to know that Burns used to attend services in St Giles'. *The Scotsman* did its best to stir up a debate, reminding its readers of the reasons why similar requests had been refused before, and the Free Church of Scotland's Edinburgh presbytery wrote objecting to the proposal. While not venturing to pronounce on the poet's final standing before God, they said, and while indeed grateful to God for Burns's literary gifts, they nonetheless considered it highly inappropriate that the Cathedral should very prominently honour someone who treated the Christian gospel so lightly. The letter was noted. When the press returned to the matter, Macmillan said firmly that the window would be a recognition of both the forgiving acceptance of people's faults as well as their virtues, and the tremendous need for the Church to recognise the importance of art.

Leifur Breidfjord, who was to become Iceland's leading stained glass artist, was chosen to design the window. He had studied at Edinburgh College of Art, where his supervisor was Sax Shaw; and now, advised by David Daiches, the distinguished literary scholar, Breidfjord produced a design which managed to please everyone at both the Cathedral and the Burns Federation. The lowest panel shows greenery, representing the natural world, with the figure of Burns in the centre, above a copy of his signature. The central panel represents the theme of common humanity which runs through so much of Burns's poetry, and at the top is a red rose against a sunburst of creativity. The rose symbolises both Christian and romantic love and recalls Burns's famous poem, 'My love is like a red, red rose' (see Plate 6).

The firm of G. King & Son, lead glaziers, Norwich was recommended by Dr Feilden to do the glazing for £13,500 and, in all, it was estimated that the window would cost in the region of £35,000. That was £10,000 more than the first figure mentioned, but it would be worth it. Unfortunately, by February 1984 the estimated total cost had risen to more than £50,000, not least because the glaziers had sent in an amended estimate of more than double their original figure. Everyone was shocked at the news, but there was no turning back. The Burns Federation had raised their promised £25,000 and the donors were eagerly anticipating the finished window. The kirk session authorised the project to proceed, with a change of glazier and the Burns Federation helped with further fundraising.

A new contract was signed with Messrs W. Derix of Rottweil in Germany in the spring of 1984. Leifur Breidfjord would supply them with all the necessary drawings and information, advise them on the types of glass to be used and visit their premises to select it. By 9 March 1985 the stonework of the wall round about the window had been cleaned, the glass of the Fanny Hamilton-Bruce memorial window was being taken out and Breidfjord was in Rottweil, painting parts of his window, helped by two of Derix's painters. The decorative memorial plaque to Fanny was left in place beneath the window. When the glass was ready, two members of Derix brought it to Edinburgh by car and installed it. In the end, the total cost was over £50,000, but everyone was most impressed and the window was dedicated at a special service on 30 June 1985. A slate panel was carved by Dick Reid with the words: 'This window celebrates Robert Burns, poet of humanity, 1985' and inserted in the floor nearby.

The following year, the shop found a new home in what had been the Ladies' Room, latterly known as St Margaret's Room. Designed by MacGibbon & Ross the architects, it had been generously donated by Sheriff Thom in 1890, but times had changed, and the ladies of the congregation no longer wore constricting crinolines and needed a couch to lie down on as well as a place to leave their voluminous cloaks on wet Sundays. The conversion into a shop was made with the help of a grant from the Scottish Tourist Board.

Less easy to solve was the worrying problem of the organ. A working party had been set up in the summer of 1984 to consider what was to be done after the abrupt end to the Charles Fisk project. In the spring of 1986 three possible organ builders were being considered but the outlook was far from encouraging, not least because the estimated cost of a new instrument was in the region of half a million pounds. The prospect of trying to raise this sum by means of yet another appeal was challenging, to say the least. However, in May 1987 Macmillan was able to tell the kirk session that an anonymous Scottish trust was offering to finance the entire cost of a new organ. This was wonderful news. The donor was in fact Alastair Salvesen, whose family had a long connection with the Cathedral. He made this gift in memory of his father, Iver Ronald Stuart Salvesen and in honour of his mother, Marion Salvesen, and was eventually persuaded to allow his name and the dedication to be made public.

With the financial burden removed, plans could speed ahead and by the autumn of 1988 it had been decided that Rieger Orgelbau of Schwarzach in Austria would build the new instrument. Messrs Campbell & Arnott were appointed architects for the project, the donor was eager for as much of the work as possible to be done in Scotland and so Douglas Laird, the partner in charge, would design the organ casework. The principal considerations were that the design should be contemporary in style, and that as much space as possible should be left around the organ, with the window behind it unblocked to allow light to flow in past it towards the sanctuary. Peter Hurford, organist and choir master at St Albans Abbey and Herrick Bunney had drawn up the specification in consultation with Rieger. There would be fifty-seven stops, three manuals, pedals with mechanical action and fully computerised stop control.

The old organ was dismantled that autumn. The console went to a Perth church, most of the pipes were taken by the Edinburgh University's McEwan Hall where Herrick Bunney was also the organist, and two would be reused in the new organ. Meanwhile, an organ was borrowed from another Edinburgh church, Lockhart Memorial, for temporary use at services. The brickwork blocking the south transept window proved more difficult to remove than had been expected, but it was done, and the floor of the south transept where the new organ would stand was strengthened. By December 1991, Macmillan and Bunney were in Austria attending events to mark the instrument's completion and work on its installation began the following February.

It took five weeks to build it on site, and eleven weeks to voice it – the fine-tuning which involves deciding on the degree of tone from one particular rank of pipes and matching it with the others. Each pipe and each stop then had to be tuned individually. The casework, made of Austrian oak stained a deep red, is of strikingly contemporary design, with decorative bronze and glass. At the top of the central pipe tower is a chromatic ring of thirty-seven hand-bells made by Whitechapel Bell Foundry, London and most of the 4,156 pipes are of tin. It was dedicated on 24 May 1992 and, shortly afterwards, Herrick Bunney declared that it was a superb instrument, of outstanding design and workmanship of a high quality. It was a joy to play, he said, and he was confident that it would rank with the finest instruments anywhere (see Plate 7).

So it has proved to be, and celebrity organists come from all over the world to give recitals. Bunney, a much loved figure, retired in 1996 after fifty years as organist and master of the music at St Giles' and was succeeded by Michael Harris, previously assistant organist of Canterbury Cathedral, whose particular interests are German Baroque and French Romantic organ music. A well-known international recitalist, he is also a lecturer in music at Napier University. In 2000 Peter Backhouse, formerly of St Mary's Episcopal Cathedral in Edinburgh, came to be assistant organist at St Giles' and in 2007 a new organisation, the Friends of the Music of St Giles', was founded to encourage the use of the Cathedral for music activities by a broad variety of groups from the wider community. The Friends also support special projects and fund the use of instrumentalists in services.

Meanwhile, a competition in 1986 for the design of a new font had failed to produce any acceptable proposal, but in 1990 the kirk session agreed to the design for a processional Cross to be carried in at the start of the 10am communion service and positioned beside the holy table, remaining there for the rest of the Sunday services. Two years later, Betty Davies designed new, oatmeal-coloured gowns for the choir and there were also various gifts to the Cathedral which helped to realise Macmillan's vision for the sanctuary. A set of lectern steps in stone and bronze, designed by Jacqueline Gruber Styger, was presented in 1991 by the Normandy Veterans' Association and in 1987 friends of Mrs Christine Miller, a member of the congregation who was celebrating her 100th birthday, had presented a special cloth for the holy table. Eric von Ibler gave another in 1994, for use during each Edinburgh Festival, its design inspired by the Cathedral windows.

There were already felt banners in colours appropriate to the different liturgical seasons of the year hanging from the four great pillars at the sanctuary, but these were becoming worn and in 1991 Sheana Stephen the artist jeweller was commissioned to design long Christmas banners with gold angels blowing trumpets. Sewn on net, they are hung to splendid effect in front of the original scarlet banners. Green banners of abstract pattern for the long Trinity season of the year were devised by the embroiderer Meriel Tilling and given in 1998 by Margot Massie to commemorate her husband, Colonel Leslie A. Massie.

Members of the congregation, including Mrs Massie, worked on the new sets, along with other skilled embroiderers, and in 2008 the first two Easter banners of a new white and yellow sequence were hung. Again designed by Sheana Stephen and sewn by members of the congregation, along with friends in the Thistle Quilters, they are made from materials generously given by Mrs Massie's daughter, Jean Barbour, in memory of her mother. Created with silks, satins, gold thread, gold braid and little mirrors, they have the sun as the focus, each time at a higher point, suggesting sunrise and the Resurrection of Christ.

Although wall space was by now very limited, several new memorials were erected at this period. The recollection of St Giles as patron saint of lepers made it particularly appropriate that a metal and stone memorial designed by James Simpson was put up in 1987 in memory of Wellesley Bailey, founder of the Leprosy Mission. In 1992 a group of Scotswomen presented the bronze sculpture of a stool 'in memory of Jenny Geddes'. For some reason it has been wrongly called 'The Cutty Stool' but that, of course, was actually the name given to the stool of repentance in the seventeenth century. Four years later, an elegant stone plaque was placed on the wall of the Moray Aisle to commemorate Sir James Young Simpson's use of chloroform anaesthesia in childbirth and when the Royal College of Surgeons celebrated their quincentenary in 2005, they obtained permission to erect in the Holy Cross Aisle a handsome stone monument showing a gloriously gilded sun, in recollection of the fact that in the early sixteenth century their qualifying examinations were for a time held in St Giles'.

Meanwhile, major roof repairs had once more become necessary. Sir Angus Grossart, the merchant banker, had by now succeeded Lord Clydesmuir as chairman of the Renewal Appeal and in June 1997 a second major phase of the Appeal was launched, with the aim of raising three million pounds. The ensuing work was planned in five phases, beginning that October, the first four concentrating on conserving the exterior, with donations from private individuals and trusts, and with large grants from Historic Scotland and from the Heritage Lottery Fund once the Church of Scotland had withdrawn its ethical objections to the latter. At the same time the Appeal established a new fundraising initiative with the creation of the 1124 Society, which took its name from the approximate date when St Giles' was founded. Invited members donate £1,124 each, and in recognition of their gift, a brass plaque inscribed with the name of the donor is placed on the back of one of the new chairs provided for the chancel and the aisles. By 2003 the society had generated over £400,000. Other donors become Guardians of St Giles', one of the first being A. S. Chambers, a great-great-grand-nephew of William Chambers.

Work on the roof, stonework and some of the interior timber of the steeple was a slow business and there was a long interlude for further fundraising, but at last in December 2005 it was complete and the scaffolding which had for so long encased different parts of the exterior could finally come down. Moreover, gilded weather vanes gleam on the crown steeple once more, replacing the long-vanished originals. They are the gift of Sir Angus and Lady Grossart, in memory of Lady Grossart's brother. The Phase Two conservation had also included extensive work on the stained glass windows. Over the years, the lead holding little pieces of stained glass in place deteriorates, the iron rusts, affecting the surrounding stones, the glass cracks and atmospheric pollution dulls the once bright colours. In 2001 the Stained Glass Design Partnership, based in Kilmaurs, Ayrshire, was therefore commissioned to make a detailed survey, in the course of which they discovered that the heraldic window next to the Montrose monument was in a dangerous state and was actually beginning to collapse under its own weight.

Beginning with it, relays of windows were boarded up as their stained glass was taken out and transported to Ayrshire. In the studio there, fading painted details were delicately retouched with acrylic pigment, dirt was removed and cracked glass was painstakingly replaced, matching the colour, texture and quality of the damaged original. Once conserved, the windows were returned to St Giles' and put back in their proper place, with new bronze horizontal support bars between their sections instead of the old weathered ones. Meanwhile masons had repaired the tracery and the adjacent stonework, and each window was given an exterior layer of protective glass. In all, the project took four years to complete, the colours once more glow with their original intensity and light streams in to illuminate the interior in a way not seen for many years. During 2008, a new inner porch at the west door, in blue glass and metal, was designed by Leifur Breidfjord, who had created the west window. It replaced the wooden porch which had been adapted from Queen Victoria's royal pew.

In 2006, after further fundraising, disabled access was provided at the west door by means of handsome ramps outside and in, designed by the Edinburgh architects Morris & Steedman Associates. At the same time, new flooring of Cadeby white limestone was laid at the west end and the firm of Charles Taylor undertook a four-month programme of conserving and polishing all the intricate woodwork in the Thistle Chapel for the first time since 1911. Once this was done, the fifth and final phase of the second Renewal Appeal could begin, but would there be enough money for a new lighting system, limewashing the roof vaults and conserving the memorials? Unfortunately, these were ineligible for Historic Scotland grants and by March 2007 the estimated cost had risen from £1.8 million to £2.8 million. As only £600,000 to £700,000 was currently available, Macmillan had to tell the kirk session on 1 June 2007 that because of the funding issues only some of the intended work could go ahead. However, with a generous grant from the Heritage Lottery Fund, work on the new lighting system was undertaken in 2008–9.

The existing mixture of old tungsten fittings in their painted metal boxes and what had been intended as temporary floodlights was inadequate, to say the least, and as long ago as 1997 a delegation from the Cathedral had visited Durham Cathedral to study its five-year-old lighting system. Now it was decided that the best solution would be to hang a chandelier in each arched bay, between the pillars, with the cabling by Arup Scotland concealed in the roof voids. There had been chandeliers before, of course, chandeliers, gasoliers and electroliers, but these would be different. Designed by the Lighting Design Partnership (subsequently named DPA Lighting) and made near Edinburgh, of stainless steel and aluminium, the twenty-four new chandeliers are in a contemporary, abstract style.

Each has multiple lighting circuits and reflecting metal fins so that it casts light both upwards, to reveal the roof carvings previously lost in the shadows, and downwards, so that the congregation can read their hymn books with greater ease. When a prototype chandelier was hung in the chancel so that its effect could be gauged, one of *The Scotsman* art critics declared that it looked like a curious cross between a satellite dish and a metallic jellyfish. However, the new chandeliers in fact resemble delicate silver lilies as they hang from the arches and are much admired as a considerable enhancement to the interior. At the same time, the long-gone medieval candles sitting on the windowsills have been replaced by twenty-nine lighting channels just beneath the sills, illuminating the stonework above (see Plate 8). With the completion of the new lighting, including lighting for the choir, and a new holy table in marble, the latest restoration was largely complete.

When Gilleasbuig Macmillan and Bernard Feilden held their first discussions in 1975, they could never have anticipated that it would take more than thirty years of devoted effort, extraordinary tenacity and generous giving to achieve what they had planned. The transformation of the interior of St Giles' during that time has intrigued, impressed and sometimes shocked the half-million or so people who come to the Cathedral each year. When services are not in progress, volunteer guides show visitors round and answer questions. Some 120 in all, the guides include members of the congregation, members of other churches and other denominations, and some who have no ecclesiastical connection at all but possess a great enthusiasm for the Cathedral. St Giles', however, is not merely an historic building but a living church which welcomes people from all over the world to its services, gives pastoral care to its members and makes regular financial contributions to local organisations, supporting the homeless, refugees, the housebound and others in difficulty.

At the same time, it develops its role as the place where services marking important civic and national events are held. The Stone of Destiny, on which Scottish and then British monarchs were crowned, was brought for a special service on its way to Edinburgh Castle after its return to Scotland from Westminster Abbey in 1996. A piece of Scottish rock 3,300 million years old, a Pictish silver chain, a nineteenth-century Gaelic Bible and a mobile phone were among the objects carried to the sanctuary at a service to mark the opening of the Museum of Scotland in 1998. The following year, the new Scottish parliament began to meet; and multifaith services are held in the Cathedral at the beginning of each session.

Following in its long tradition, St Giles' and its minister are indeed playing a vital part in the ecumenical movement which began with the World Missionary Conference in Edinburgh in 1910 and is now of such importance to the Christian Church. As we have seen, the focus was at first on uniting the rival Reformed churches which had divided in the nineteenth century, but now the Roman Catholic Church is also a major player in international ecumenism. The ensuing dialogues are not undertaken as some sort of attempt to combine shrinking congregations. They are inspired by a genuine desire to heal the breaches of the past. There are many difficulties, of course, and there is a long way to go, but there are promising initiatives, both local and national, and interfaith dialogue is also a vital part of the work. In the early twenty-first century both Cardinal Keith O'Brien, Roman Catholic Archbishop of St Andrews and Edinburgh, and Dr Richard Holloway, formerly Primus of the Scottish Episcopal Church, may be seen from time to time in the pulpit of St Giles', while Dr Bashir Maan, Convener of the Muslim Council of Scotland, is an equally familiar figure as he gives one of his addresses at special services.

All this is part of the present chapter in the long and complex history of St Giles'. As we have seen, many men and women have been involved in the evolution of the great building over the centuries – priests, parishioners, benefactors and architects, famous men like John Knox and anonymous women like the unnamed water wife. A multitude of others have come to mark the defining moments in their lives and find consolation in time of crisis, be it after the Battle of Flodden in 1513 or in the wake of the terrorist attacks on New York and Washington on 11 September 2001. Thinking about how to worship God has shaped the building, and the building has inspired and strengthened faith. Tourists may arrive out of curiosity rather than from any spiritual considerations but many, like the young Australian at the start of this book, are impressed by the unique atmosphere of a great church and find their thoughts turning to time and eternity.

Some people believe that a church is made holy by a service of consecration, while others are of the opinion that it is sanctified by the prayers of generations of worshippers. However one likes to explain it, St Giles' truly comes into its own on Sunday mornings when sunlight slants in through the south windows, dappling the medieval walls with the red, blue and yellow of the stained glass, anthems float upwards to the shadowy Gothic arches, sermons are preached, prayers are said and, at communion, in utter stillness, the congregation hear those same words which have been spoken in that sacred space, in Latin or in English, for nearly 900 years: 'Take, eat, this is my body ...'.

Sources

Much of the research for this book has been based on documentary sources. Past kirk session records of St Giles' are preserved in the National Archives of Scotland, as are records of the Edinburgh Ecclesiastical Commissioners. The early charters, Edinburgh dean of guild accounts and town council minutes all contain significant material and are to be found in Edinburgh City Archives. The Latin charters have been published in *Registrum Cartarum Ecclesiae Sancti Egidii de Edinburgh MCCCXLIV–MDLXVII,* ed. David Laing (Bannatyne Club 1859), while selections of the council minutes are printed in the Burgh Records Society series *Extracts from the Records of the Burgh of Edinburgh* AD *1403–1718,* (Edinburgh 1869–1967). The personal papers of Dr Charles Warr, Dr Harry Whitley, the Chambers Papers and the records of St Giles' Managing Board are in the National Library of Scotland. I have also drawn upon the St Giles' Conservation Plan of 2001 and other records at the Cathedral.

Important background reading includes Margo Todd, *The Culture of Protestantism in Early Modern Scotland* (New Haven and London 2002), Gordon Donaldson, *The Faith of the Scots* (London 1990) and Peter Hammond, *Liturgy and Architecture* (London 1960). James Cameron Lees, *St Giles', Edinburgh: Church, College, and Cathedral* (Edinburgh and London 1889) is characteristic of nineteenth-century historical writing, with voluminous appendices, and William Chambers described his own major restoration of St Giles' in his little *Historical Sketch of St Giles' Cathedral* (Edinburgh 1884). Alan R. MacDonald discusses parliament's use of the west end of the nave in *The Burghs and Parliament in Scotland c.1550–1651* (Aldershot 2007), and other aspects of the building are addressed in *The Thistle Chapel, within St Giles' Cathedral, Edinburgh*, ed. Elizabeth Roads (Edinburgh 2009), Charles J. Burnett, *Stall Plates of the Most Ancient and Most Noble Order of the Thistle in the Chapel of the Order within St Giles' Cathedral, the High Kirk of Edinburgh* (Edinburgh 2001) and Lynne Gladstone-Millar, *Medieval Carved Stones in St Giles'* (Edinburgh 2006). Jo Penney and John Knight, *St Giles' Cathedral: a Guide's Handbook* (Edinburgh 2005) provides a concise and useful architectural chronology.

Biographies and autobiographies of the ministers include Rosalind K. Marshall, *John Knox* (Edinburgh 2000), Norman MacLean, *The Life of James Cameron Lees KCVO, DD, LLD* (Glasgow 1922), Christopher N. Johnston (Lord Sands), *Life of Andrew Wallace Williamson* (Edinburgh and London 1929), Charles Warr, *The Glimmering Landscape* (London 1960) and Henry C. Whitley, *Laughter in Heaven* (London 1962). For prominent personalities mentioned fleetingly in the text, the *Oxford Dictionary of National Biography* (Oxford 2004) is available online to subscribers and through libraries at http://www.oxforddnb.com, *The Scotsman* Archive, http://archive. scotsman.com, covers the period 1817–1950 and includes a vast array of detail about St Giles', while a wealth of useful doctrinal information is given by the Church of Scotland website, http://churchofscotland.org. uk, the official Vatican website, http://www.vatican.va and The Catholic Encyclopaedia, http://www.newadvent.org.

Sources of Quotations

Abbreviations and Acknowledgements

BL   British Library. (This item is reproduced with permission of the Trustees of the British Library.)

ECA   Edinburgh City Archives. (These items are reproduced with permission of Edinburgh City Archives.)

NAS   National Archives of Scotland. (These items are reproduced with permission of the National Archives of Scotland.)

NLS   National Library of Scotland. (These items are reproduced with permission of the Trustees of the National Library of Scotland.)

Scotsman *The Scotsman* newspaper. (These items are reproduced with permission of *The Scotsman*.)

Abbreviated Book Titles

Extracts   *Extracts from the Records of the Burgh of Edinburgh* (Edinburgh 1869–1967)

Lees, *St Giles'* James Cameron Lees, *St Giles', Edinburgh: Church, College, and Cathedral* (Edinburgh and London 1889)

page 9   *Scotichronicon*, ed. D. E. R. Watt, vii (Aberdeen 1994), 407, 520

page 10   *Charters and Other Documents relating to the City of Edinburgh AD 1134–1540* (Scottish Burgh Records Society 1871), 35

page 15   Same volume, 79

page 16 para 1 last line   *Edinburgh Records: The Burgh Accounts* ii, *Dean of Guild Accounts, 1552–1567*, ed. Robert Adam (Edinburgh 1899), 26; **para 2 line 7** *Charters and Other Documents*, 79

pages 18, 19   Helen Sarah Brown, 'Lay Piety in Later Medieval Lothian, c.1306–c.1513' (unpublished Edinburgh University PhD thesis, 2007), 207, citing NAS, Dalhousie Muniments, GD45/13.123.1, f. 7

page 26   *Registrum Cartarum Ecclesiae Sancti Egidii de Edinburgh MCCCXLIV-MDLXVII*, ed. David Laing (Bannatyne Club 1859), 129

page 29   Same volume, 227

pages 30–1   *Charters and Other Documents*, 142

page 32   NLS, Dep 341/556, Chambers Papers, letter of William Hay to William Chambers, 4 October 1882

page 35   *Edinburgh Records: Dean of Guild's Accounts, 1552–1567*, 58

page 40 para 2 line 3   *Dean of Guild's Accounts, 1552–1567*, 45, 76; 73

page 45   *The Works of John Knox*, ed. D. Laing (Edinburgh 1854), vi, p. lxxxvii

page 52 para 2 lines 6–7   *Edinburgh Records: The Burgh Accounts* i, *Town Treasurer's Accounts 1552–67*, ed. Robert Adam (Edinburgh 1899), 324; **para 2 lines 8–9** *Edinburgh Records: Dean of Guild's Accounts, 1552–67*, 132

page 53 para 2 lines 14–15   Same volume, 196; **para 3 lines 10–12** *Extracts 1557–71*, 71

page 55 para 2 line 5   National Archives of Scotland, CC8/8/7, Edinburgh Register of Testaments, Edward Henderson (Henryson), 15 August 1579; **para 3 lines 7–8** *Extracts 1655–65*, 64

page 58   *Extracts 1573–89*, 214

page 62   George Dalgleish and Henry Steuart Fothringham, *Silver: Made in Scotland* (Edinburgh 2008), 143; The *Scots Confession of 1560*, ed. G. D. Henderson (Edinburgh 1960), 42

page 63   *Dean of Guild's Accounts 1552–67*, 236

page 64   *Extracts 1557–71*, 129

page 68 para 3 lines 3–4   *The Autobiography and Diary of Mr James Melville*, ed. R. Pitcairn (Wodrow Society 1842), 60;

para **3** **lines** **7–8** *The Works of John Knox*, ed. D. Laing, vi (Edinburgh 1854), p. lxxxiii; **line 10** Margaret H. B. Sanderson, 'Service and Survival: the clergy in late sixteenth-century Scotland' in *Records of the Scottish Church History Society*, xxxvi (Edinburgh 2008), 96, citing NAS CC8/8/7, Edinburgh Register of Testaments, Adam Foulis, 17 February 1575

page 69 para 2 last line ECA, Dean of Guild Manuscript Accounts, 1568–1626, 126; **para 3 last 2 lines** P. Hume Brown, *Early Travellers in Scotland* (Edinburgh 1891), 84

page 71 David Calderwood, *The History of the Kirk of Scotland* (Wodrow Society 1843–9), v, 81–2

page 72 ECA, Dean of Guild Manuscript Accounts, 1568–1626, 399

page 73 *Extracts 1573–89*, 539

pages 74 and 75 John Row, *History of the Kirk of Scotland from the Year 1558 to August 1637*, ed. David Laing (Edinburgh 1942), 115–16

page 76 para 2 line 3 ECA, Dean of Guild Manuscript Accounts, 1568–1626, 530; **para 2 line 4** same volume, 532; *Extracts 1604–26*, 134; **para 3 line 6** ECA, Dean of Guild Manuscript Accounts, 1568–1626, unpaginated, item under 1623–4; **para 3 last lines** Same volume, page 177

page 77 Same volume, 330

page 78 Alexander Baillie, *A True Information* (Wirtsburgh 1628), 26

page 81 William Maitland, *The History of Edinburgh from its foundation to the present time* (Edinburgh 1753), 184

page 82 *The Book of Common Prayer* (Edinburgh 1637), Section 13, The Order of the Administration of the Lord's Supper, or Holy Communion, introduction

page 83 Row, *History of the Kirk of Scotland*, 409

page 85 *Letters and Journals of Robert Baillie, AM, Principal of the University of Glasgow, 1637–62*, ed. D. Laing (Edinburgh 1841), i, 24

page 91 Poem inscribed on memorial to James Graham, Marquis of Montrose, in St Giles' Cathedral; **last para lines 2–3** J. Nicoll, *A Diary of Public Transactions and other Occurrences*, ed. D. Laing (Bannatyne Club 1836), 13

page 93 para 3 line 2   *Extracts 1642–55*, 253; **last para line 5** Nicol, *Diary*, 68

page 94   *Extracts, 1655–65*, 376

page 96   Same volume, 334, 353

page 97   *Extracts 1681–89*, 339

page 98   NAS, CH2/136/1, St Giles' Kirk Session Minutes, 1704–5, unpaginated

page 100   *Extracts 1689–1701*, 242, 259; 252

page 104   ECA, Dean of Guild Manuscript Tradesmen's Accounts, 1735–81, 479

page 105   Lees, *St Giles'*, 213, quoting Robert Chambers, *Traditions of Edinburgh* (Edinburgh, n.d.), 257

pages 106–7   *Letters of John Ramsay of Ochtertyre 1799–1812*, ed. B. L. H. Horn (Scottish History Society 1966), 33

page 112   NAS, Exchequer Records, E 342/39/5, letter of William Burn to William Trotter, Lord Provost of Edinburgh, 20 December 1826

page 113 para 2 line 7   NAS, 342/39/13, letter of Robert Reid to Sir Henry Jardine, 27 November 1827; **para 2 lines 11, 15–17** NAS,E 342/39/21, Exchequer Records, letter of William Burn to Sir William Rae, the Lord Advocate, 31 January 1828; **para 3 lines 9–10** NAS, CH12/134/3, St Giles' Kirk Session Minutes, 1816–35, 26

page 116   Lees, *St Giles'*, 264

page 118   William Chambers, *Historical Sketch of St Giles' Cathedral* (Edinburgh and London 1884), xlii-xliii

page 119   William Chambers, *Story of a Long and Busy Life* (Edinburgh and London 1882), 16, 21

page 120   *Scotsman*, 2 November 1867, report of Chambers's speech

page 121   NAS, CH2/136/4, St Giles' Kirk Session Minutes, 1863–79, 52

page 122   *Scotsman*, 14 November 1871, reports of meetings of 13 November 1871 and 21 February 1872

page 124 para 2 lines 2–3   NLS, Dep 341/565, Chambers Papers, letter of William Chambers to [William Hay], 9 April 1883; **para 3 lines 1–2** *Scotsman*, 24 February 1875

page 125 para 1 lines 5–6   *Scotsman*, 7 March 1873, journalist's report; **para 3 lines 3–4, 6–8** Same 4 March 1873, report of public meeting

page 126 NAS, CH2/136/4, St Giles' Kirk Session Minutes, 1863–79, 185

page 129 NLS, Dep 341/565, Chambers Papers, letter of Lindsay Mackersy to William Chambers, 5 June 1882

page 130 *Scotsman*, 6 April and 14 August 1880, letter from William Chambers and journalist's report

page 134 para 2 lines 4–7 NLS, Dep 341/565, Chambers Papers, letters of Lindsay Mackersy to William Chambers, 5 June 1882; **para 2 lines 8–10** William Hay to William Chambers, 4 July 1882; **para 3 lines 2–5** Lindsay Mackersy to William Chambers, 27 July 1882; **para 3 second last line** Same, letters of William Hay to William Chambers, 27 July and 8 August 1882

page 135 para 2 lines 5–6 Same, letter of Lindsay Mackersy to William Chambers, 7 September 1882; **para 3 lines 4–5, last 2 lines** Same, letters of Lindsay Mackersy to William Chambers, 6 and 17 July 1882; **para 4 line 8** Same, William Hay to William Chambers, 12 September 1882

page 136 para 1 line 3 Same, letters of William Hay to William Chambers, 17 July 1882; **para 2 lines 5–6** Lindsay Mackersy to William Chambers, 7 September 1882 and **para 2 lines 7–10** William Hay to Chambers, 13 September 1882; **para 4 last line** Lees, *St Giles'*, 269

pages 137–8 *Scotsman*, 24 May 1883, report of sermon by Dr James Cameron Lees

pages 138–9 *Scotsman*, 24 May 1883, journalist's report.

page 143 para 4 lines 4–8 A. Charles Sewter, *The Stained Glass of William Morris and His Circle: Volume 2, A Catalogue* (Yale University Press: New Haven and London, 1975), 69; **para 3 last 2 lines** *The Collected Letters of William Morris, 1885–1888*, ed. Norman Kelvin, ii, 1885–8 (Princeton, 1987), 578–9, quoting BL add. mss 45339, letter of William Morris to Jenny Morris

page 146 NAS, CH2/136/78, St Giles' Kirk Session Minutes, 1901–11, 74

page 147 Same volume, 311–12

page 150 *Scotsman*, 28 June 1913, appreciation of James Cameron Lees

page 151 Christopher N. Johnston, Lord Sands, *Life of Andrew Wallace Williamson* (Edinburgh and London 1929), 98

page 154 para 1 lines 2–3 *Scotsman*, 20 February 1939, journalist's report; **last para lines 4–5** NAS, CH2/136/80, St Giles' Kirk Session Minutes, 1920–8, 10 July 1926, 372

page 157 Same volume, 465

page 159 Same series, CH2/136/82, 1945–52, 314–16

page 167 Minute of the meeting of the St Giles' Cathedral and Manse Buildings Committee, 1 July 1971, 33

page 168 St Giles' Cathedral, St Giles' Kirk Session Minutes, 1970–83, 184

page 169 Muriel Armstrong, 'At the Helm of the High Kirk', in *Life & Work*, August 2003, 15

pages 171–2 St Giles' Cathedral, Paper and Renewal Sermon by the Very Reverend Gilleasbuig Macmillan in Feilden Report, June 1976, in St Giles' Conservation Plan, Appendix D

page 184 St Giles' Cathedral, St Giles' Appeal Office Papers, unpaginated, 'The New Organ', undated

Index